Collective Resistance in China

THE WALTER H. SHORENSTEIN
ASIA-PACIFIC RESEARCH CENTER

Studies of the Walter H. Shorenstein Asia-Pacific Research Center

Andrew G. Walder, General Editor

The Walter H. Shorenstein Asia-Pacific Research Center in the Freeman Spogli Institute for International Studies at Stanford University sponsors interdisciplinary research on the politics, economies, and societies of contemporary Asia. This monograph series features academic and policy-oriented research by Stanford faculty and other scholars associated with the Center.

Collective Resistance in China

WHY POPULAR PROTESTS SUCCEED OR FAIL

Yongshun Cai

Stanford University Press

Stanford, California

Stanford University Press
Stanford, California

Printed in the United States of America on acid-free, archival-quality paper

Library of Congress Cataloging-in-Publication Data
Cai, Yongshun.
  Collective resistance in China : why popular protests succeed or fail / Yongshun
Cai.
       p. cm. — (Studies of the Walter H. Shorenstein Asia-Pacific Research Center)
  Includes bibliographical references and index.
          ISBN 978-0-8047-6339-4 (cloth : alk. paper) –
          ISBN 978-0-8047-6340-0 (pbk. : alk. paper)
   1. Social movements—China. 2. Protest movements—China. 3. Political
participation—China. 4. China—Politics and government—1976–2002.
5. China—Politics and government—2002– I. Title. II. Series: Studies of the
Walter H. Shorenstein Asia-Pacific Research Center.
   HN733.5.C365 2010
   303.60951'09045—dc22

                                                                    2009019445

Typeset by Thompson Type in 11/14 Adobe Garamond

For Wang Chen and Xinyu

Contents

Figures and Tables

Figures

Tables

Acknowledgments

I received help from many people during the process of writing this book. Over the years, Jean Oi has never hesitated to give me intellectual support and encouragement, and she has continued to be a patient reader of my manuscripts and to offer comments and suggestions. I would also like to thank Andrew Walder for his suggestions on the manuscript and for his encouragement. Ever since I became interested in contentious politics in China, I have benefited from, among many others, the works by Kevin O'Brien and Lianjiang Li and from my communications with them. When the book manuscript was under review at the Stanford University Press, Kevin O'Brien was one of the two anonymous reviewers. His comments and suggestions helped me to place the case of China in a broader theoretical context. I also wish to thank the other anonymous reviewer whose insightful suggestions helped me to clarify issues about my framework as well as the process of interactions among the different parties involved in collective resistance in China.

I would like to thank Shi Fayong, Guo Jiguang, and Li Siliang for their assistance in collecting the data for this book. I also wish to thank Virginia Unkefer and Margaret Pinette for their editorial assistance. Research for this book was partly financed by the Research Grants Council of Hong Kong (640108) and the Chiang Ching-kuo Foundation (RG008-P-07).

At Stanford University Press, I wish to thank Stacy Wagner and Jessica Walsh for their patience and their support for the book.

Part of Chapter Five originally appeared in "Disaggregating the State: Networks and Collective Resistance in Shanghai" (by Fayong Shi and Yongshun

Cai), *The China Quarterly* (published by Cambridge University Press), volume 186: pp. 314–332 (2006). I wish to thank Cambridge University Press and Fayong Shi for allowing me to include this article in Chapter Five.

Finally, I would like to thank my family for their support for my research over the years. My wife, Wang Chen, has been the source of support and encouragement ever since I began my academic life. I also wish to thank my daughter, Xinyu, for the joyful moments she has given me. Although she believed that I should write interesting books for kids, she tolerated my spending much time on the research for this project. This book is dedicated to them.

Collective Resistance in China

ONE

Introduction

Popular resistance has become an important mode of political participation in China since the early 1990s. Various groups of people, including workers, peasants, and homeowners, have resorted to this mode of action to protect or pursue their interests.[1] Numerous contentious incidents have put serious pressure on the party-state. It is against this background that building a so-called harmonious society has recently become a top priority of the central party-state.[2] The collective acts of resistance have occurred not only because there have been widespread violations of citizens' rights but also because this mode of action helps citizens to defend or pursue their legitimate rights. As elsewhere, people stage collective resistance not simply because they want to send a signal of impatience or frustration but also because "they have some reason to think it will help their cause."[3] In China, some protestors have been successful in their resistance,[4] and, more importantly, their resistance has also led or contributed to changes in some unfavorable policies.

On the other hand, popular contention is by no means an easy or safe undertaking in China. In recent years, many participants in non-regime-threatening collective resistance have been detained, arrested, or imprisoned.[5] For example, in a county in the Guangxi Autonomous Region, peasants from a village resisted a 2004 court ruling regarding ownership of a piece of land. In January 2005, the local government arrested twenty-seven peasant activists. When more than 200 villagers approached the local authorities demanding the release of the activists, they were accused of attacking state agencies, and about 110 were detained. Seventeen villagers were sentenced to jail terms of up to eight years, ten were sent to labor camps for up to two years, and another eighty-two were released on bail after paying between 2,000 and 8,000 yuan.[6] The limitations to popular resistance also lie in the fact that the government may refuse to adjust policies that disadvantage certain groups despite their grievances and resistance.

That authoritarian governments should use suppression to deal with disobedient citizens is not surprising: In democracies, politicians face the pressure of (re)election and therefore have to be cautious when using repressive tactics. They are, thus, more tolerant of nonviolent dissident behavior and may use a mix of concessions and repression to suppress such actions when necessary. In contrast, political leaders in authoritarian regimes, who are less concerned with election, rely more on repression to demonstrate the state's power and determination to protect the political system.[7] In the communist regimes of Eastern Europe, for example, "legalized repression" was used to silence citizens.[8] "By and large, popular resentment, though profound, did not manifest itself openly," Kecskemeti explains, as "protesting in public was not only prohibitively risky but also futile, since no potential alternative to the prevailing system was visible."[9]

This mixed picture of the outcome of popular resistance in China raises two important questions. Why do some instances of resistance succeed while others fail in this nondemocratic regime? When is popular resistance more likely to contribute to policy changes? This study aims to answer these questions and promote an understanding of the operation of the Chinese political system and of contentious politics in a nondemocratic setting. To explain why some actions succeed while others fail, we need to examine the mechanisms through which people staging resistance exercise influence or the factors that affect the outcomes of their actions. This study shows that both the government, which is responsible for dealing with popular resistance, and the resisters face constraints in their interactions with each other. The resisters' chance of success lies in their ability to exploit the constraints facing the government or to (re)shape the latter's cost-benefit calculations in a way that suppressing or ignoring an act of resistance is not a feasible or desirable option.

Protest Outcomes in China

As the ultimate end of collective action such as social movements is to bring about change, recent research on collective action has paid increasing attention to outcomes.[10] Gamson suggests that the outcomes of social movements or protests fall into two basic clusters, "one concerned with the fate of the challenging group as an organization and one with the distribution of new advantages to the group's beneficiary."[11] Subsequent research has expanded on Gamson's work.[12] The current consensus is that the outcomes of collective action may take different forms, including political, economic, social, and cultural changes.[13] Consequently, the outcomes of social protests can be divided into three categories: (1) the outcome of individual incidents of collective action; (2) the aggregate impact of collective action staged by members of a social group; and (3) the enduring or indirect effect of social protests. This book explores the factors that affect these three types of outcomes of popular contention in China.

Research on social movements or protests has pointed to the different factors that affect the effectiveness and outcomes. One is the political opportunity structure that determines whether social movements can rise or develop in the first place.[14] A second group of factors is the power of a protesting group, which has to do with the protesting group's solidarity, organizational bases, and resources.[15] Collective action tactics are also found to influence the effectiveness of protests, especially among politically weak groups.[16] Finally, the chance of success has much to do with the protesters' demands, which determine the cost of making concessions on the part of the actor being targeted. For example, groups that intend to displace those in power or make broad changes in the political system are unlikely to succeed.[17]

All these findings shed important light on the outcomes of social protests in China by pointing to some of the basic conditions for successful action. But many of these findings are based on research on social movements in democracies. One factor that makes the handling of social protests in China different from that of many social movements in democracies is the role of the government. Social movements in democracies may not directly target the government or may not have a specific target at all. Governments in democracies are thus less sensitive to such actions if they do not seriously violate the law. Indeed, citizens in these regimes can even get permission for holding demonstrations. In contrast, governments in authoritarian regimes are much more sensitive to popular resistance. The occurrence of such incidents may signal problems with social control or the weakness of the government because such events are not supposed to occur in a regime where citizens are denied the right to disrupt the system.[18]

Authoritarian governments' high sensitivity to popular resistance implies that they are more committed to the settlement of collective action than are their counterparts in democracies. In research on the settlement of protests in democracies, the strategies used by the police are an important focus.[19] In research on protests in China, more attention needs to be paid to the interactions between the governments and the protesters. This does not mean that the police in China do not play an important role in dealing with collective action.[20] However, the decision on how to handle collective incidents, especially large ones, is generally made by the government. For example, a survey of more than 1,000 police officers in Fujian province in 2005 showed that 80 percent reported that the ultimate decision on the settlement of collective incidents was made by the party committee and/ or the government or their top leaders and not by the police.[21] Therefore, protest outcomes in China are often directly affected or determined by the response of the government at the local or central level.

The Rationale behind Government Response in China

Research on the government's reaction to collective action in democracies reveals the following modes of response: tolerance, repression, concessions, or a combination of concessions and repression.[22] However, this research has generally focused on one level of the government (e.g., the national level). In China, local governments rather than the central government have most frequently been targeted by protesters. This is the case because, first, local authorities may directly violate citizens' rights, distort the central government's policies, or fail to protect citizens' rights.[23] County, township, or city governments or their agencies are much more frequently sued by citizens than is the provincial or central government.[24] Second, the concentration of power implies the concentration of responsibility. Local authorities are targeted because they are responsible for daily governance and are believed to have the power and responsibility to address citizens' grievances.[25] Given the power of the local government, when competing groups fight against each other (businesses versus citizens, for example),[26] the outcome is largely determined by the government, which has decisive influence over the legal system and commerce at each level.

On the other hand, local governments in China are embedded in the political hierarchy topped by the central government. This political system grants local governments conditional autonomy: They have considerable autonomy in dealing with popular resistance while facing constraints imposed by the central government. Therefore, the chance of success depends not only on the particular local governments that are targeted by protestors but also on the interaction between different levels of state authorities.

Many studies on popular resistance in China have shown that a favorable environment for protest in the Chinese context does not necessarily result from significant changes in the political system that create political opportunities.[27] Instead, opportunities for resistance in China normally arise from the divide between state authorities at different levels (i.e., the central versus the local). Given the political hierarchy, it has been commonly accepted that intervention from the central government or upper-level local governments is a crucial way of achieving successful resistance in China.[28] But what has been inadequately explored is under what circumstances such intervention is possible. In other words, why have some instances been subject to intervention while many others have not? Under what circumstances is successful resistance possible in the absence of intervention from above? Why has the government changed certain policies but not others, although both kinds of policy have caused grievances and resistance? Answering these questions requires a systematic examination of the constraints and power of the governments at different levels, in particular the costs of concessions incurred by the government in dealing with popular contention.

This book suggests that the governments at different levels may have different perceptions of costs and benefits in addressing citizens' resistance and that their perceptions shape their choice of the mode of response, thereby determining not only the opportunity for resistance but also the outcome. For analytical convenience, I divide the state authorities in China into the central government and local governments. Both levels of government may adopt one of the following modes of response to deal with popular resistance: (1) concessions (i.e., citizens' demands are met); (2) concessions with discipline (i.e., citizens' demands are met, but some or all participants are punished); (3) tolerance (i.e., citizens' demands are ignored, but the government also tolerates their resistance); and (4) repression (i.e., citizens' demands are ignored, and some or all participants are punished).

A crucial factor that makes the central government behave differently than local governments is its greater interest in protecting the regime's legitimacy.[29] Legitimacy is about the political system's worthiness to be recognized.[30] Given that the central government is more responsible for the operation of the political system or it largely represents the regime, it has a greater interest in protecting the regime's legitimacy. In contrast, local officials in

China are more concerned with policy implementation or task fulfillment (e.g., maintaining social stability) and local issues; thus, legitimacy is not their main concern.[31] A simple comparison of the incentive structures faced by the two levels of government reveals that the central government's more serious concern about legitimacy helps to make it more tolerant than local governments of non-regime-threatening popular resistance.

The central and local governments incur two types of costs when concessions are made: (1) economic and/or political costs; and (2) signs of weakness (Table 1.1). Addressing citizens' complaints may require the expenditure of financial resources (economic costs). It may also require the government to correct its practices or policies or discipline state agents deemed responsible for the grievances or resistance (political costs). The cost of showing weakness is that making concessions may trigger more demands or actions. If the cost of showing weakness is considered to be the same for the two levels of government, then the central government incurs a smaller cost than the local government does when making concessions. First, when the central government intervenes in a dispute and makes concessions, it often requires the local government to address citizens' grievances with local financial resources. Thus, the local government has to shoulder the cost. Second, when malfeasant or irresponsible local officials are disciplined, the local government incurs a heavier loss because it relies more directly on these officials for local governance than the central government does. As far as the benefits are concerned, if stopping resistance is equally desirable to the two levels of government, the central government gains more because legitimacy is more important to the central government than to the local government.

In the case of repression, the two levels of government also incur two types of costs: (1) loss of legitimacy and (2) risk from repression (Table 1.1). Repressing citizens' resistance with legitimate claims damages the regime's legitimacy. For the reasons discussed above, the central government faces a higher cost from losing legitimacy than does the local government when repression is used.

The other type of cost incurred from repression is the risk arising from ineffective or failed repressive measures. For the central government, the risk is that ineffective repression leads to more serious or regime-threatening resistance. This possibility (or the risk) is rather small given the power of the central party-state in China. In contrast, the local government faces a more serious risk in repressing resistance. For one, ineffective repression may cause the escalation of resistance, which signals the local government's

TABLE I.I
Costs and Benefits in Concessions and Repression

	Benefits	Costs
Concessions	a. Stopping resistance b. Gaining legitimacy	a. Economic and/or political costs b. Signs of weakness
Repression	Deterring resistance	a. Loss of legitimacy b. Risks in repressive measures

SOURCE: Author's summary.

failure in maintaining social stability. For another, forceful repression that results in serious casualties will damage regime legitimacy.[32] In either situation, the central government will intervene, and local officials may be punished. However, the local government will face a small cost from repression if it is able to use the modes of repression that carry little risk (given that legitimacy is not its main concern). Hence, when the risk from repression is low for both levels of government, the local government is more likely to use repression than is the central government.

Nonetheless, although the central government is more tolerant of citizens' resistance, its concessions are conditional. When the central government decides to make concessions to citizens, it often means that it will intervene in the conflict between citizens and the local government. This is likely when the central government feels pressure to stop the resistance and protect regime legitimacy. Conversely, the central government is very unlikely to intervene in disputes that are peaceful and small in scale simply because the pressure for intervention is small.

These conditions for the central government's intervention affect the local governments' responses. Local governments will use concessions or concessions with discipline to stop citizens' resistance quickly when facing intervention or a threat of intervention from the central government. However, in the absence of intervention or when the likelihood of intervention is negligibly small, local governments assume considerable autonomy in choosing the mode of response. Concessions will be difficult if (1) the local government faces high economic or political costs; and (2) partial concessions or tolerance results in persistent resistance that threatens social stability or the images of local leaders. In these circumstances, repression is a low-cost option.

The incentive structure faced by the two levels of government in China is crucial to our understanding of the outcomes of collective resistance. From the perspective of protesters or resisters, their chance of success, either in individual instances of resistance or in the case of policy change, is jointly determined by the type of demand, which determines the costs of concessions incurred by the government, and the forcefulness of their resistance. Their ability to achieve successful resistance thus depends on whether they can effectively exploit the constraints faced by the two levels of government. In this book, I define the success or failure of citizen resistance in light of the goals claimed by the participants. An instance is seen as successful if the participants achieve their goal entirely or partly.

Seeking Success

It is not new to apply the cost-benefit approach to analyzing government responses to popular contention.[33] What needs to be stressed is that neither the cost nor the benefits to the government should be treated as fixed or predetermined. The government's perception of the cost and benefits is weighed against the power of the resisters or the forcefulness of their action. In China, although the citizens are generally weak in relation to the government, the nonmonolithic nature of the party-state implies that there does exist the political space for successful resistance. Therefore, the outcome of popular resistance should be viewed as the result of a dynamic interaction between the government and the protestors. This is crucial to understanding the resisters' chance of success because it points to the importance of strategies, resources, and other factors that affect the power of the participants. The dynamic interaction can also be understood as a process of creating or expanding opportunities for resistance. Political opportunities are found to affect the efficacy of social movements,[34] but the opportunities may not be predetermined. They can be created when protestors resort to certain modes of action or strategies.[35]

In China, citizens' resistance is mostly directed at local governments; or at least it starts by targeting local governments. The incentive structure discussed above suggests that it is inaccurate to assume that local governments in China are always reluctant to make concessions if the cost of doing so is small. The difficulty of making concessions lies in those cases with high-cost demands. However, because the most serious constraint on local officials is that imposed by upper-level authorities, the citizens can stage successful action if they are able to make the local government eager to stop popular contention while preventing it from relying on suppression. A fundamental way of achieving this goal is to seek or threaten to seek favorable intervention from higher authorities. This is possible when participants are able to gain extra leverage over local officials, generate support from within the state, or stage powerful disruptive action to strengthen their intervention-seeking ability.

GAINING EXTRA LEVERAGE

In China, a protesting group can seek intervention from upper-level authorities, including the central government, through permitted channels (e.g., petitions) or noninstitutionalized action, such as protests. In using permitted channels, a groups' intervention-seeking ability is affected by the timing of its action in the sense that, if an issue is high on the agenda of the central or provincial government, the window of opportunity is more accessible. But not all citizens' issues are high on the agenda of the central or provincial government. Moreover, citizen resistance may still be ignored even if an issue is of high importance. For example, when citizen complaints are numerous, the threshold for central or provincial government intervention is inevitably raised. Therefore, an important factor that affects a group's ability to seek intervention is whether it can find extra leverage over malfeasant or irresponsive local officials.

Resisters' extra leverage means extra constraints on local officials, which may make the local officials more responsive or accountable. In China, it is not uncommon for malfeasant or irresponsive local officials to be exempted by upper-level authorities despite citizens' complaints or resistance. This is because, in addition to the financial resources needed to address citizens' grievances, the disciplining of local state agencies or their officials is a sensitive political issue, and the political cost involved may deter upper-level authorities from doing so. As a result, many of the grievances sent by citizens through "rightful resistance" may simply be ignored by upper-level state authorities.[36] This is the fundamental reason why the violation of citizens' rights or the ignorance of citizens' injustices by state authorities has recurred in China despite the enactment of laws or regulations.

One method for the disgruntled to prevent upper-level authorities from ignoring lower-level agents' misconduct or irresponsiveness is to lower the political cost of discipline. Other things being equal, the upper-level authority is more willing to punish agents who have committed multiple acts of misconduct as opposed to those who have committed fewer. The authority is also more willing to punish those who have committed serious misconduct. When possible, protesters can highlight the multiple acts of misconduct of local officials, their serious misconduct, or even their crimes (e.g., corruption), although some of the misconduct may not be the causes of the protesters' grievances. As a result, if local officials fail to address citizens' grievances or try to repress their demands, the citizens can reveal or threaten to reveal local officials' other types of malfeasance to upper-level authorities. This method of issue connection poses risks or threats to targeted officials because some of the reported misconduct may be seen as unacceptable by upper-level authorities, thereby triggering intervention. Consequently, those local officials who are worried about citizens' reporting on their misconduct may be more responsive to the citizens' grievances and even make concessions to silence them.

SEEKING SUPPORT FROM WITHIN THE STATE

A second way for resisters to achieve success in popular contention is to receive external support or to seek alliances in or outside the political system. Allies can provide resources and make the system more open to protest demands, thereby providing important aid to weak groups. Lipsky points out that the essence of political protest consists of activating third parties to participate in a controversy in ways that are favorable to the protest's goals.[37] As a matter of fact, gaining external support has been seen as a precondition for weak groups' success. Jenkins and Perrow argue: "When deprived groups do mobilize, it is due to the interjection of external resources . . . Success comes when there is a combination of sustained outside support and disunity and/or tolerance on the part of political elites."[38] This can be true for weak groups regardless of the political system.

In China, there may also be external support, such as media exposure, that provides significant help to the people in defense of their rights. Nevertheless, because the state controls political power and most political resources, seeking support from within the state is often necessary. This is also possible because the Chinese state is not monolithic, and there are differences not only between different levels of government but also between different state agencies at the same level. These differences imply that some state actors may be more receptive to the demands of the disgruntled than others will be. In other words, these differences may create latent opportunities for successful resistance, but participants have to activate such latent opportunities through effective means.

O'Brien and Li show that some state agents may support citizens' claims because the enforcement of certain policies benefits their agencies.[39] At other times, an alliance with state agents may not be based on state agencies' organizational interests. In Chinese society, where politics is less institutionalized than in well-established democracies, individuals have important influence in the operation of the political system. This creates the possibility for some citizens to generate support from within the state through personal networks. Chinese society is characterized by the permeation of personal connections, or *guanxi*, in social and political settings.[40] Therefore, an important channel through which the disgruntled seek support from inside the state is to mobilize their personal connections with people who have either political power (e.g., government officials) or political influence (e.g., journalists). Social networks or connections are important political assets of the citizens. Certainly, not all citizens have such connections, and their access to political resources based on networks may vary considerably.

STAGING FORCEFUL ACTION

Not all citizens whose interests are violated can gain extra leverage or obtain support from within the state, but some of these people may resort to more disruptive modes of action to succeed. Certainly, such success is also conditional. Piven and Cloward believe that "to be ignored or punished is what the poor ordinarily expect from government."[41] This is the case because the costs and risks involved in repressing a weak target are small compared with those associated with the repression of a powerful opponent.[42] By the same token, powerful or better-organized groups have enhanced opportunities. This helps to explain the efficacy of organized action. For example, Shorter and Tilly find that, in France (from 1915 through 1935), strikes with unions present were less likely to fail than strikes that lacked union backing.[43] Organizational bases are seen as an important indicator of group strength. McAdam, Tarrow, and Tilly argue that, in democracies, "would-be activists must either create an organizational vehicle or utilize an existing one and transform it into an instrument of contention."[44]

In China, more often than not, the disgruntled lack an organizational basis for understandable reasons. But this does not mean that Chinese citizens are unable to stage powerful action such as protests or demonstrations. As detailed in subsequent chapters, there has been successful disruptive or noninstitutionalized action in China in recent years. The recurrence of such incidents reveals the existence of mobilization mechanisms despite the political system. When resorting to noninstitutionalized action, a protesting group's intervention-seeking ability is determined by its power to prevent the government from ignoring its demands. A few factors often make the upper-level government regard intervention as necessary: (1) casualties from the resistance (e.g., deaths of participants), (2) media exposure, and (3) the number of participants in the resistance. Casualties and media exposure can generate serious pressure on regime legitimacy, while the number of people indicates the scope of resentment and the potential disruptive consequences. Hence, a combination of casualties with media exposure or with a large number of participants is very likely to invite intervention from the central government or upper-level local governments. At other times, when citizens' resistance is forceful, local governments may make concessions without intervention from above because they have felt the threat of such intervention.

It is also found that collective action tactics may contribute to the effectiveness of a protest. McAdam writes: "Lacking institutionalized power, challengers must devise protest techniques that offset their powerlessness."[45] The effectiveness of the same tactics varies across issues, protesters, places, and times. This is especially true of disruptive tactics or violence, in the sense that studies on the effectiveness of these tactics yield mixed results.[46] Consider research on the use of violence in strikes. Snyder and Kelly show that violent strikes by Italian workers were much more likely to fail than were peaceful work stoppages.[47] This observation contradicts the findings by Shorter and Tilly, who concluded from their study of strikes in France that workers' use of violence tended to have a positive effect on strike outcomes.[48] Others suggest that violence does not have an independent effect on the outcome of protests.[49]

Like protesters elsewhere, Chinese citizens have also used certain tactics to increase their chance of success. Yet not all tactics are acceptable to the government. Innovative peaceful tactics may increase the chance of success when they place pressure on the government while denying it legitimate grounds for suppression. Some disruptive tactics are also acceptable by the government if they are not destructive. However, the use of violence tends to be less tolerated by the government. As a matter of fact, in resistance with demands that are difficult to meet, the use of violence is often counterproductive and increases the likelihood of suppression and thereby the risks to participants, especially when the scale of resistance is small.

It must be pointed out that the conditions for intervention from above also determine that many cases of resistance are ignored by state authorities. The central or provincial government is unlikely to intervene in disputes that are peaceful and small in scale, simply because the pressure to do so is small. The central government may also fail to intervene in some large-scale incidents when the political costs of disciplining local governments or their officials are high. Specifically, the central government is less willing to intervene in cases that involve high-ranking local officials, particularly at the provincial level, as opposed to low-ranking local officials at the township or county level.[50] Therefore, citizens tend to encounter serious or insurmountable difficulties in mounting successful resistance if their cases involve local governments at the city and provincial levels.

Social Protests and Policy Adjustment

Popular resistance in China, as elsewhere, not only helps participants achieve success specific to them but also exerts influence on matters of government policy. In a pioneering study on the impact of popular contention in rural China, O'Brien and Li found that collective action affects policy implementation in a number of ways: Popular protests against the poor implementation of government policies can provide central authorities with crucial intelligence about policy violations and help them correct problems, or popular contention may improve policy implementation by mobilizing sympathetic and powerful advocates who have a stake in seeing that a policy is upheld.[51] In this book, I show that in addition to its influence on policy *implementation*, citizen resistance also contributes or leads to policy *adjustment* on the part of the government. I define policy adjustment as the revision or abolition of policies that have directly caused or failed to address citizens' grievances, as well as the creation of new policies to address the problems that have triggered resistance or to accommodate protesters' demands.

Collective action may need to meet a number of conditions to be effective. But when it succeeds (and sometimes even when it fails), it can have other important impacts, in addition to bringing success to individual protesting groups. To the extent that "social movements are formed to express dissatisfaction with existing policy in a given area," as della Porta and Diani maintain,[52] one area in which their effects can be felt is public policy. Amenta and Young hold that instances of collective action produce "collective benefits," groupwise goods made available to all group members.

They explain, "the greater the value and type of such goods achieved by any challenge or challenger, the greater the impact."[53] Policy changes are thus significant accomplishments of popular resistance.[54]

Yet the rationales behind policy adjustment can be complex. In democracies, policy outcomes are likely to be the result of a number of contingent and interactive forces.[55] In other words, many different factors or intervening variables, such as movement activists, public opinion, interest groups, parties, and executives, may combine to shape movement outcomes. Therefore, it is not easy to assess the impact of citizen resistance on policy changes or, more generally, on movement outcomes. As Giugni suggests, the principal difficulty is finding a way to establish a causal relationship between a series of events that can reasonably classify as social movement actions and an observed change in society, be it minor or fundamental, durable or temporary.[56] "While it is possible to correlate outcomes with movement efforts," Tarrow also points out, "it is not as easy to identify particular movement actions as the cause for a specific outcome."[57]

The difficulty of isolating the effect of movements has led some scholars to propose cross-national comparisons to identify the link between movement actions and those consequences.[58] Perhaps a comparative approach can shed even more light on cases that occur in the same country because of the shared socioeconomic, cultural, and political contexts.[59] This book addresses the relationship between popular contention and policy changes in China by comparing five social groups that staged resistance in light of their demands and the forcefulness of their resistance.

In China, national policies that do not favor certain social groups are made by the central government. Some policies may place certain groups of people at a disadvantage or provide too many loopholes through which local governments can abuse power. Likewise, an ostensible absence of policies may grant local governments too much autonomy. Citizen resistance highlights these inequities and points to the need of policy adjustment. As in the case of dealing with individual instances of resistance, the government's decision regarding policy adjustment is shaped by two sets of factors, the cost of adjustment and the forcefulness of resistance. These two sets of factors affect the occurrence, pace, and degree of policy adjustment.

Research on policy outcomes in democracies addresses the relationship between movement and policy outcomes by examining the mechanism of legislation—the relationship among movements, their characteristics, and legislative results.[60] In this approach, public opinion is an intervening variable given that, in democracies, politicians or legislators tend to modify their policy preferences to fit shifting public opinion and thereby retain electoral support.[61] Because such research is based on the voting behavior of legislators in democracies, the cost of making such policy changes has not been adequately analyzed. In contrast, in the case of China, the concentration of the decision-making power in the hands of the central government makes it feasible to analyze the impact of popular contention on policy adjustment by examining the pressures faced by the government as well as the costs it is willing to pay to bring an end to social grievances and popular resistance.

As far as the forcefulness of resistance is concerned, it is determined by a social group's power to stage powerful action and its access to external support or extra leverage. A group that is able to stage widespread, frequent, and large-scale (often disruptive but not necessarily destructive) resistance is better able to put pressure on the government. Forceful resistance not only threatens the social order, but it also enhances the salience of an issue. In democracies, legislators have a strong incentive to obtain accurate information about what voters really want.[62] Like politicians in democracies, the upper-level government in an authoritarian regime desires to know about the local situation. But a government that does not allow a free press has a harder time acquiring accurate information about the situation at the grassroots level.[63] This difficulty, however, does not always put authoritarian governments at a disadvantage. When enacting certain policies or addressing citizen grievances is costly, government officials can pretend not to know about the problem, thereby diffusing blame or directing it to the local government. Forceful resistance prevents the government from pretending not to know about a problem because the resistance makes the problem common knowledge to both the government and the general public.

Some groups may not be able to stage powerful disruptive action, but their issue may still become salient enough to trigger a policy adjustment. This happens under two circumstances. First, these groups receive support from other parties. As mentioned earlier, theorists of the political opportunity structure stress the importance of political alliances to the effectiveness of social movements. In China, the media are perhaps the most crucial third party in citizens' resistance, despite the party's control. Second, the salience of citizens' complaints is also affected by the complaints' relationship to other issues. A social group's position will be strengthened if its issue is tied to other salient issues in a mutually beneficial way (that is, solving one issue helps to solve the others) and will be weakened if it is tied to other salient issues in a mutually exclusive way (as when the government can afford to solve only one problem). When different social groups compete for attention and resources from the government, the impact of a group's resistance is determined not only by the forcefulness of its resistance but also by that of other groups.

Though salient grievances tend to be addressed by the government through policy adjustment, the pace and degree of such policy adjustment will be determined by the costs involved. As a result, the government sometimes adjusts a policy without making any fundamental changes to it. Likewise, it could postpone important changes because of a lack of resources or a consensus among the decision makers. In other instances, the government simply abolishes an existing policy and makes a new one. The cost of policy adjustment, together with the forcefulness of popular resistance, allows us to examine why some groups are better able than others to receive favorable policy responses from the government.

Government and the Indirect Effect of Popular Resistance

As elsewhere, the consequences of popular resistance in China are not limited to success or failure specific to a protesting group or policy adjustment;[64] there can be indirect or enduring consequences that are unintended or unanticipated. But such consequences are even more difficult to assess. In his study of civil rights movements in Mississippi, Andrews tries to establish a causal relationship between movements and social change by combining quantitative analysis and case studies. He proposes a three-part movement infrastructure model that evaluates leadership, organizational structure, and resources to explain the enduring impacts of movements.[65] Andrews finds that the characteristics of the movement infrastructures in different counties in Mississippi in earlier years influenced a number of local issues in subsequent years, including voter registration, poverty alleviation, and school desegregation. Organizational strength is thus an important indicator of a movement's enduring impact.

In contrast, protesting groups in China are mostly temporary communities without an organizational base. They protest when an issue arises and are no longer closely connected to one another once the issue disappears, although popular resistance may affect individual activists in some communities.[66] In this book, I show that collective resistance has also had an important indirect impact in China—the influence on state–citizen relations. Both the government and the citizens learn lessons from previous resistance. Popular resistance is changing how citizens and government officials view each other. Local officials are no longer constrained by ideological rhetoric when dealing with resistance. Depending on their past experiences, local governments may become more suppressive or more tolerant. Those citizens who encounter injustice, on the other hand, have little expectation that local officials will act solely on the basis of their moral responsibility, and they have limited confidence in a socialist government that claims to "serve the people's interests wholeheartedly." Instead, because they wish to see a law-observing government, they tend to frame their demands in legal language.[67]

Equally important, collective resistance has affected the central party-state's attitude toward interactions between the citizens and the local government. The central government has tried to make local officials more responsive to citizens' grievances by expending efforts to institutionalize state–citizen interactions and strengthen legal institutions.[68] At the same time, the central party-state remains tolerant (sometimes unbelievably so) toward local governments' suppression of popular resistance because too much tolerance or concession is believed to trigger more resistance, especially when the society is replete with grievances. Therefore, the government's concerns about legitimacy can be compromised by the cost of concessions at both the central and local levels. However, persistent resistance remains a pressure on the government because, if government agencies fail to follow the law, citizens may also resort to illegal means of action.

Notes on the Data

In recent years, there have been many reports on incidents of collective action in China, but most of these reports do not provide enough information for systematic study. Indeed, there is very limited information on the outcome of these incidents. This study does not overcome the problem of limited cases, but it reduces it by tapping different sources. The data used in this book come from several different sources, including a survey, fieldwork, and secondary sources.[69] A national general social survey (China General Social Survey 2005) of 10,372 residents in twenty-eight provinces or cities (at the administrative level of the province) was conducted in 2005 (see Appendix A). Its results are used here mainly to examine the magnitude of social conflicts and the modes of conflict resolution in China.

Another important source of data used in this book is my collection of 266 cases of collective action (see Appendix B). Five of the 266 cases were riots in which participants did not have clearly specified goals, and these five cases are included only in the analysis of the occurrence of violence in Chapter Seven. The 266 cases were collected from about fifty newspapers, including overseas newspapers, nine books and journals, and more than fifty websites, in addition to my fieldwork in China. It must be pointed out that publications permitted by the government at different levels in China are not necessarily biased against protesters. It is not rare for reports to be sympathetic to protesters and to be critical of the methods local governments employ to handle collective action. The 266 cases were selected using the criterion that there is information on the type of participants, the number of participants, the mode of action, the presence or absence of leaders, and the outcome of the action. All these cases are nonpolitical in the sense that the participants did not raise political demands that challenged the political system.[70] Cases concerning religious issues or ethnical conflicts were excluded.

Needless to say, this collection of 266 cases is rather small in comparison to the large number of instances of collective acts in China. They may not be systematically enough for rigorous statistical tests either. This collection, however, includes cases that occurred in twenty-seven provinces or provincial-level cities in China between 1994 and 2007. Moreover, my collection of large-scale protests is relatively comprehensive because such protests are now difficult to cover up as a result of the emergence of new technologies, especially the Internet (see Appendix C).

A third major source is the collective petitions reported in the yearbooks of some cities and provinces (see Appendices D through F). These are perhaps the only publicly accessible sources on collective resistance that are relatively systematic for a comparison between different cities.

The Organization of the Book

The chapters that follow investigate citizen resistance in China in a number of different contexts to develop the argument about the conditions for effective resistance laid out here. I begin by assessing the magnitude of social conflicts in China based on the national survey and discussing the modes of conflict resolution in China in Chapter Two. I show that there is a discrepancy between the people's intentions and their actual actions in addressing social conflicts. Facing disputes with state agencies, some citizens choose to tolerate them, whereas others may escalate their actions. Collective resistance becomes an option because it is believed to increase the odds of success or because citizens lack other alternatives.

Chapter Three discusses the conditions for successful resistance and the difficulties or obstacles resisters encounter in staging successful resistance. I show that the cost of making concessions and the forcefulness of citizens' resistance significantly shape local governments' behaviors. The difficulties in successful resistance lie in the fact that local governments are generally unwilling to make concessions to participants when the disputes are caused by the governments themselves. This is particularly true when citizens' resistance is not forceful enough. Moreover, staging resistance can be risky because local governments have considerable discretion in punishing participants. I use the case of peasant resistance to rural land use to illustrate these difficulties.

I then turn to cases of successful resistance in the following three chapters. Chapter Four shows that Chinese citizens who stage resistance may gain extra leverage over local officials by applying multiple constraints on the latter. More specifically, citizens may strengthen their position versus that of local officials by linking their grievances to other issues that local officials are also responsible for. An effective use of issue linkage can prevent local officials from using suppression because it will prompt citizens to pursue other related issues that threaten local officials' reputations.

In Chapter Five, I show how citizens can seek favorable intervention from above by using another nonconfrontational tactic. I demonstrate that personal connections with people who have political influence or resources prove to be an important weapon for citizens. Such connections, of course, are not available to many people in Chinese society. As Chapter Six demonstrates, a more common mode of action is to place pressure on local governments and officials through disruptive collective action. This mode of action can be effective because it poses a threat to local officials, paralyzes public order, or both, but it often requires a large number of participants to succeed and has accompanying risks. I also demonstrate that intervention from higher authorities in disruptive action is highly conditional.

Chapter Seven discusses the limits of the state's tolerance of citizens' use of disruptive tactics by focusing on the use of violence. The use of violence is generally illegal in China, but it has frequently occurred in popular resistance. I explain why participants use this method despite the corresponding high risk by proposing a group-structure approach. This approach argues that participants' perceptions of risks are affected by the structure of the protesting groups. Violence is mostly frequently used in those protesting groups whose participants face little constraint and have a weak sense of risk. Nonetheless, because the use of violence is not necessarily a strategic choice, I show that, among the cases I collected, the use of violence seems to reduce the odds of success.

Chapter Eight examines an important issue in popular resistance—the relationship between resistance and the government's policy response. I identify the factors that affect policy adjustments by comparing five social groups that have complained about their respective problems. While popular resistance in China almost always leads to some policy changes, the cost of policy adjustment and the forcefulness of the resistance affect the occurrence, the pace, and the degree of policy adjustment. Those groups that are able to stage powerful resistance tend to receive a fast policy response. Weak groups need to gain extra support to obtain a favorable policy response. Finally, Chapter Nine discusses the evolution of state–citizen relations in China as a result of citizen resistance.

TWO

Social Conflicts and Collective Resistance in China

China has witnessed numerous social conflicts in recent years. While the reasons for the conflicts are complex, perhaps the most important one is that citizens' legitimate or legal rights have been ignored by state agencies or businesses in the fast-changing socioeconomic context.[1] As in other non-democracies, such as the former Soviet Union,[2] China has multiple channels for political participation, including elections, petitions or contacting officials, lawsuits, reporting to the media, the use of personal networks, and noninstitutionalized actions, such as protests, demonstrations, strikes, or even attacks on state agencies.[3] But the availability of multiple channels by no means implies that they are effective. Factors such as the degree of accessibility, cost, and required knowledge account for the differences not only in the frequency of use of participation channels but also in the effectiveness of modes of action.

Using data from the China General Social Survey carried out in 2005 (see Appendix A), this chapter examines the magnitude of social conflicts in China in recent years as well as the modes of conflict resolution used in state–citizen conflicts. As elsewhere, an important rationale behind Chinese citizens' choice of the mode of political participation is the desire to increase their chance of success. Collective resistance becomes a choice of some citizens because they believe that this mode of action can increase the chance of success or because they do not have other alternative channels after they have failed in permitted channels. However, according to pertinent laws and government regulations, most modes of collective resistance in China are illegal. Despite this illegality, the recurrence of the many incidents of collective action reveals not only the political space for popular resistance but also the possible mechanisms of mobilization in this nondemocratic regime.

Social Conflicts in China: The Magnitude

Piven and Cloward explain that "protest movements do not arise during ordinary periods; they arise when large-scale changes undermine political stability." Such shifts, they explain, "giv[e] the poor hope and mak[e] insurgency possible in the first place."[4] Much of the literature on political opportunity structures has stressed this idea.[5] The increase in collective resistance in China does not fit this pattern well. It mainly has to do with the broad socioeconomic changes and reform measures that have threatened the interests of a vast number of people. Very few transitional economies have undergone industrial restructuring, urbanization, and the adoption of various market-oriented reforms simultaneously, as China is now doing. For example, the unprecedented reform of public enterprises in China from the second half of 1990s to the early 2000s threatened the interests of tens of millions of workers.[6] On the other hand, the lack of a strong legal system that can effectively restrain state power has led to state agents' repeated abuse of power at the expense of citizens.

Available statistics on social conflicts in China over the years are not systematic for understandable reasons, but available ones can still point to the drastic rise in the number of conflicts in recent years. For example, the courts accepted 4.26 million lawsuits in 1994, and this number rose by 90 percent to more than 8 million in 2003.[7] Most (around 86 percent) of these lawsuits are civil cases, but the number of administrative litigation cases in which state agencies were sued also increased from 35,000 to 87,900, or by 1.5 times, during this period of time. State agencies at both the central and local levels have been sued by citizens from almost all social groups.

Petitions are perhaps more indicative of the magnitude of conflicts in Chinese society.[8] The petition system was established in the 1950s. Over the years, the party organizations (e.g., the discipline inspection committee), the governments, the people's congresses, the courts, the procuracies, and the public security bureaus at the county level and higher have established reception offices or complaint departments to handle citizens' complaints. Citizens can present petitions by sending letters to pertinent authorities or by presenting petitions in person individually or collectively (to be discussed later). When petitioners fail to receive meaningful responses from local state authorities to whom they have appealed, some of them may choose to present petitions to upper-level authorities at the provincial or national level.[9]

Presenting petitions to upper-level state authorities has remained the most commonly used mode of action employed by citizens who have conflicts with state authorities ever since the system was established in the early 1950s.[10] Therefore, the number of petitions has been an important indicator of social change in China. Figure 2.1 shows the fluctuations in the number of petitions received by the General Office of the State Council in selected years between 1952 and 2005. Right after the Cultural Revolution, petitions were the dominant mode used by citizens seeking justice. Not surprisingly, the number of petitions rose drastically at that time. In 1978 and 1979, the numbers of petitions submitted to the central government were 510,000 and 570,000, respectively, as opposed to 209,300 in 1965. With the problems caused by the Cultural Revolution addressed, the number of petitions declined over the years and dropped to 297,900 in 1984. However, this number began to rise in 1994 and reached 586,400 in 2000 and 603,000 in 2005.[11] Nationwide, the number of petitions directed to the complaint agencies at the county level and above was 4.79 million in 1995, and it rose to

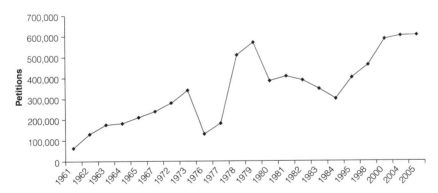

FIGURE 2.1 Petitions to the Central Government in Selected Years. SOURCES: Diao Jiecheng, *Renmin xinfang shilue* (A brief history of people's petitions) (Beijng: Beijng Jingji Xueyuan Chubanshe, 1996); Xiong Yihan, "Xinfang xiang hequchu?) (Where is the petition system heading?), *Ershi yi shiji* (The 21st century) 6 (2005): 91–95; http://news .sohu. com/20060429/n243070831.shtml (accessed May 1, 2006).

10.24 million in 2000 and 13.73 million in 2004.[12] These petitions include all kinds of problems that have occurred during the transitional period.

The China General Social Survey conducted in 2005 (hereafter the China GSS 2005) is also suggestive of the magnitude or frequency of social conflicts in China in recent years. This national survey covered more than 10,000 residents in twenty-eight provinces or provincial-level cities. In this survey, interviewees were asked to report whether or not they had had conflicts with other citizens or state authorities in the past four years (i.e., 2001 through 2004). Of the 10,372 people surveyed, urban residents accounted for 58.8 percent (or 6,098) and rural residents accounted for 41.2 percent (or 4,274). More than 9 percent reported that they had conflicts with other citizens in the past four years, while 2.5 percent reported conflicts with state authorities (Table 2.1). The data thus show that there were proportionally more civil conflicts than state–citizen disputes. The data also reveal that there is no significantly large difference between rural and urban residents in terms of the frequency of their disputes with state agencies.

The China GSS 2005 seems to suggest that the number of people who had conflicts with state authorities was rather limited. Landry and Tong's survey of about 7,710 people in 2003 found that roughly 6 percent (most of them peasants) reported that they had had one or more grievances against government agencies in the past twenty years.[13] The China GSS 2005 covers a much shorter time span, and therefore the proportion is understandably smaller. But this small percentage does not necessarily imply that the pressure of maintaining social stability faced by the party-state is not serious. For one, the data do not show the degree of confrontation of such conflicts. As discussed in subsequent chapters, there have been large-scale and even deadly confrontations between citizens and local governments in recent years. For another, state–citizen disputes are only part of the many conflicts in society. For example, a survey of about 1,000 police officers in

TABLE 2.1
Social Conflicts in China

	People Surveyed	Civil Disputes	Percent (%)	State-Citizen Disputes	Percent (%)
Urban residents	6,098	489	8.0	140	2.3
Rural residents	4,274	458	10.7	121	2.8
Total	10,372	947	9.1	261	2.5

SOURCE: China General Social Survey, 2005.

Fujian province in 2005 found that 54 percent reported incidents of collective action were primarily triggered by the inappropriate conduct of the government.[14] This finding, while pointing out government behavior as the major cause of social unrest, also reveals that other types of disputes may have also caused social disruptions.

The Choice of the Mode of Action

Chinese citizens have adopted different modes of action to address their disputes with state agencies or other social actors. An examination of their choice of the mode of action reveals citizens' propensities as well as the limitations of the existing mechanisms of conflict resolution. This section discusses citizens' modes of action as revealed in the China GSS 2005. Table 2.2 shows that, among those citizens who had conflicts with state authorities, going to the courts is the most commonly used method (i.e., 27 percent) despite the many problems associated with suing the state in China.[15] Approaching upper-level leaders was the second most commonly used method (i.e., 26.8 percent). Given that there have been a limited number of lawsuits against state agencies and large numbers of petitions to upper-level authorities or leaders, this finding is not expected. But because appealing to upper-level leaders and collective petitions are categorized as petitions, it can be concluded that petitioning pertinent agencies or leaders remains to be the most commonly used mode of action (i.e., 40.2 percent), which is in line with the findings of other studies.[16]

The survey data suggest that Chinese citizens tend to use the courts more frequently in addressing state–citizen disputes than in civil disputes (i.e.,

TABLE 2.2
Modes of Resolving State–Citizen Disputes

Modes of action	Total (%)	Urban (%)	Rural (%)
Law	27.1	32.9	21.5
Approaching upper-level leaders	26.8	29.3	24.0
No action	26.0	14.3	39.5
Approaching leaders of the agency concerned	18.3	22.1	16.5
Collective petition	13.4	16.4	9.9
Approaching the media	4.6	5.7	3.3
Miscellaneous	3.8	4.3	3.3
Total number of cases	261	140	121

SOURCE: China General Social Survey 2005.

NOTE: Some people took two or more modes of action.

27 percent versus 16 percent). In addressing civil disputes, about 31 percent of the people reported mediation by acquaintances, followed by approaching state authorities (e.g., village authorities) (i.e., 20 percent) and the use of law (i.e., 16 percent). In contrast, in addressing state–citizen disputes, the more frequent use of the law may be because mediation is less feasible in state–citizen disputes in the sense that it is not easy to find a third party. On the other hand, when state–citizen disputes arise, appealing to upper-level authorities may be less effective than lawsuits. For example, a survey of 632 peasants who made petitions in Beijing suggests that fewer than one percent of them reported successful petitions.[17] Before 2005 when the new directive on petitions was issued, complaint agencies could afford to be less responsive, which seriously damaged petitioners' confidence in the petition system. By comparison, one advantage of using the courts is that citizens receive a reply, whether or not it is the reply they want.

While the media have played an important role in helping citizens seeking justice in China,[18] the survey shows that only fewer than 5 percent of citizens chose to approach the media when they had conflicts with state authorities, perhaps because the media still face serious constraints in dealing with state authorities. While sensational incidents are likely to attract the attention of the media and the public, not all disputes are sensational.[19] As a matter of fact, citizens have great difficulties in gaining access to influential media like Chinese Central Television (CCTV). For example, the *Focus* program produced by CCTV is influential in the sense that the problems it uncovers are almost always immediately addressed.[20] It is thus frequently approached by people seeking justice. In the early 2000s, the program received about 300 letters and 200 telephone calls every day. While the total number of contacts was huge, the number of grievances investigated and broadcasted was negligible.[21]

What merits mentioning is that 26 percent of the respondents reported that they did not take action in disputes with state authorities or that they tolerated the disputes.[22] Given the power of state authorities in China, citizens' lack of confidence and the potential cost are perhaps the most important reasons for their lack of action. Citizens often encounter difficulties in dealing with state authorities regardless of the modes of action they take. As mentioned earlier, petitions may be useless. Lawsuits against state authorities may not be accepted by the courts or may not be fairly decided by the courts.[23] Although these hurdles do not always deter disgruntled citizens, they do discourage some citizens from taking action.

The survey also reveals some differences between rural and urban residents in terms of their choice of the mode of action. First, there is a difference in the frequency of using lawsuits between these two groups of people. While 33 percent of urban residents who had disputes with state authorities reported the use of lawsuits, only about 22 percent of rural residents reported using the courts (Table 2.2). It must be pointed out that the percentage of peasants is not small, but it is smaller than that of urban residents. This may not be surprising in that using lawsuits requires not only money but also legal knowledge. Compared with urban residents, rural residents are more likely to lack financial resources and the necessary legal knowledge. These disadvantages may also be an important reason for the second and also the biggest difference between these two groups of residents—almost 40 percent of rural residents chose not to take any action when disputes with state authorities, including the village authority, arose, as opposed to 14.3 percent of urban residents.

The above discussion points out the continuities and changes in citizens' use of the modes of conflict resolution in China. On one hand, some traditional methods, especially petitions, remain important tools for addressing state–citizen disputes. But suing state authorities has also become an important option, although this method has been more commonly used in urban areas than in rural areas. While these different mechanisms have helped resolve social conflicts in China, a large portion of citizens (i.e., 26 percent) who had conflicts with state authorities did not take any action. The lack of action is likely the result of the difficulties or costs involved in taking action, which reflects the problems with the existing mechanisms of conflict resolution.

THE DISCREPANCY BETWEEN BEHAVIORAL INTENTION AND ACTION

This section discusses the problems with the existing mechanisms by comparing citizens' behavioral intention and their actual actions to examine to what extent their intentions differ from the actual modes of action they have taken. As mentioned earlier, the China GSS 2005 reveals that most of the respondents reported that they did not have conflicts with other citizens or state authorities. In the survey, they were asked a hypothetical question of what they would do if there was such a conflict. A comparison between the answers to the hypothetical questions and the actual modes of action by those who did have disputes provides important clues regarding the rationale behind citizens' responses to disputes and thereby the inadequacies of certain mechanisms.

Table 2.3 shows three significant differences between people's behavioral intentions and their actual actions. The first concerns the use of the law. While 41.1 percent of the 10,111 people reported that they would use the courts if they had a conflict with state authorities, only 27 percent of those who did have such conflicts chose the courts in reality. The difference is particularly large among urban residents. While 50.5 percent of the 5,959 urban residents said they would use this method, only 33 percent of those who encountered such disputes actually went to court. To be sure, 33 percent of urban residents is by no means a small portion, but the difference of 17 percent may still suggest that the difficulty or cost of using the courts to deal with state authorities is a challenge to citizens. This difference (i.e., 6.8 percent) is not as large among rural residents. Therefore, although the use of the legal channel has become an important method used by citizens to deal with state agencies, the total number of administrative litigation cases is rather limited. Since 1990, when the Administrative Litigation Law took

TABLE 2.3
Behavioral Intention in State–Citizen Disputes

Rural Modes	Total		Urban		Rural	
	Intention (%)	Action (%)	Intention (%)	Action (%)	Intention (%)	Action (%)
Law	41.3	27.1	50.5	32.9	28.3	21.5
Approaching leaders of this agency	14.4	18.3	15.2	22.1	13.2	16.5
Approaching upper-level leaders	25.1	26.8	17.5	29.3	40.0	24.0
Collective Petition	2.3	13.4	2.0	16.4	2.7	9.9
Approaching media	4.2	4.6	5.8	5.7	1.8	3.3
No action	11.8	26.0	8.3	14.3	16.8	39.5
Miscellaneous	1.0	3.8	0.8	4.3	1.3	3.3
Total cases	10,111	261	5,958	140	4153	121

SOURCE: China General Social Survey 2005.

NOTE: Some people reported or took two or more modes of action.

effect, the number of administrative litigation cases has never exceeded 2 percent of the total number of lawsuits heard by the courts.[24]

A second significant difference is between the reported use of collective petitions and the actual use of this mode of action. Among the 10,111 respondents who did not have conflicts with state authorities, only 2.3 percent reported that they would use this method. However, among those who did have disputes with state authorities, 13.4 percent used it. This is particularly the case among urban residents. While 2 percent of the 5,958 urban residents said they would use this method, 16.4 percent of those who did have such disputes actually used it. A likely reason is that people used this method because of the ineffectiveness or high costs of alternative approaches.

The third large difference is between the reported use of tolerance and actual inaction, which has a significant implication for understanding popular resentment in China. While fewer than 12 percent of the 10,110 people reported that they would tolerate disputes with state authorities or take no action, the percentage was as high as 26 percent among those who had actual conflicts with state authorities. This is particularly obvious among rural residents. While 16.8 percent of them reported that they would tolerate such disputes, 39.5 percent of those who had actual conflicts with state authorities took no action. In other words, the difference is as large as 22.7 percent. In addition, 40 percent reported that they would approach upper-level leaders if they had conflicts with state authorities, while 24 percent of those who actually had such disputes used this method; the difference is as large as 16 percent.

It may not be surprising that there are differences between people's behavioral intention and their actual action. Unanticipated difficulties lead to such results.[25] Hence, the discrepancy between people's intentions and their actual actions is suggestive of the problems with the conflict-resolution mechanisms in China today. In addressing state–citizen disputes, although the courts are considered an important mechanism by citizens, various reasons deter them from using the courts. More significantly, the limited effectiveness of these redress mechanisms has driven citizens to choose two opposite options. One is that a large proportion of the people did not take any action. People's tolerance of injustice from state authorities does not mean that they are satisfied with the situation; instead, they may not take action because they lack resources or confidence. If this is the case, their resentment will not disappear and may erupt when opportunities arise. As discussed in subsequent chapters, such pent-up resentment has a powerful effect on mobilization, and it has been an important reason for some seemingly trivial incidents triggering large-scale riots with participation by people from different walks of life in recent years.

The other tendency is the escalation of action, such as the use of collective petitions. As discussed below, collective petitions are the basic mode of collective action in China. That proportionally more people used this mode of action in reality is crucial to understanding the occurrence of numerous incidents of collective action during the reform period. In the China GSS 2005, about 13.3 percent of 261 respondents (or thirty-five cases) used two or more methods to address their disputes with state authorities. Collective petitions were used in twelve of the thirty-five cases (i.e., 34 percent), which points to a scenario in which citizens who have a high stake in addressing the disputes may resort to more forceful modes of action, including other modes of collective action.[26] As a matter of fact, the numerous confrontations between resisters and the government or businesses suggest that the escalation of action has always been possible in popular resistance in China. The escalation of action suggests that what Schock has said is also true in China: "Participation in a nondemocratic regime's channels of political participation is not likely to succeed unless combined with noninstitutional pressure."[27] In this sense, the escalation of action may be seen as tactical escalation.

Collective Action in China

From 1993 to 2004, the number of incidents of collective action recorded nationwide rose from 8,700 to 74,000, or by 8.5 times.[28] The Ministry of Public Security revealed that the police investigated 87,000 cases of social disruption in 2005, which implies that these cases possibly involved violations of the law.[29] According to the Chinese Ministry of Public Security, an instance of disruptive action is an action that violates laws or regulations, disrupts the social order, threatens public security or other citizens' personal security, or damages public or private property. Such action includes disruptive collective petitions, strikes, protests, sit-ins, gatherings, demonstrations, traffic blockades, office blockades, attacks on state agencies, and confrontations with officials or the police, among other forms.[30]

In my collection of 266 cases that occurred in twenty-seven provinces between 1994 and 2007 (Appendix B), participants' modes of collective action are divided into the following categories: collective petitions (39 percent), protests or demonstrations (including strikes and riots) (32 percent), confrontations with the police, officials, or the business (24 percent), and attacks on state agencies (19 percent).[31] Participants in these incidents come from almost all social groups, including workers, retired workers, farmers, homeowners, demobilized soldiers, students, and business people.

China is not the only transitional economy that has seen an increase in collective action, but the increase of collective action in other transitional economies has largely been due to regime changes that relaxed constraints on participants. In Poland, for example, there were 7,443 strikes in 1993, as compared to 894 in 1989 (or 8.3 times more); similarly, workers in the former Soviet Union went on strike 3.5 times more often in 1992 (6,273 times) than they did in 1990 (1,771).[32] The large increase in the instances of resistance in China, on the other hand, has occurred without regime change. Moreover, most modes of collective action in China are illegal. Strikes are illegal according to the constitution; demonstrations require the approval of the police department; and the number of participants in a collective petition cannot exceed five. Confrontations with state agents or attacks on state agencies are certainly seen as crimes. Therefore, the occurrence of the many incidents of collective action reflects both the political space for resistance as well as the available mechanisms for mobilization among participants.

POLITICAL SPACE FOR COLLECTIVE ACTION

Changes within the administrative system are credited for creating this new political space for resistance in China. Bernstein and Lu hold that a decline in the effectiveness of state control has "weakened the ability of rural public security to control protests, crime, and social disorder."[33] Bianco also states that the ability of the authorities to exercise control over local society "has undergone a long-term fading away under Mao's successors, which is a . . . factor behind the resurgence of rural disturbances during the reform era."[34] But although the government may fail to prevent illegal modes of resistance, it is still able to impose harsh punishment after such resistance has occurred, which would act as a deterrent to other potential resisters. Hence, the increased frequency of resistance in China also reflects the government's greater tolerance. Authors della Porta and Reiter argue that under enforcement of the law against protesters is common in democracies: "Law breaking, which is implicit in several forms of protest, tends to be tolerated by the police. Law enforcement is usually considered as less important than peacekeeping."[35] This is also now true in China when citizen resistance has a legitimate or legal basis (e.g., rightful resistance).[36]

In China, state tolerance or the political space for popular resistance has much to do with the differences between the central and local governments. As discussed in the previous chapter, the central government is more seriously constrained by its concern for the protection of regime legitimacy than are local governments. As a result, the central government is more tolerant of citizens' non-regime-threatening resistance, although this does not necessarily mean that the central government will always intervene to address citizens' grievances, as discussed in subsequent chapters.[37] The central government's tolerance places constraints on local officials by preventing them from always relying on suppression in dealing with popular resistance.

The government's tolerance has been reflected in its handling of collective petitions. In recent years, the number of collective petitions directed at the authorities at local and central levels has increased significantly. In 2000, the number of collective petitions was 245,700, or 2.8 times that of the 1995 figure.[38] According to statistics from five provinces that I collected, this number increased from 0.27 per 10,000 citizens in 1990 to 2.09 in 2002, or by 7.7 times.[39] Collective petitions create a problem for the government because they can easily escalate into disruptive action; disruptive collective petitions are the basic mode of social disruption in China. In Fujian province in 1999, 74 percent of the 827 instances of social unrest took the form of collective petitions, 6 percent were strikes, and the remainder were demonstrations, gatherings, sit-in protests, and riots. Similarly, more than 63 percent of the 297 instances of disruptive action that occurred in Qinghai province between 1998 and 1999 were collective petitions or appeals, whereas 17.5 percent were gatherings.[40]

On numerous occasions, collective petitions to state authorities have escalated into blockades of traffic or government office compounds or even attacks on state agencies. A Liaoning province official states that 80 percent of the collective petitions directed at the provincial authority involved "drastic action."[41] Participants resorted to disruptive action to attract attention in 53 percent of the 108 collective petitions (with more than fifty participants in each) made in Zhejiang province in the early 2000s.[42]

In theory, disruptive collective petitions are not supposed to occur because they are illegal. According to the regulation of the State Council,

collective petitions are allowed only if there are no more than five participants.[43] But according to the statistics I collected on collective petitions to
the provincial authorities in ten provinces in 2002, the average number of
participants ranged from twenty-three to thirty-nine—far more than the
number allowed. This is also true of petitions to authorities at the city and
county levels (see Appendices D through F).[44] Consider what happened in
Zhengzhou, the capital city of Henan province. In 1995, the participants in
collective petitions blocked the office compounds of the city and provincial
authorities forty-six times and blocked traffic eight times. Forty-eight times,
the participants in collective petitions broke into the office compounds of
city authorities, on one occasion staying for as long as forty-two hours and
on another occasion parking more than a hundred vehicles within the office compound or in front of the gates of government offices. Twenty-five of
these collective petitions had between fifty and one hundred participants,
and thirty-one had more than one hundred.[45]

Such evidence makes it clear that the boundary between collective petitions and protests, demonstrations, or gatherings is easily blurred in contemporary China.[46] The large numbers of participants in collective petitions
reflect citizens' belief that a larger number of participants can exert more
pressure on the local government because more participants are able to create larger-scale chaos.[47] A larger number is also believed to enhance the security of individual participants, in that "legal punishment does not apply
to participants in large-scale action" (*fa bu ze zhong*).[48] Consequently, when
citizens present petitions in person, they tend to do so collectively. Nationwide, 60 percent of the total number of people making petitions in person
in 1998 did so as members of groups. The proportion rose steadily from
71.2 percent in 2000 to 75.6 percent in 2001.[49] The proportion reached 90
percent in Jilin province in 2002. In Henan, it increased from 49 percent in
1993 to 90 percent in 2002.[50]

If tolerance of illegal collective petitions becomes the government's
method to appease participants and maintain social order, other modes of
disruptive action become possible. For example, strikes are illegal, but they
are frequently used in China. In the years between 1990 and 1994, the
numbers of people participating in strikes were 234,000, 288,600, 268,400,
310,030, and 495,600, respectively.[51] As a matter of fact, strikes have been
repeatedly used by workers, especially in private and foreign enterprise, in

recent years. The relaxed enforcement of the law is an important reason for the occurrence of illegal modes of collective resistance.

MOBILIZATION

The opportunity for resistance will remain latent if prospective participants fail to coordinate themselves. Literature on social movements has highlighted the role of organizations in mobilizing participants and making collective action possible. In China, for understandable reasons, organizations that are able to mobilize citizens to take action against the will of the state are nonexistent. Hence, instead of relying on organizations for mobilization, collective resistance in China largely depends on the mobilization efforts of organizers or leaders and other context-contingent factors that facilitate mobilization, such as the living environment in which potential participants interact with one another.[52] A basic pattern of collective resistance in China consists of three types of actors: (1) organizers or leaders, (2) activists, and (3) common participants. While not all collective action requires leaders or even activists, it is useful to analyze the reasons for the emergence of leaders as well as the mechanisms that facilitate coordination or information dissemination among potential participants.

Leaders and Activists

Leaders play an important and sometimes indispensable role in collective action.[53] Schumpeter suggests that "collectives act almost exclusively by accepting leadership—this is the dominant mechanism of practically any collective action."[54] Research on collective resistance in China has pointed to the preeminent role of leaders in initiating collective resistance and making it successful. Specifically, leaders play several roles in Chinese citizens' collective action: (1) They mobilize participants; (2) they disseminate information; (3) they inspire confidence in participants; (4) they take the greatest risk and reduce that for average participants; and (5) they negotiate with the government or other social actors on behalf of participants.[55] It is a common finding that leaders of collective action in China are often those people who know about relevant government policies and enjoy a certain degree of respect and prestige in their communities. In rural areas, leaders of peasant resistance include village cadres, rural teachers, demobilized soldiers, or other better-educated members of the community and respected villagers not in office.[56] In urban areas, leaders in worker resistance include managerial personnel, demobilized soldiers, and other respected workers.[57]

Research on social movements suggests that a sense of moral responsibility is an important reason for the emergence of movement leaders.[58] Studies on collective action in China have identified a number of factors that may turn some people into leaders of collective action, such as personalities, career benefits, a sense of moral responsibility, community pressure, and personal stake or self-interest in the collective goal.[59] Some individuals mobilize collective resistance because of their personal interests, and they see collective action as a means to achieve their personal goals. Such goals may or may not be the same as those of other participants. For example, one instance in a city in Henan province in 1997 was instigated by a person who was resentful of the government for executing his grandfather during the land reform of the 1950s.[60]

Instances of civil resistance in China also suggest that some people become the leaders because of their strong sense of justice and moral responsibility. As will be discussed in subsequent chapters, leading resistance against the state authority not only incurs risks but also consumes time, energy, and financial resources. But these leaders do not normally receive more benefits than an average participant or even a nonparticipant does. In this circumstance, leaders emerge because of a combination of their sense of justice and moral responsibility, community pressure, and sometimes their personal interests in the collective goal. This has happened in Chinese peasant communities.[61] In one example, a peasant leader sacrificed his time and family business to lead peasants to fight against corrupt local cadres in a village in Hebei province in the 1990s. When the village cadres wanted to buy him off by offering the position of the village party secretary, he rejected it.[62] In peasants' resistance to tax and fee collections, some people who became peasants' representatives had little personal gain because they were not peasants and only happened to live in the peasant community.[63]

Leaders are especially important to sustained collective action.[64] The factors leading to the emergence of leaders may not be the same as those sustaining their leadership. Some people are willing to sustain the leadership because of community pressure. In sustained resistance, it takes courage, energy, time, and sacrifice for some people to continue their roles as leaders. For this to be possible, leaders need the support of their family members and their communities. In rural China, some peasant leaders received strong support not only from their family members but also from village communities. Cognizant of the risk the leaders incur and their importance to the success of their action, some peasants defended their leaders from the local government. In the 1990s, there were a number of cases in which peasants confronted local officials or the police to protect their leaders from being arrested.[65] Once peasants are willing to support and defend their leaders, community pressure rises.

For example, in a village in Hunan province in 1998, a peasant leader led villagers to resist fee collection by township cadres. The villagers fought the cadres physically and overturned their jeep. That peasant leader was then sentenced to three years in prison on the charge of "organizing riots and disrupting the social order." When this person was jailed, his family received help from many other villagers, including those who had not met the family before. At one time, it was raining heavily, and a peasant who lived more than ten kilometers away from this peasant leader's village came to his home to help repair the house. Such instances may have an emotional impact on the leaders and put strong community pressure on them. When this peasant leader was released, he continued to organize peasant resistance. He admitted, "The people treat us representatives in such a way, if we fail to fight for their justice, how can we face them?"[66]

A second reason for some leaders to sustain their leadership is that they become locked into the action. Some leaders think that they will lose face if they stop the resistance before achieving any success. Others feel that they have been mistreated by local authorities, or they believe that only successful resistance will justify their action against local authorities and protect them from being persecuted. As a result, these leaders are trapped in collective resistance in that their personal security is tied to sustaining the resistance. In one case in the Three Gorges area, the construction of a dam in the 1970s for electricity generation led to the migration of some peasants from a village and affected their interests.[67] Throughout the 1980s, the peasants in the village lodged persistent complaints with state authorities at different levels. An important leader of the resistance was a local schoolteacher who was motivated by community interest and his own personal gain. But once he was involved in the resistance, it was difficult for him to stop. Seen as a "thorn in their side" by local officials, this leader was punished in various ways. For example, despite his wife's poor heath, the township government forced her to have a sterilization operation in 1983, which required three years of recovery. This circumstance fomented his deep hatred toward the local officials. In the ensuing years, fighting against and removing the local cadres became the most important goal of this organizer. He sustained the resistance also because of possible retaliation from the cadres. By sustaining the resistance, the leader could receive support from the peasants, and he did not have to face local officials individually. Another peasant leader in this case continued to act as a leader also because he could not easily remove himself. This person once went to Beijing to appeal, but he was detained there. His miserable experience in a detention station almost deterred him from continuing his participation. But after he returned to the village, he worried that if the resistance did not achieve any positive result, he could be accused of filing false charges against local officials.

Information Dissemination

The emergence of leaders may not be sufficient for successful resistance. Forceful collective action requires as many participants as possible. An important characteristic of collective resistance in China is the voluntary participation of individuals. Although a lack of selective incentives or sanctions may lead to free riding, the ever-present collective action suggests that this is not an insurmountable problem. There can be many mechanisms to overcome the free-rider problem, including private incentives and a sense of moral responsibility.[68] In some circumstances, the priority of potential participants is the success of their resistance, and nonparticipation will likely lead to the lack of resistance in the first place. As a result, individuals' desires to achieve particular goals can also motivate their participation.[69] But this is premised on the condition that information dissemination or consensus building among prospective participants is possible. Individuals will participate in collective action only when they know that others will do the same.

In China, there are several ways through which information can be disseminated so that participants who agree on an action can be mobilized. One method is the traditional way of face-to-face briefing. While this method carries risks, it may also inspire confidence in participants and encourage more participation if the leaders are believed to be capable. Other tools, such as telephones, have also been used to organize collective action. In a relatively small community like a village or a residential community, the people may also use gongs, bells, or fireworks as a signal of action as agreed beforehand.

In a village in Hebei province, peasants had the norm that fireworks would be set off if there was an important issue to be addressed. When villagers heard the fireworks, they would go to meet in a particular place in the village. In the evening of September 8, 2000, a few activists set off fireworks, and villagers gathered in front of a small shop. The purpose of this gathering was to have villagers sign a petition letter concerning the alleviation of their financial burdens. The next morning, after fireworks were set off, more than forty villagers gathered and approached the township government to complain about their financial burdens and the village cadres' mismanagement of village affairs. But major township leaders avoided meeting the "troublemakers" the whole day. In the evening, fireworks were set off again, and villagers gathered and marched to the township government. The demonstration turned into a riot after peasants from neighboring villages also joined. Some participants set fire to the offices, burning some rooms, files, a fire truck, and seven motorcycles. The riot ended with the punishment of a few activists and township officials.[70]

A second method of information dissemination is to post notices. This mode has been common in workers' resistance during the reform period. A factory in Shaanxi province, for instance, adopted ownership reforms that affected workers' interests in 2004. Workers strongly suspected that the reforms involved corruption, so they launched collective action to demand the intervention of higher-level authorities. The workers organized their action by publicizing the venue and time of their gathering in a letter entitled "A Letter to All the Employees," which was posted on the wall of the factory. The letter listed workers' problems and their causes as well as their demand that higher-level authorities investigate the management of the factory. It then indicated the time and venue for their gathering:

> Venue of gathering: in front of the company office building.
> Please bring with you small stools, banners, and slogans.
> Time: 9:00 A.M., 13 September 2004.
>
> Our wishes:
> The security department of the company should also think about workers' interests and should not tear down this post. Those workers who have this post should try their best to disseminate, post, and photocopy them. Those who have access to the Internet should try to send this message to websites of the central and provincial discipline inspection committees. Workers and middle- and high-level cadres who have a conscience and know about inside information about the company should report and disseminate such information.[71]

On September 13, 2004, about 1,000 workers showed up at the arranged venue and initiated a collective action by blocking the traffic on the road in front of the factory. Subsequently, some of their demands were met by the factory's management and the local authorities.[72]

Given the potential risk or punishment imposed by the government, an important characteristic of the dissemination of information is that it is often done anonymously. For example, in Hefei, the capital city of Anhui province, taxi drivers anonymously organized a collective action in March 2000. The serious encroachment on taxi drivers' rights, such as unauthorized fines, by the local police had aroused strong resentment among taxi drivers. On March 16, 2000, taxi drivers received a notice of a collective appeal to the city government at 9 o'clock on the morning of March 20. That notice was issued by the Association of Taxis of Hefei, an organization that did not exist. Many taxi drivers supported the collective action by joining the strike or participating in the collective petition.[73]

Third, with the development of new technologies, the Internet, e-mail, and cell phones have become increasingly important tools for citizens to disseminate information. The minister of the Ministry of Public Security acknowledged: "The development of information technology, while facilitating social and economic development, has also posed a serious pressure on maintaining social stability."[74] This mode of mobilization is likely to persist given the number of people who have access to such technologies. The number of Internet users in China reached 210 million, and cell phone users totaled 515 million by the end of 2007.[75] The advantage of new information technologies is that they can mobilize previously unconnected people at a low cost.

The power of the Internet has been reflected in several large-scale social protests in China, one of which occurred in Xiamen in Fujian province in 2007. In 2006, the city government of Xiamen allowed the construction of a 10-billion-yuan chemical plant that had a Taiwanese investor. The local government had a strong incentive to complete this project because the plant would almost double the GDP of the city and generate a large amount of revenue, and it would be a great achievement of the local leaders. Local newspapers and television news programs repeatedly reported the economic benefits that would be brought to the city because of the new factory. Although this investment was strongly opposed by some experts and local people because of the potential for serious pollution, their opposition did not change the minds of local officials.

However, things changed after large-scale protests occurred in the city. The protests were initiated by residents through the Internet and cell phones. On May 28, 2007, an Internet user posted a message entitled "Antipollution: A Million Citizens Spread the Word through SMS Like Crazy" on a website whose server was located in Guangdong province. The message stated:

> Xianglu Company has started the construction of a chemical project in Hai-chang district. When the massive toxic chemical products go into production, it will mean an atomic bomb has been released over all Xiamen Island. It will cause leukemia and deformed babies among the Xiamen people. We want to live, and we want our health. International organizations say that such projects should be located more than 100 kilometers away from a city. But this project is only sixteen kilometers away from Xiamen. For the sake of future generations, please pass this message to all your Xiamen friends. For the sake of our descendents, please take action and join the 10,000-people demonstration. It will start at 8 o'clock on June 1. Please go to the city government from where you live. Send this message to all your friends.[76]

Whether a million people spread this message was not important; what was important was that this posted message informed people of the time of the demonstration. The local police tried to block the cell phone mobilization but failed. In the ensuing two days, thousands of people participated in the demonstrations regardless of the city government's warnings and the presence of a large number of uniformed and plainclothes police. On June 1, people went to the city government from all directions, and the number was estimated to exceed 10,000 at its peak. The next day, the number declined, but it still reached thousands at its peak.

Interestingly, citizen journalists carrying cell phones sent text messages and pictures about the demonstrations to bloggers in Guangzhou and other cities who then posted real-time reports for the entire country to see.[77] Hundreds of pictures of the demonstrations were also posted on the Internet.[78] All this made it difficult for the local government to use harsh repressive measures. The demonstrations put serious pressure on the local government and directly contributed to the suspension of the project. The frustrated government in Xiamen city then stipulated that Internet users must use their real names when they posted messages on the Internet. This regulation was unlikely to be enforced simply because it was technically unfeasible to do so, especially if the servers were located outside the city.

Certainly, not all collective acts need mobilization or even information dissemination. Some are triggered by unanticipated factors, what can be called catalytic factors or events. As Piven and Cloward suggest, "Riots require little more by way of organization than numbers, propinquity, and some communication."[79] In my collection, as discussed in Chapters Six and Seven, a number of riots occurred without much mobilization. The gathering of a large number of disgruntled people can be sufficient to trigger riots. For example, in a county in Hunan province, a township government held a mass meeting in 1999 to discipline six peasant representatives for their resistance to fee and tax collection. The six peasants were shackled and brought to a site where many other peasants were present. In the course of the meeting, the son of one of the shackled peasants made his way into the area to rescue his father. His action triggered the participation of the other peasants present, resulting in a large-scale confrontation between the cadres and peasants. Outnumbered by the peasants, dozens of cadres fled.[80]

Conclusion

Unlike most other transitional economies, the Chinese party-state has seen a drastic increase in social protests while the Communist Party remains in power. While these incidents reveal the regime's resilience,[81] they also point to the limitations of the existing mechanisms of conflict resolution. In China today, citizens are allowed to use a number of channels, including lawsuits and petitions, to voice or address their grievances. But the problem lies in the effectiveness of these channels. As revealed in the China GSS 2005 discussed in this chapter, there is a significant discrepancy between people's behavioral intentions and their actual actions, which, to some extent, points out the problems that participants may encounter when they resort to certain modes of action in reality. For example, in dealing with disputes with state agencies, many more people choose to tolerate the disputes in reality. A very likely reason is that it takes serious effort and wisdom to fight against state agencies.

The inadequacies of the conflict-resolving mechanisms may lead to the escalation of action. As revealed by the China GSS 2005, the portion of people who had disputes with state authorities and used collective petitions is much larger than those who did not have disputes and reported their intentions to use this method. This rationale of tactical escalation also applies to other modes of collective action that are even illegal. This begs the question of how such collective action is possible in this nondemocratic system. As discussed in Chapter One, the crucial reason is the difference between different levels of state authorities in terms of their tolerance of popular resistance with nonpolitical claims.[82] Upper-level authorities' higher tolerance places constraints on lower-level authorities, resulting in the relaxed enforcement of laws and thereby creating political space for popular resistance. On the other hand, the existence of those factors that facilitate mobilization, such as the presence of leaders and new methods of mobilization, also makes collective action possible.

It must be stressed that the occurrence of popular resistance in China does not necessarily indicate the power of its participants. On the contrary, it often indicates the weakness of the people. Chinese central authorities admit that participants' demands in most cases of resistance are reasonable and that their problems should have been addressed by local governments.[83] Chinese citizens often resort to noninstitutionalized action because their rights have been violated; so, they take action to *defend* their rights or because they do not have alternative channels. Moreover, it is one thing that collective resistance is possible in China and entirely another whether such resistance can succeed. As subsequent chapters show, successful resistance in China is highly conditional.

THREE

Obstacles to Successful Resistance in China

China has enacted many laws and regulations that are supposed to protect its citizens' legitimate rights. It is also common for central authorities to promulgate directives warning local officials against abusing power at the expense of citizens. Such directives become the foundation of citizens' "rightful resistance";[1] however, there is no guarantee that these favorable directives are actually meaningful commitments on the part of the state rather than half-hearted promises, lip service, or political rhetoric. O'Brien and Li assert that "the divide between the central government and its local representatives creates an opening for rightful resistance—so long as the Center really means what it says."[2] How do local officials or citizens know whether the central government really means what it says? One obvious indicator is whether or not those officials who violate government regulations are disciplined. When the central government's punishment is credible, the citizens' intervention-seeking ability is enhanced. The reverse is also true: If malfeasant local officials are often exempted from punishment, then the central–local divide regarding the accommodation of citizens' rights is narrowed. As a result, the opportunity for successful resistance becomes largely nonexistent.

It is certainly inaccurate to assume that Chinese local governments do not have any intention to help citizens address their grievances. The problem lies in the costs involved. Based on the 261 cases I collected (see Appendix B), this chapter examines the difficulties in staging collective resistance in China. It shows that because most incidents of collective resistance are not forceful enough and are thereby exclusively handled by local governments, they have significant autonomy in choosing the modes of response.

Local governments may make concessions when popular resistance is forceful and/or citizens' demands are less difficult to meet. However, ignorance or suppression becomes the option when the local governments believe that the cost of making concessions is high and that the citizens' resistance is weak. The nonagricultural use of farmland is used as an example to illustrate the obstacles to staging successful resistance in China.

Successful Resistance in China: The Difficulties

In China, the concentration of power in the hands of the party-state also means the concentration of responsibility. The government is responsible for addressing popular resistance even though some incidents are not caused by state agencies. This section analyzes the rationale behind government response in light of the participants' demands and the forcefulness of their resistance, based on my collection of 261 cases.

For analytical convenience, I divide the participants' claims into high-cost demands and low-cost demands. A demand is seen as costly to meet if it creates a zero-sum game between the government and protesters in the sense that the protesters' gain is the government's loss (i.e., economic or political cost); otherwise, a demand is seen as less costly to meet (e.g., addressing citizen grievances caused by a third party). The forcefulness of resistance depends on the degree of threat it poses to social stability or regime legitimacy. For local governments, forceful resistance also means a high possibility of intervention from their superiors. More specifically, an action is categorized as forceful if it has more than 500 participants,[3] involves casualties, or receives media coverage (see also Chapter 1); otherwise, an action is seen as less forceful. Needless to say, these criteria are relative, but they serve as a very useful tool in the analysis of the government's behavior.

Figure 3.1 presents the outcomes of the 261 incidents of collective resistance collected for this study. It shows clearly the influence of the type of demands as well as the forcefulness of citizens' resistance. Citizens are most likely to succeed when the cost of accommodating their demands is low and their resistance is powerful (i.e., the Low/Forceful cell). Nineteen of the twenty-two cases (i.e., 86.4 percent) succeeded. In contrast, those who stage resistance are most likely to be repressed when their demands are difficult to meet and their resistance is not forceful. In 129 such cases, the action failed in 114 (i.e., 88.4 percent). In cases with high-cost demands,

Forcefulness of Action

		Forceful				Not Forceful	
		a. Concessions	17		a. Concessions	10
Low		b. *a* + discipline	2		b. *a* + discipline	2
		c. Repression	2		c. Repression	17
		d. Tolerance	1		d. Tolerance	13
		a. Concessions	26		a. Concessions	7
High		b. *a* + discipline	12		b. *a* + discipline	2
		c. Repression	24		c. Repression	114
		d. Tolerance	6		d. Tolerance	6

FIGURE 3.1 State Response and Protest Outcomes (N = 261 cases) SOURCE: Author's collection.

forceful action increases the odds of success. Among the sixty-eight cases (i.e., the High/Forceful cell), the participants achieved success in thirty-eight cases (i.e., 56 percent) and were repressed in twenty-four cases (i.e., 35.3 percent). However, the success in resistance with high-cost demands can be costly because the local government commonly uses concessions with discipline to deal with some participants (i.e., twelve out of thirty-eight successful cases).

The data show that some cases of less forceful resistance also succeeded, but the odds of success are much smaller. Participants who staged less forceful resistance succeeded in only nine of the 129 cases with high-cost demands (i.e., 7 percent). As discussed in subsequent chapters, success in such cases is highly conditional (five of the nine cases succeeded because of intervention from above). Certainly, because my collection includes only 261 cases, it is not possible to assess whether or not they are representative. For example, the collection does not include many cases that were ignored by state authorities, mainly because such cases have been less frequently reported. However, the collection does indicate the importance of the forcefulness of resistance and the type of demands. These two types of factors point to the difficulties in achieving successful resistance in China.

COSTS OF CONCESSIONS

Chapter 1 shows that local governments may face different costs when making concessions. Two major costs are financial costs and political costs.

Subsequent chapters will demonstrate that many instances of collective resistance in China focus on economic benefits, and participants face difficulties in obtaining these benefits when local governments lack the necessary financial resources. Local governments may also refuse to make concessions if they believe that the participants' demands threaten local governments' important goals, such as revenue generation and/or local development (e.g., antipollution or conversion of farmland into nonagricultural uses).

Another serious cost of concessions for party or government leaders at each level is the political cost paid to discipline irresponsible, irresponsive, or malfeasant agents who ignore, violate, or fail to protect the citizens' legitimate rights. Disciplining state agents is a complex political issue in China. A leader of the National Inspection Bureau stresses the party's need to be lenient toward cadres, whose training requires significant investment from the party. He said that it is not easy for a person to become a cadre or for the party to train a cadre. The party cannot turn a person into a cadre overnight; instead, it takes much time, money, and energy to do so. If a person who commits a mistake can correct his or her mistakes, it means that he or she has some immunity. "We should stick to the party policy of being strict with those who refuse to acknowledge their crimes and of being lenient to those who are willing to acknowledge their misconduct."[4]

If government officials at the central level hold this view, it is not surprising that such leniency exists at the local level. Grassroots officials are not directly accountable to central or provincial authorities; instead, they answer to their local leaders. Higher-level local leaders may be reluctant to punish their subordinates for various reasons, including political considerations (protecting their own images by covering up their agents' misconduct, for example), patron–client relations, personal connections, faction politics, and corruption.[5] After all, local leaders rely on lower-level agents for local governance and policy implementation.

The high cost of disciplining local officials has resulted in the "nice-man theory" (*haoren zhuyi*) within the party and the government, which means that major leaders are reluctant to punish their subordinates for infractions concerning laws or regulations. A survey of 13,300 cadres and party members in Sichuan province in 2003 found that more than 53 percent reported that the nice-man theory was a serious problem among local leaders.[6] In 2000, Jiang Zemin also acknowledged that some cadres adopt the nice-man theory and stress secular personal networks: "They are especially reluctant to punish the following people: their acquaintances, capable people, celebrities, people holding important posts, those with strong backgrounds, and their relatives."[7] Chinese local officials are particularly unlikely to be punished if they violate citizens' rights in the name of community interest, such as local development.[8]

These obstacles become barriers or the so-called protective umbrellas that protect malfeasant or unresponsive local officials.[9] In China, the discipline inspection committee of the party and the inspection bureau of the government work together to investigate the misconduct of party cadres and public employees for infractions, including corruption, abuse of power, malfeasance, and violation of citizens' rights. Citizens' reports are the dominant channel through which these two organizations obtain information on the misconduct of officials. In recent years, about 1.5 million to 1.8 million reports on the misconduct of state agents have been made annually by citizens to discipline agencies, but many of these reports are not investigated.[10] According to the statistical data that I collected from twenty-two provinces, only about 13.8 percent of the 956,389 cases reported in 2002 were investigated.[11] Some reported cases were most likely not investigated because the information provided to the discipline agencies was false or incomplete, but officials in these agencies admit that they are also cautious in carrying out investigations of some officials, especially those holding important positions.[12]

Furthermore, officials found to be malfeasant may not be seriously punished. In China, both the party and the government are responsible for disciplining party members and officials. As a matter of fact, malfeasant officials are generally first given party or administrative discipline and then are given legal punishment if necessary. Within the party, a member who violates party discipline may receive one of five modes of punishment ranging from being warned to expulsion from the party. Similarly, in the government sector, a malfeasant public employee or official may receive one of six modes of punishment ranging from a warning to being fired. As long as a cadre is not expelled from the party or fired from the public sector, he or she may be able to restore his or her political and administrative status by performing well at a later time.

In contrast, punishment through the courts often means the end of a cadre's political career. However, the number of officials given legal punishment is rather small. It seems that party or government discipline, rather than the law, is usually used to deal with malfeasant state agents.[13] For example, about 846,000 public employees were subject to party or administrative discipline between 1997 and 2002, and only about 4.5 percent of them were punished through the courts.[14] Between 2003 and 2004, about 1.8 of every 1,000 party members were disciplined each year, and those who were tried in courts accounted for only 2.7 percent of the total number of officials disciplined.[15] The punishment of higher-ranking local officials is particularly difficult.[16]

The implication of abusive local officials being exempted from punishment is self-evident. It not only allows government officials to ignore citizens' rights and grievances but also increases the difficulty for citizens to achieve success. Moreover, local officials may be emboldened to abuse power and become even more irresponsible. As will be discussed in subsequent chapters, the cost of disciplining officials not only shapes the behavior of upper-level local authorities but also affects the central government's behavior.[17]

THE FORCEFULNESS OF RESISTANCE

Another difficulty in successful resistance has to do with the participants' ability to stage forceful resistance. Less forceful resistance allows local governments to use suppression. Ceteris paribus, the smaller in scale a collective action is, the less likely it is to succeed. Most instances of resistance in China can be classified as small in scale, although the number of participants in collective resistance ranges from dozens to tens of thousands. An account of 3,600 cases of collective resistance in seven provinces shows that, in 1999, the average number of participants was eighty-one.[18] Nationwide, it was estimated that 730,000 people were involved in 8,700 instances of collective action in 1993, or an average of eighty-four participants per incident; 3.07 million people were involved in 58,000 instances in 2003, or an average of fifty-two participants per incident; and 3.76 million people in 74,000 collective actions in 2004, or an average of fifty-one participants per incident.[19] The decline in the average number of participants is largely due to the increasing number of small-scale actions.

According to the police department, an action with more than 500 participants is regarded as a large-scale action, and actions with more than 1,000 participants are regarded as especially large in scale. If this criterion is used, most instances of disruptive action fall into the small-scale category. According to a count of 1,117 instances of social unrest in three provinces, those cases with more than 500 participants in each accounted for 7 percent, whereas those cases involving fewer than 100 participants accounted for 76 percent. The number of cases that involved more than 1,000 participants accounted for only 2.2 percent of the total number of instances.[20] This is also true of collective petitions, the most basic mode of collective resistance in China. In Zhejiang province between July 2000 and June 2001, there were 58,600 petitions in person, including both collective (19.3 percent or 11,300) and individual ones (80.7 percent). The number of collective petitions with more than fifty participants totaled 1,140, or 10 percent of the total number.[21]

Table 3.1 shows that instances of collective action with 100 or more participants accounted for less than 15 percent of the total number of collective action cases in recent years. In 1999, only 125 cases had more than 1,000 participants, accounting for less than 0.4 percent of the total number of disruptive actions.[22] Certainly, the actual number of large-scale actions is not small. Nationwide, the number of instances with 100 or more participants in each increased from 1,400 in 1994 to 7,000 in 2003.[23] However, it is impossible for the central and provincial governments to intervene in most of these cases. In other words, the intervention-seeking ability of most groups of participants is limited by their group size. This does not necessarily mean that small protest groups always fail, but they do need to make extra efforts or receive external support, such as media coverage, to succeed.

RISKS IN RESISTANCE

The preceding discussion by no means implies that local officials face no pressure in dealing with incidents of collective action. As a matter of fact, some "hard targets," such as maintaining social stability, have been assigned to local officials at different levels and must be accomplished.[24] The failure of lower-level agents to achieve those targets also negatively affects

TABLE 3.1
Instances of Social Unrest in China

Year	Number of cases	Proportion of cases with 100 or more participants (%)
1993	8,700	16.1
1994	10,000	13.6
2000	30,000[a]	14.5
2001	—	15.6
2002	51,130	—
2003	58,500	12.0

SOURCE: He Zhuowen, "Zhengque renshi he chuli woguo xianjieduan de liyi guanxi maodun" (Properly handling conflicts of interests in our country), *Kexue shehui zhuyi* (Scientific socialism) 2 (2005): 8–11; Chen Jinsheng, *Quntixingshijian yanjiu baogao* (Research report on instances of collective action) (Beijing: Qunzhong chubanshe, 2004), 62.

[a]Between January and September 2000.

higher-level leaders. Take collective petitioning as an example: Lower-level government agents regularly sign responsibility contracts with the next higher ranking authority to prevent the local people under their jurisdiction from making petitions to higher-level authorities, especially at the central and provincial levels.[25] The central authority also links the number of petitions from a province to local officials' efforts to prevent social conflict.[26] But this pressure does not necessarily force local governments to make concessions to resisters. Instead, it may prompt them to use suppression, though local officials face some constraints in the choice of the mode of suppression.

As the Chinese government has claimed, most instances of collective resistance in China are "internal conflicts among the people."[27] Therefore, the central government has made strict regulations on the use of force in dealing with popular resistance. The most important criterion for the use of force is the nature and mode of the resistance. The central government reiterated its policy in 1998 when the State Council issued a directive stipulating the methods of handling gatherings, demonstrations, protests, and petitions.[28] An act is seen as "political" or destructive and therefore intolerable if it is an attempt to overthrow the political system or the party, if it threatens the territorial integrity of the country, if it attacks state agencies, or if it destroys important infrastructures or facilities. Hence, state agencies should handle popular resistance based on the following considerations: (1) whether the participants' demands are political, (2) whether there is organized violence, (3) whether there is intentional confrontation, and (4) whether there is support from overseas.

In dealing with collective action, the authorities need to know the aims of the action, the main organizers and their political backgrounds, and whether the action crosses work units or places. Police officers are expected to protect important facilities and important party and government agencies with force if necessary. Yet force should not be used to deal with peaceful action with legitimate demands. As repeated in the directive on the settlement of social unrest issued by the Ministry of Public Security in 2002, the mobilization of police officers and the use of equipment and weapons must strictly follow regulated procedures.[29] There should be "caution in employing armed force, in using weapons, and in employing compulsory measures."[30] This is so the police will avoid misusing force and exacerbating popular ire.[31] Higher-level local governments have also restricted the use of force in dealing with citizen resistance.[32]

Nevertheless, these regulations have not entirely prevented the use of force that causes serious casualties. There have been several cases in which the police opened fire on citizens.[33] But because opening fire on unarmed citizens in non-regime-threatening resistance is unacceptable to the central party-state, local officials incur serious risks.[34] Violent crackdowns are thus exceptions instead of being the norm. In many cases, serious casualties are not the result of local governments' intentional use of bloody suppression but of the unanticipated escalation of the confrontation between participants and local officials and/or police officers.

Given the risk of violent suppression, a more commonly used mode is to impose punishment on selective participants, the activists or the leaders in most cases. As discussed in Chapter Two, the lack of organizations for mobilizing participants in collective resistance in China sometimes leads individual participants to act as organizers or coordinators. Therefore, an important way of deterring resistance is to impose "exemplary punishment" by selectively punishing protest organizers, leaders, or activists.[35] It is also the central government's policy to limit the punishment to activists in mass actions—to isolate and punish the minority and to win over, divide, and educate the majority.[36]

Local governments have adopted two approaches in dealing with activists or leaders in collective action.[37] One is that some grassroots officials resort to the illegal method of hiring thugs to harass or attack the activists or leaders in collective resistance. For example, some local governments commonly hire local thugs to attack homeowners who resist housing demolition or peasants who resist the occupation of their farmland. Sometimes, local governments tolerate the business's use of this method in dealing with resisters whose interests are ignored by the government and/or the business. According to a survey of 632 peasants making petitions in Beijing, 54 percent reported that local officials hired local thugs to harass or hurt them.[38]

More commonly, local governments use legal punishment to deal with organizers or activists of collective action. The existing law and regulations provide a convenient basis for imposing punishment because most instances of collective action are illegal. According to Article 290 of the criminal law, a person commits the crime of assembling the masses to attack state agencies if the action she or he has organized prevents the state agency's operation *and* causes serious losses; a person commits the crime of assembling the masses to disrupt social order if the consequence of the action is serious, disrupting the order of work, production, business, or school *and* causing serious losses. In the case of attacking state agencies, the leader can be sentenced to five to ten years in jail, whereas the other activists can be sentenced to up to five years in jail. In the case of disrupting the social order, the leader can be sentenced to three to seven years in jail, whereas the other activists are sentenced to up to three years in jail.

Participants stage resistance precisely to prompt the government to pay attention to their grievances. It is natural for them to target the government or to disrupt the social order so as to generate sufficient pressure. However, the participants face risks when taking such actions. In 175 of the 261 cases I collected (Table 3.2), 1,115 participants were beaten, detained, arrested, or jailed for up to fifteen years while one was sentenced to death. In more than 70 percent of the 175 cases, the activists were accused of organizing the people to attack state agencies or disrupting the social order, including the traffic. Sometimes, these are lumped together with other crimes.[39] Participants are normally unable to defend themselves successfully in the courts. China adopts a two-instance system in which a litigant or a defendant can appeal to the upper-level court for a retrial if the ruling in the first hearing is not acceptable. In the 175 cases, only in thirteen cases were the results of the appeals to the appellate courts reported, and all thirteen appeals were rejected.

The Case of Rural Land Use

The hurdles to successful resistance have been fully reflected in Chinese peasants' resistance to external land users' occupation of their farmland. In recent years after the rural tax reform, the nonagricultural use of farmland

TABLE 3.2
Criminal Charges against Participants

	Cases	Frequency (%)	People
Assembling the masses			
to attack state agencies (a)	60	34.3	310
to disrupt social order (b)	45	25.7	289
Multiple accusations:			
(a), (b), or others	6	3.4	124
(a) and others	10	5.7	59
(b) and others	6	3.4	57
Miscellaneous	15	8.6	45
Detained for unspecified reasons	33	18.9	231
Total	175	100.0	1,115

SOURCE: Author's collection

has become the most conflict-generating issue in rural China.[40] According to the Land Law, ownership of farmland resides with the "rural collective." But the law stops short of defining who makes up the rural collective. In practice, the small production group, the administrative village, and sometimes the township government can all be regarded as the rural collective.[41] As a result of its emphasis on the management of rural land, the government has tried to unify rural land ownership by delegating the authority over farmland management to the administrative village.[42]

One problem faced by peasants is that the village cadres who control village administration may abuse power in their management of the land. Village cadres have the deciding vote regarding land use within a village, although some of their decisions require the approval of higher-level government agents. Village cadres abuse this power in land use in various ways. Some occupy village land to build extra housing, others allocate land to people outside the village for their personal benefit, and still others embezzle or misappropriate compensation funds.[43] For example, in a village in Guizhou province, eleven village cadres embezzled 11 million yuan reaped from land leases between 2000 and 2003.[44] In Shantou city in Guangdong province in 2007, villagers' suspicion of the village cadres' corruption in land sales led to a series of riots in which peasants attacked and looted the homes of village cadres in more than ten villages in a township.[45]

A more serious problem faced by peasants is external land users, such as the government or government-supported businesses, because peasants possess little leverage over them. The central government stipulates that the conversion of farmland for nonagricultural purposes requires the approval of the government at the provincial or central level, depending on the amount of land to be converted. In other words, the government must first nationalize the farmland to change its ownership. There is nothing wrong with this policy per se, given the necessity of converting land for public use. Rather, it is the issue of compensation that causes discontent among peasants. Over the years, two modes of compensation have remained dominant, though new modes of compensation are also emerging.[46] The first method is job allocation. If the amount of land per capita of the rural collective is reduced to a certain level, the land users (often the government) must turn some peasants into urban residents and provide them with jobs.

The other method is the provision of lump-sum cash compensation. This method of compensation severs the relationship between peasants and land users to prevent future conflict. Job allocation is costly, so providing lump-sum cash compensation is the dominant mode of compensation in many places. For example, in Fuzhou in Fujian province, about 82 percent of the 23,400 peasants who lost their land received lump-sum cash compensation, as opposed to just 1.2 percent who were allocated jobs by land users.[47] The problem with lump-sum compensation is that peasants either are not compensated or are undercompensated.[48]

Local governments have taken land from peasants not only for the construction of public projects but also for the purpose of attracting investors by providing cheap land.[49] Local governments have also raised revenues through the lease or sale of farmland. In a number of cities and counties, the amount of revenue generated from land lease or sale accounts for 30 percent of the fiscal revenue, and it is as high as 70 percent in some places.[50] It is estimated that between 60 and 70 percent of the profits from farmland conversion go to the government or government agencies above the township level, approximately 25 to 30 percent to village governments, and only about 10 percent to peasants in compensation for their loss.[51]

The small cost of obtaining farmland and the huge resulting benefits serve as a strong incentive for local governments to take land from peasants. But the limited compensation has also threatened the livelihood of many peasants. Between 1990 and 2000, about 50 million peasants lost part or all of their farmland, and many failed to receive reasonable compensation.[52] The limited compensation or its absence has led many of these peasants to incur an income decrease, which has given rise to their grievances, frustration, and anger.[53] As a result, the nonagricultural use of farmland has generated numerous conflicts across the country in recent years.

PEASANT RESISTANCE AND ITS LIMITED EFFECTIVENESS

In defending their farmland, peasants have taken both preemptive and reactive measures. Preemptive or *ex ante* resistance is aimed at preventing the encroachment from occurring, serving as an institutional arrangement that restrains powerful actors. For example, some peasants have used a land shareholding system to resist external land users. Under this system, villages translate peasants' rights to land usage into shares indicating their percentage of ownership of the collective land. They divide the pooled land into different usage categories, including industrial development, commercial housing construction, and grain production.[54] As shareholders, the peasants receive the profits from the land, whether these are from agricultural or nonagricultural business.[55] By pooling the land of all individual peasants, the rural collective binds the interests of villagers together because land is no longer distributed within each small group. Although the government may still require villagers to turn in some land for public use, such as road construction, this method reduces the odds of the local government occupying farmland at will for its own fundraising purposes. All of the land has a designated purpose, so the government will face difficulties in forcing villagers—who can easily be mobilized by village cadres—to turn in more land without reasonable compensation.[56]

However, while peasants' preemptive resistance is more effective, this is difficult because it often requires active participation and organizing by village cadres, who may play a significant role in peasants' confrontations with the state. Village cadres, as a result of their position in the village community, have the resources as well as the prestige to make coordinated action possible, and they thereby act as political entrepreneurs.[57] But not all village cadres are willing or able to protect community rights by offending upper-level authorities. For example, among a selection of 837 complaint letters regarding land use addressed to a central media agency, 60 percent focused on the occupation of farmland. Among the 837 letters, about 40 percent were directed against either city-level authorities or their agencies (12.9 percent) or county-level authorities or their agencies (26.4 percent), and nearly 26 percent were directed against township governments and their cadres.[58] The actual conflicts caused by state authorities at the county level and above could be larger than 40 percent because these authorities sometimes require township or village governments to implement their plans.

In addition to the fact that some village cadres themselves are corrupt, seeing land use as a good opportunity to reap personal gain, village cadres have little power when dealing with upper-level authorities even if they want to. As a result, peasants often defend their land without the help of village cadres. Among the 837 letters, 75 percent were submitted by peasants as a collective. While a small number of complaint letters were sent by village committees (4 percent) or production groups (14 percent), they accounted for just 18 percent of the cases.

Village cadres' unwillingness or inability to organize preemptive action implies that peasant resistance to the occupation of land is mostly reactive in the sense that they take defensive action after their interests have been encroached or are being encroached. Regardless of their modes of action, peasants face serious hurdles. For example, like other groups of citizens who fight against the government or government-supported businesses, peasants have encountered serious difficulties in going to courts. Some local justice departments have even convened meetings of lawyers to warn them against accepting such administrative litigation cases.[59] Local courts may refuse to accept peasants' lawsuits against local governments.[60] Therefore, peasants have mainly relied on extrajudicial modes of resistance, including collective petitions and other modes of collective action.

Petitions remain the mode of action most commonly used by peasants when they have conflicts with state agencies over issues including land use.[61] As presented in Table 3.3, the number of letters and petitions to the Ministry of Land and Resources has increased in recent years, involving more than 12,000 petitioners in 2005. In the first half of 2002, petitions regarding the illegal occupation of land accounted for 73 percent of the total petitions received by the ministry.[62] According to a research group's analysis of 62,450 messages sent by citizens to a central media organization in the first half of 2004, 36 percent concerned rural issues, with 69 percent of these being about rural land use. It was also found that peasants who went to Beijing to present petitions mostly complained about the issue of rural land use, especially after the rural tax reform.[63]

Peasants have also resorted to disruptive actions. For example, in Inner Mongolia, seventy-two instances of social unrest occurred between January 2004 and March 2004 ,involving 10,476 participants, or 146 on the average in each instance. Twenty-six (or 36 percent) of the cases occurred because of land use in rural and urban areas.[64] According to a 2004 account of 130

TABLE 3.3
Petitions to the Ministry of Land and Resources in Selected Years

	2002	2003	2005[a]
Letters	3,380	5,250	8,930
Petitions in person	1,760	2,350	3,640
Petitioners	5,870	8,890	12,120
Collective Petitions	193	402	
Average participants	15	12	

SOURCES: The website of the Ministry of Land and Resources, retrieved on June 2, 2006 from www.mlr.ov.cn/zt/mlr youth/xxyd/xxyd_4.htm; the website of Nanyang Bureau of Land and Resources, retrieved on June 5, 2006 from www.nygtzy.gov.cn.

[a]Between January and November.

mass confrontations between peasants and police reported by Yu Jianrong, eighty-seven were due to land use. Forty-eight occurred when peasants tried to stop the occupation of their land by confronting police officers. In those confrontations, hundreds of peasants were wounded, three were killed, and more than 160 were detained.[65] Such incidents have recurred in recent years. In a township in Guangdong in 2006, more than 5,000 peasants from several villages blocked traffic to protest against low compensation for their lost land. Violent confrontation occurred when more than 1,000 police officers tried to drive away the protesters. Reportedly, a thirteen-year-old girl was killed in the clash, and some police officers and villagers were also injured.[66] Subsequent chapters will show that some of the largest protests that have occurred in the communist era were the direct result of peasants' complaints about the low compensation for land use.

Nevertheless, peasants have encountered tremendous difficulties in protecting their rights against land users. For example, according to a survey of 500 peasants who lost land in seventeen provinces in 2005, thirty-two peasants reported that they were not satisfied with the compensation and appealed to pertinent authorities through letters or petitions in person. Only three reported that the compensation was raised to a satisfactory level, whereas twenty-two, or 69 percent, reported that the compensation was not increased or that authorities did not take any action. Five peasants reported the use of lawsuits, but only one of them succeeded.[67]

Among the 261 cases I collected, sixty-six concerned farmers' collective resistance to land use, and ten of them succeeded. In six of the ten successful cases, peasants succeeded because of the intervention from the central or provincial governments. As detailed in Chapter Six, intervention from above was possible in some cases largely because of the large number of participants or because of the serious casualties or death of peasants. Certainly, the collection of sixty-six cases may not be representative in terms of the proportion of successful collective action, but these cases do reveal the significant hurdles faced by Chinese citizens when they stage resistance against local governments or officials. A combination of local governments' power with the high cost of concessions determines the small chance of success in peasant resistance to the occupation of their farmland.

CAUSES OF THE DIFFICULTIES

The obstacles to success faced by peasants resisting land use are many, but the most fundamental one is that the high costs of addressing peasants' grievances seriously undermine upper-level state authorities' willingness to intervene. Once farmland is taken, it is difficult to convert it back because it has often been used for construction. Technically, the central government is unable to prevent land acquisition because the land may be used for legitimate purposes or for projects approved by the central or provincial governments. In consequence, local officials in China tend to see "violating the law for public interests" as a fairly low-risk activity.[68] Farmland is often appropriated by local government officials who claim that doing so will speed up local development in line with the goals of the central government, although the land may in reality be used to generate revenue or for other purposes.

An official of the Ministry of Land and Resources acknowledged in 2006 that "almost all serious law violations in land use involve [local] governments or the leaders."[69] Local governments were responsible for 80 percent of the land illegally taken.[70] The previous chapters have shown that punishing local leaders, especially at higher levels, is difficult. Table 3.4 shows that, from 2000 to 2004, 616,360 cases of law- or regulation-violating cases were investigated, but only 4,705 people were disciplined by the party or the government, and just 521 people were tried in court for their corruption in land use. As a result, although the central government may urge local governments to respect peasants' rights, the small likelihood of being punished makes it easy for local officials to ignore upper-level authorities' instructions, which renders it more difficult for peasants to resist their abuses of power. In my collection, petitions were the most important mode of action used by the peasants. But only in five of the cases did peasants receive meaningful response from upper-level authorities. In addition, local cadres were punished in only six of the sixty-six cases, thus implying a rather small risk in abusing power.

The small chance of success undermines the peasants' confidence in the party-state. Chinese citizens often blame local governments for their problems, as opposed to the central government, either because they believe that the central government is unaware of local government misconduct or because local government agents have directly caused their suffering.[71] But this perception is formed by local people who have not approached the central authorities with their problems. Once they have done so, their disappointment in the central government becomes pronounced.[72] In one case, a peasant representative from Fujian province spent months crafting appeals to the authorities in Beijing about the loss of farmland, but to no avail. He

TABLE 3.4
Officials Disciplined in Land Use

	Cases		State Agents Disciplined	
	Detected	Investigated	Party/Administrative	Criminal
2000	184,000	172,000	622	49
2001	125,200	117,360	958	107
2002	140,000	114,000	1,223	168
2003	178,000	128,000	925	132
2004	111,000	85,000	977	65
Total	738,200	616,360	4,705	521

sources: *Jingji ribao*, April 27, 2002; *Renmin ribao*, April 12, 2003; *Beijing chenbao*, March 24, 2004; *Fazhi ribao*, April 17, 2005.

approached all the central agencies that could be helpful and more than ten news agencies. He explains why he finally gave up:

> I was fed up with the ignorance and indifference I experienced. Local people hate corruption and had a boundless expectation of and trust in the Center (*zhong yang*). We thought that local officials abused power without the knowledge of the center, and the center would never tolerate it had it known it. How could we expect that central agencies would deal with our complaints perfunctorily? Almost all of them would tell a few irresponsible officials to talk with us and accept our petitions and then refer them back to local authorities. Having experienced this once or twice, many people come to believe that central agencies do not have the authority or capacity to require lower-level authorities to address our problems at all.[73]

The provincial government tends to be even less willing than the central government to intervene because it is more closely tied to lower-level governments. In a city in Sichuan province, the city government occupied peasants' farmland to establish a so-called high-technology development zone in 1993 without adequately compensating the peasants. More than 30,000 peasants were affected, either because they lost land or because their homes were dismantled. They appealed to the authorities and the courts at both the central and local levels, but to no avail. In July 2002, 1,300 peasants jointly applied to the government of Sichuan province for an administrative reconsideration of the local government's decision to occupy their farmland, but they were ignored by the provincial authority. The local authority eventually felt pressure when the case was exposed on the central television network in 2003. By the time the media disclosed the case, the deadline for the provincial authority to reply to the peasants' application for an administrative reconsideration had passed. The provincial authority then issued a formal rejection and closed the case.[74]

Desperate peasants have exhausted almost all possible avenues in their fight for their rights. Some have appealed to the foreign media or organizations in Beijing and even Hong Kong.[75] Others have even committed suicide to attract attention to their grievances. Petitioners have also embarrassed central state authorities, such as the National People's Congress (NPC). In 2004, more than 100 petitioners in Beijing sued the NPC on the grounds that it had made laws with loopholes that allowed local governments to abuse power and thus encroach on citizens' rights. The congress was also accused of failing to prevent local governments and legal departments from abusing power. Not surprisingly, when petitioners filed the lawsuit with the high court in Beijing and the Supreme Court, they were rejected. Peasants who lost land have also embarrassed local officials by signing appeals to the people's congresses at both the local and national levels, requesting that the congresses rescind the memberships of their local officials.[76] These actions certainly challenged the legitimacy of the party-state.

SUPPRESSION AS A MODE OF RESPONSE

Upper-level governments' reluctance to intervene does not imply that local governments are thereby absolved of responding to peasant grievances. Peasants' resistance damages the image or performance of the local government. This pressure, as discussed above, may drive local governments to use repression if the cost of concessions is too high, while peasant resistance is likely to persist. In the sixty-six cases I collected, more than 320 peasants were detained, arrested, or put in jail because of their resistance (Table 3.5). Leaders or activists were mostly charged with the crime of assembling the masses to disrupt the social order, attack state agencies, or prevent law enforcement. It is not rare for peasants to be wounded when protecting their land through confrontation. In my collection, at least 120 peasants were injured in their confrontations with local officials and/or police officers.

In Yulin city in Shaanxi province, the local government took a piece of farmland from a village in 2003 and met with strong resistance from the villagers. The local government sent hundreds of police officers to the village to suppress the resistance several times, but the peasants confronted the police each time. In the end, the local government arrested twenty-seven villagers and put them in jail for up to fifteen years.[77] In another case in

TABLE 3.5
Major Modes of Peasant Resistance to Land Seizure

Modes of Action	Cases*a*	Crimes	People Punished
Collective Petitions	39	Attacking state agencies (a)	82
Confrontation	23	Disrupting social order (b)	87
Protests/demonstrations	15	*a*, *b*, and others	102
Attacking state agencies	4	Unspecified	52
Lawsuits	3		
Cases or people	66		323

SOURCE: Author's collection.
*a*Some participants adopted more than one mode of action.

Sichuan province, a district government did not follow the compensation plan approved by the provincial government. It took away a piece of land from a village by force by sending 700 police officers and public employees. In the process, eighteen peasants were wounded, seventy were detained for questioning for more than ten hours, and eleven of them were arrested.[78]

Peasants may also be punished when they attempt to approach upper-level authorities because this is damaging to local officials' images. In a number of cases, peasants were detained, beaten, or arrested because of their petitions to upper-level authorities. In the eighty-seven cases of confrontation reported by Yu Jianrong, thirty-one occurred because the police, at the behest of local government officials, tried to prevent peasants from making petitions to higher-level authorities.[79] Similarly, in twenty of the sixty-six cases I collected, peasants were arrested or put in jail because of their petitions to upper-level authorities. In one case, two peasants were jailed for one year and then released on probation only because they threatened to present a petition. In another case in a village in Zhengzhou, the capital city of Henan province, peasants lodged complaints with the governments at the district, city, provincial, and central levels over their loss of farmland. Upset by these petitions, the city authority sent hundreds of police to storm the village to arrest the leaders in July 2004, leaving dozens wounded.[80]

Local governments have considerable autonomy in punishing disobedient peasants and may even receive support from upper-level authorities. As a matter of fact, upper-level authorities, including the provincial and even central authorities, may turn a blind eye to how local officials deal with petitioners as long as they can stop petitioners from approaching the central authorities in Beijing.[81] Some provincial governments have not only tolerated but also encouraged local government repression of peasants who presented petitions in Beijing.[82] Consequently, petitioners in China now have a difficult time traveling to the national capital because of the harassment of local governments. In addition, even though some petitioners can travel to Beijing, they may still be prevented from submitting their petitions if they are found out by their local officials, sent there to stop them.[83] All these obstacles are reflected in the case presented below.

THE MIGRANTS' RESISTANCE IN HEBEI PROVINCE

In 2004, there were several influential cases in which a large number of peasants who lost land signed collective appeals to the people's congresses at the local and national levels, requesting them to remove their local leaders and to rescind their memberships in the people's congresses. Two of these cases occurred in Hebei province and another two in Fujian province.[84] Peasants chose to delegitimize local officials because they had failed after repeated petitions to central and local authorities. This section presents the case of the peasants' collective appeal in Tangshan city in Hebei province to show the obstacles to successful resistance as discussed above.

Background of the Dispute

In 1986, the provincial government of Hubei decided to construct a reservoir in a county in Qinhuangdao city. It was expected that the reservoir would not only address the water shortage in the eastern part of the province but also bring economic benefits (i.e., water fees) to local governments. According to the plan, more than 40,000 people in thirty-six villages of eight townships in this county had to be relocated in two cities that would benefit from the reservoir. More than 17,000 people were relocated in Qinhuangdao city, and more people (i.e., 23,000) were relocated in Tangshan city because Tangshan was expected to benefit more from the reservoir.[85]

The relocation of the peasants was carried out between 1992 and 1997. According to the compensation plan made by the provincial government, each peasant should be paid about 13,000 yuan in compensation.[86] As for the sources of funding, the provincial government provided 62 million yuan, and the two cities were expected to raise more than 200 million yuan. By the end of 1998 when the reservoir was completed; however, the local governments were able to raise only about two-thirds of the funds. As a result, the peasants were inadequately paid, and each person was owed thousands of yuan. One migrant reported,

> The land seizure destroyed my home and ruined my family [his parents died because of frustration]. The 1,400 fruit trees and 8,235 trees my family owned were flooded. According to Directive No. 55 of Hebei Province, the minimum compensation for the trees was 518,378 yuan. But we were given only 1,500 yuan. Our family was forced to move to Fengnan county in Tangshan city. The provincial government stipulated that each person should receive 13,000 yuan in compensation, but the actual amount we received was only about 4,000 yuan because the money was deducted by the government at each level.[87]

As a result, some relocated migrants could not afford to construct new houses in designated villages because of the inadequate compensation. The migrants not only suffered serious economic losses but also incurred other problems when they tried to settle in new communities. Some migrants returned to their hometowns because they had been unfairly treated by the local authorities responsible for relocating migrants. But because the environment in their hometowns had been destroyed, their life was very difficult.

While migrants were inadequately paid, the compensation funds were mismanaged by the city and county governments. According to the audit report released by the National Audit Office of the State Council in 1999, local governments misappropriated 220 million yuan for departmental or personal uses. The money was used to make investments, make loans, and construct office buildings. For example, the head of the Relocation Office of Tangshan city misappropriated 8.9 million yuan.[88] Some officials deposited the money in their personal bank accounts to collect the interests, while others simply embezzled the money.

Migrants' Resistance and Government Response

The miserable situation faced by the migrants gave rise to their strong resentment and resistance. The migrants in Tangshan were relocated in 152 townships in six counties, but this did not prevent their collective action. The massive migration affected not only peasants but also some local cadres. Some migrants had been vice township heads, village party secretaries, village directors, or heads of township government departments, such as the land management station, the finance station, and the justice station, before the migration. For example, one activist, Zhang Youren, had been the head of the justice station of a township, and another activist, Qiao Zhanke, used to be a vice township head. These cadres, mostly aged between 40 and 60, knew government policies and enjoyed prestige among the migrants. They became the representatives of the migrants in their resistance.[89]

Like peasants seeking justice elsewhere in China, the migrants in Tangshan city began their resistance in 1996 by presenting petitions to almost all pertinent authorities at the provincial and national levels, including the Central Discipline Inspection Commission, the General Office of the central party committee, and the General Office of the State Council. They had also approached legal departments, including the courts. But also like many peasants elsewhere in China, the migrants did not receive any meaningful responses after they had appealed for years.

Although these migrants failed to obtain intervention from upper-level authorities, their resistance upset the city government in Tangshan. Reluctant to make concessions, local officials used repression to silence or deter the migrants. A number of migrants were detained, beaten, wounded, or even disabled because of their resistance. On April 1, 2000, when more than 100 migrants went to Shijiazhuang, the provincial capital city, to present petitions, they were detained as Falungong practitioners. In addition to being fined tens of thousands of yuan, the migrants were beaten, and some were seriously wounded. Four participants were put in jail for three to five years on the charge of attacking state agencies.

By 2004, the migrants had exhausted almost all possible means of resistance, but they did not achieve any success. The representatives then decided to delegitimize the city party secretary who had been seen as the culprit of the migrants' sufferings. They believed that, according to law, citizens have the right to remove unqualified members of the people's congress. Therefore, they decided to collect the signatures of migrants to present a collective appeal to rescind the city party secretary's memberships in the National People's Congress (NPC) and the provincial people's congress.[90] Zhang Youren gave a reason for their appeal to the NPC:

> We hope that the people's congress will send a team to take a look at people's life in the reservoir area. You cannot find a place like this in any other part of the world. Life there is worse than in the slums in the United States. In the slums, black people at least have bread. But in the reservoir area, the people cannot afford even to have corn cake. More than 60 million yuan in compensation has been misappropriated and embezzled by government officials. There is

simply no difference between these officials and the rulers of autocratic societies who "kill the poor to amass wealth."[91]

On January 31, 2004, thirty representatives met and discussed the collection of signatures. It was decided that, in each township, there would be one or two people responsible for collecting signatures, and the total number of such activists was about 300. From February 1, 2004, the activists began to approach the migrants in their respective townships to collect their signatures. To avoid the suspicion of local officials, the representatives normally went to collect signatures during the night. Some of the representatives also went back to their hometowns to collect the signatures of those who had moved back. Each peasant who agreed to the appeal was asked to write down his or her name and identification card number, and sign it with his or her fingerprint. Within two weeks, the activists collected 11,200 signatures.

However, because of the large scale of the action, the news of petition reached some local cadres. Local officials and the police began to keep an eye on the activists. Under this circumstance, the representatives decided to go to Beijing ahead of their original schedule in case local officials took action against them. On the nights of February 26 and 27, ten representatives, including Zhang Youren, went to Beijing with the signatures that the activists had collected. Local police began to check the passengers who were going to Beijing in the local bus and railway stations, so the representatives had to leave for Tianjin first and then go to Beijing from there. When the city authority learned that the representatives had departed for Beijing, a large number of local police and officials from the six counties, including township and village cadres, were sent to Beijing to stop the representatives.

By February 28, all the ten representatives had arrived in Beijing. The next day, the representatives combined all the signatures they had collected and made five copies. On the same day, one representative returned to Tangshan to get another 2,000 signatures that were ready for collection, and the other nine representatives approached *Guangming Daily*, an influential national newspaper, to report their appeal. Journalists showed a strong interest in their case because appealing to rescind the congress membership of a city leader had never occurred in China before. They promised that the newspaper would cover their story when they presented their appeal to the NPC that would be convened soon.

Nevertheless, on March 1, seven representatives were found and caught in a small hotel by the police and officials from Tangshan. Fortunately, the appeal materials were not kept by the seven representatives; they were kept by Zhang Youren and Qiao Zhanke who, at that time, happened to be staying with Yu Meisun, a former government official in Beijing.[92] Zhang and Qiao thus took the responsibility of presenting the appeal.

When the news that the representatives were detained reached the migrants in Tangshan, they were angered and planned to go to Beijing to present petitions. Zhang Youren sent an urgent application for demonstration to the Ministry of Public Security on March 1 by express. The application stated the following:

> We are representatives of 20,000 migrants in Tangshan city in Hebei province. We come to Beijing to appeal to the National People's Congress to rescind the congress membership of Zhang He, the city party secretary of Tangshan, in light of the law. In Shouchang Lu Hotel in Beijing, the police from Tangshan arrested seven representatives, while two fled and went to hiding. The 20,000 migrants in Tangshan are angered, and 5,000 of them are coming to Beijing to report the criminal conduct of the party committee of Tangshan city to the people's congress. According to the Law on Demonstrations and Protests, we make a particularly urgent application to the ministry, requesting it to provide protection for the petitioners along the road.[93]

Zhang Youren did not expect that the ministry would approve their application. But he certainly hoped that the application could inform central authorities of their case and encourage their intervention. It was unclear whether the ministry informed the Tangshan city government of the collective petition. In the end, the petition did not occur.

Given that the local officials were still searching for Zhang and Qiao, they had to hide themselves. In this circumstance, Yu Meisun sent the collective appeal to the National People's Congress on March 4, by express, on behalf of Zhang and Qiao. Yu then reported this incident online and made it known to the public. Not surprisingly, the National People's Congress did not reply to the migrants' appeal. On March 19, Zhang Youren was caught by the police from Tangshan and was brought back to the city. He was then detained without justifiable reasons and was released on June 30, 2004, only after he went on a hunger strike. But the police placed him under surveillance as a suspect for "violating other peoples' personal honor."

The migrants' resistance thus failed again. The central and provincial governments refused to intervene, perhaps because they did not want to provide economic assistance and/or punish the city leaders. The lack of intervention from above allowed the local governments to use suppression with immunity. In Qinhuangdao city, more than 10,000 migrants who complained about the low compensation also signed an appeal to remove the mayor, but failed. When the government in Qinhuangdao learned about the appeal, it quickly repressed it. In the case of Tangshan, although local officials failed to prevent the migrants' appeal to the NPC, they did not face serious consequences. Having experienced these failures, the migrants' disappointment with central authorities was pronounced.

Conclusion

This chapter discusses the conditions for successful resistance by presenting the outcomes of the 261 cases of resistance I collected. These cases provide strong evidence for the conditions of successful resistance outlined in Chapter One: Participants are most likely to succeed when their demands are less costly and their action is forceful. By the same token, they are least likely to succeed when their demands are costly and their action is less forceful. A cost-benefit analysis of state response to popular resistance is not new,[94] but this approach may lead to a tautological argument without defining the cost and benefit. In this chapter, I have shown that the financial resources required for addressing citizens' grievances as well as the discipline of government officials are two major types of cost that affect state response to popular resistance in China.

These factors point to the difficulties in staging successful resistance in China. First, Chinese citizens stage resistance in many cases because their interests have been directly violated by state agencies. This implies that the cost of concession is high for the government because disciplining these agencies can be politically costly or because the government is reluctant to give up its economic benefits. Second, if the number of participants is used to assess the forcefulness of collective resistance, the participants in most instances are unable to stage powerful action because their resistance is often small in scale (i.e., with fewer than 100 participants). Therefore, most protesting groups have rather limited intervention-seeking abilities.

The difficulties in successful resistance have been fully reflected in peasant resistance to the nonagricultural use of farmland, which shows that the high cost of making concessions determines a small chance of success in peasant resistance. Given the benefits reaped by local governments and their officials from the nonagricultural use of farmland, there is often a zero-sum game between local governments and peasants. As a result, local governments are often reluctant to make concessions. Worse still, land use involves local governments or local leaders, so upper-level authorities face a high political cost when they intervene to mete out punishment. Effective intervention from above is rather rare in land use cases, which implies that most incidents of peasant resistance are exclusively handled by local governments, which may resort to suppression when necessary. The case of rural land use thus suggests that weak groups need to receive extra support or find extra leverage to achieve success.

FOUR

Issue Linkage and Effective Resistance

A common problem or the fundamental hurdle encountered by Chinese citizens who defend their legitimate rights is the high threshold of intervention from upper-level authorities. As discussed in the previous chapter, the lack of intervention from above often means failure when the cost of concessions incurred by local governments is high. The pivotal issue is how citizens can overcome the hurdle or get upper-level authorities involved in the settlement of their grievances. Earlier chapters have shown that protesting groups' intervention-seeking ability is largely affected by the forcefulness of their resistance. Therefore, some protesting groups can achieve success by staging powerful disruptive actions. This will be discussed in detail in Chapters Six and Seven. However, given the conditions for effective disruptive tactics (e.g., a large number of participants) and the risk of punishment imposed by the government, Chinese citizens tend to use less confrontational modes of resistance when possible (also see Chapter Two). Needless to say, the success of nondisruptive tactics is highly conditional, depending on whether citizens can place effective constraints on local officials.

This chapter and the next chapter show that, when using nondisruptive tactics, Chinese citizens may improve their chance of success by exploiting the political space embedded in the political system with means that are acceptable to the state. Chapter Five focuses on citizens seeking support from within the state through personal networks. In this chapter, I demonstrate that some citizens increase their chance of success by applying multiple constraints on local officials. Usually, intervention from upper-level authorities is more likely when local officials' malfeasance is serious. This happens when local officials violate a law or a government regulation to a degree that is unacceptable to upper-level authorities. Local officials' malfeasance may also be seen as serious when they simultaneously violate different laws and government regulations. In these circumstances, citizens can place multiple pressures on local officials by relating their grievances to other problems that are tied to the same local governments. When local governments fail to address citizens' grievances or try to repress their demands, the citizens can reveal or threaten to reveal local officials' other types of malfeasance to upper-level authorities. Depending on the seriousness of those issues, local officials may need to make concessions to silence the citizens. In this way, issue linkage expands the opportunity for resistance and strengthens citizens' bargaining power.

Applying Constraints on Chinese Local Officials

In a political system with multiple levels of governance like China's, there is a high possibility of the leakage of authority, a problem that occurs when orders pass down through various levels of the hierarchy. Downs explains how such a leakage occurs: Official A issues an order to B, but B's own goals indicate that his commands to his subordinate C should encompass only 90 percent of what he believes A actually has in mind. If C thinks in the same way, by the time A's order reaches D-level officials, they will receive commands that encompass only 81 percent (90 percent of 90 percent) of what A really intends.[1] Such a leakage accumulates when many levels are involved and can have a striking impact on the effectiveness of orders issued by top-level officials in a multiple-level hierarchy.[2] In China, the degree of leakage of authority has important implications for popular resistance because it shapes the opportunity for successful resistance.

Existing research on social protests has found that political opportunities may vary across issues and groups and that there can be issue- and group-specific opportunities.[3] Such opportunities sometimes mean that certain institutional arrangements are more likely to produce protests by certain groups, or that, over a relatively long time span, certain changes in the society may strengthen some groups' positions and create better opportunities for action.[4] In China, group-specific opportunities have much to do with the central government's commitment to the solution of the group's issue. A strong commitment means less leakage of authority because higher-level local officials will expend more effort to enforce an order that they recognize as important to the central government. For citizens who stage resistance, the government's strong commitment to the issue they have raised increases the possibility of intervention from above and, therefore, the odds of successful resistance. By the same token, the government's weak commitment means a small chance of success. The nonagricultural use of farmland discussed in the previous chapter is an illuminating example of the impact of the leakage of authority on peasants' chance of success in the sense that local officials do not believe that upper-level authorities are serious about the protection of peasants' right.

The government's commitment is affected by the importance of a grievance (the number of people affected by the issue, for example) and the cost of intervention. Given that the importance and cost vary across issues, the willingness of upper-level governments to intervene in different issues also varies. Their willingness to intervene is not always as weak as it is in the case of the nonagricultural use of farmland. Certainly, when citizens' complaints are not high on the agenda of the government, their chance of success is low. Alternatively, when complaints or grievances become numerous, the threshold of intervention from above is also raised. In these circumstances, the citizens' chance of success will be improved if they are able to link their grievances to issues for which the leakage of authority is less serious. For example, the central or upper-level local government is more tolerant of local officials' malfeasance or abuse of power for so-called public interest,[5] but they are less tolerant of officials' abuse of power for personal gain (e.g., corruption), other things being equal. If citizens link their grievances about a particular issue with local officials' self-interested malfeasance or failures in performing some other important duties, the threat they pose to the officials is likely to be serious.

Issue linkage thus expands the political space for successful resistance by placing local officials in a difficult situation: If they suppress certain demands from citizens, they also prompt the latter to pursue other demands that are more likely to trigger intervention from above. As a result, issue linkage increases the risk to local officials who use or intend to use suppression. Needless to say, the use of this mode of resistance is conditional, depending on whether citizens are able to find issues that are important to upper-level authorities and can be linked to the same local governments that are being targeted.

In the remainder of this chapter, I demonstrate how issue linkage creates opportunities for successful resistance with the case of peasant resistance to tax collection prior to the abolition of the agricultural tax in rural China. Financial burdens were a cause of peasant grievances across the country until the early 2000s, when the agricultural tax was abolished.[6] Unlike in the case of nonagricultural use of farmland, the punishment of malfeasant local officials is more credible or serious in cases of tax collection. Many local officials, including provincial-level officials, were punished for their abuse of power in tax and fee collection or for their failure to discipline lower-level officials. The central government was especially intolerant of local officials whose behavior led to casualties or large-scale confrontations. However, despite the central government's serious attention to this issue, there was a still a threshold that peasants needed to cross to have their grievances heard. Thus, they used a number of methods to increase their chance of success. Staging large-scale disruptive actions was an option, but not all peasants were able to take such action. Some peasants resorted to issue linkage by connecting the payment of taxes and fees to the solution of other issues, thereby applying multiple constraints on local officials. Issue linkage proved effective when local officials were reluctant to have upper-level authorities see their misconduct in tax collection and other areas.

The Case of Peasant Resistance to Tax Collection

In the 1990s, peasants' financial burdens became a dominant issue that affected the relationship between peasants and the government in China, especially at the local level. Rural China was in large part economically segregated from the urban areas, in the sense that peasants were mostly responsible for financing public institutions in rural areas, such as education. Rural cadres, especially at the township level, were politically answerable to higher-level authorities and had to fulfill the various responsibilities assigned to them.[7] When rural governments lacked adequate funding to fulfill these responsibilities, they often turned to the peasants. The fiscal pressure on local governments worsened after 1994, when fiscal reform was initiated and a majority of revenues were collected by the central government.[8]

Figure 4.1 shows that, before 1998, peasants' financial burdens remained at relatively high levels in terms of the proportion that taxes and fees took from their total income.[9] Between 1994 and 1997, the average income of peasants was 1.9 times that of 1993, but they paid fees that were nine times as high as they had been between 1990 and 1993.[10] Peasants, especially those in agricultural areas, seriously suffered from this financial burden.[11] In a county in Hubei province, one peasant, an ex-prisoner, wrote a letter to the county magistrate in 1996 and complained, "The living standard of a prisoner is better than that of a peasant like me."[12] Michelson's survey of 2,970 peasant households in seven counties found that "peasants' burdens exert a dramatic and detrimental effect on overall life satisfaction." He elaborated: "Burdens not only produce grievances, but, together with these grievances, they also erode the general happiness of those who are subjected to them."[13]

On the other hand, township and village cadres widely acknowledged that tax collection was perhaps the most difficult job in rural China in the 1990s.[14] Tax evasion by peasants was by no means rare. According to a study based on twenty townships in fifteen counties in ten provinces, an estimated 10 to 20 percent of peasant households owed taxes or fees.[15] In some places, 20 to 40 percent of taxes and fees were not collected, largely because of the peasants' resistance.[16] In a city in Guangdong province, the government could collect only about 60 percent of taxes.[17] In some places, village and township governments had to borrow money to make payments when peasants refused to pay.[18] According to a survey of 182 villages in Hubei province, the taxes and fees owed by peasants accounted for, on average, 34 percent of the net assets of each village.[19] By 2005, peasants nationwide owed an estimated total of 60 billion yuan.[20]

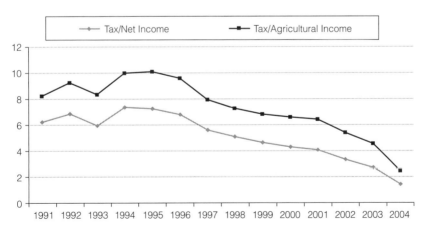

FIGURE 4.1 Peasants' Financial Burdens in China (1991–2004). SOURCE: Calculated from the National Statistical Bureau, *Zhongguo nongcun zhuhu diaocha nianjian 2005* (2005 yearbook of Chinese rural households) (Beijing Zhongguo tongji chubanshe, 2005), 35–39.

Peasants refused to pay taxes and fees because they were too poor, to be sure, but they sometimes refused to pay also because simply they did not want to. For example, of the twenty-six cases in which peasants refused to pay taxes in Hunan province, 54 percent cited reasons other than not being able to afford to pay.[21] They resisted tax or fee payment in various ways.[22] Some gave up their contracted land and refused to farm; others managed to obtain certificates of disability to avoid paying taxes or fees; and still others cancelled their household registration so as to be excluded from the taxed population.[23] Peasants also staged high-profile resistance, including protests, demonstrations, and attacks on the local government. Bernstein and Lu report a number of cases of individual and collective peasant resistance to tax and fee collection.[24] Available reports indicate that some instances of resistance involved thousands of participants (see Appendix C).

In explaining the occurrence of peasant resistance to tax and fee collection in rural China, the role of the central government is crucial. Bernstein and Lu write, "The most important resource that emboldened villagers to engage in strategic, rational collective action was the belief that the central authorities themselves opposed excessive burdens and therefore sided with them against their own agents."[25] Such a belief, supported by the favorable policies issued by the central authorities, inspired "rightful resistance."[26] However, this central–local divide did not ensure success on the part of the peasants because of the high threshold of intervention from upper-level authorities.

POLICY-BASED RESISTANCE AND THE THRESHOLD OF INTERVENTION

In rural China before the tax reform, the taxes and fees peasants were required to pay included: (1) state taxes, (2) township-retained fees and village-retained fees, (3) obligatory labor and cumulative labor, and (4) ad hoc fees. The state tax was not heavy; rather, peasants complained most about the second and fourth types.[27] In 1991, the Chinese central government decreed that the township-retained fees and village-retained fees paid by peasants could not exceed 5 percent of their income in the previous year (on a township basis before 1998 and on a village basis after 1998).[28] This limit became the legal basis for peasant resistance to local cadres who were responsible for tax and fee collection.

According to the Chinese Tax Law, government officials at each level do not have the right to collect taxes (taxes can be collected only by the tax collection department). However, tax collection in rural China became the responsibility of rural cadres, contributing to peasant–cadre contention. The higher-level government assigned the job of tax collection to rural cadres at the township and village levels rather than relying on tax collection departments. Moreover, the higher-level government linked the fulfillment of this task to the performance evaluations and salaries of rural cadres.[29] Given the limited staffing of the township government, village cadres played an important role in the collection of taxes and fees. In village governments that depended entirely on tax payments for income, cadres' salaries were taken from the tax pool.

Originally, township governments in many areas collected taxes and fees through the grain station when peasants sold grain. The central government stopped this practice because some local governments also collected unauthorized fees in this way.[30] As a result, the cadres' only option became door-to-door collection. Usually, township cadres assigned the task of tax and fee collection to the village authority, who then asked the head of each production group to collect fees and taxes in his or her respective group. In other cases, the village-level cadres collected the fees themselves. Township cadres were also involved in tax and fee collection. Given the difficulty of the job, the township party committee and the government commonly assigned each township cadre to a few villages to help fulfill the task. This arrangement naturally led to an interest alignment between township and village cadres.[31]

People comply with laws not only to avoid punishment for failing to do so but also because of their belief in the legitimacy of the law.[32] The reverse is also true. If the policies or the people who implement the policies lack legitimacy, then it will be difficult to achieve voluntary compliance. In rural China, some cadres abused power or were believed to have abused power in tax collection, so peasants were often reluctant to pay. The difficulties in collecting taxes in turn prompted many rural cadres to use force, leading to further complaints and resistance from peasants. The Ministry of Agriculture received 2,770 letters and petitions concerning peasants' financial burdens in 1998. About 20 percent of the letters focused on cadres' abuse of power in collecting taxes. This complaint was second only to the complaint that cadres imposed unauthorized fees (29 percent).[33] When employing force, rural cadres confiscated property such as television sets, grain, and even livestock from peasant households that refused to pay their taxes and/or fees.[34]

From the mid-1990s, the use of force became increasingly unacceptable to the central government.[35] Central authorities showed unprecedented determination to prohibit the use of force in tax and fee collection, claiming that if serious incidents occurred (for example, peasants' deaths or large-scale confrontations between peasants and cadres), cadres would be punished.[36] The central government stressed that tragic events resulting from resistance to taxation must be thoroughly investigated and those responsible punished. Additionally, the central government indicated that the investigation and punishment of offending cadres should be publicized for the purposes of the democratic and legal education of the masses. Specifically, the "one-item-veto" system was adopted to deal with local officials, which meant that when serious incidents occurred, the performance of the responsible cadres would be censured regardless of their other achievements. Further, those who covered up or failed to investigate such events or retaliated against people who reported serious incidents would be severely punished, and major party and government leaders at the county and city levels would be held responsible for serious incidents and their promotion halted. If serious incidents repeatedly occurred in a place and caused significant social impact, party and government leaders at the provincial level would also be considered liable.

The central government also issued an annual statement to local officials about the serious incidents of resistance that had occurred in tax collection from the early 1990s. Table 4.1 charts the serious incidents reported by central authorities from 1992 to 2004. Not all casualties were caused by force. In fact, many rural cadres were very cautious when dealing with peasants. Some peasants committed suicide because of their financial burdens. Of the twelve peasants who died in 1995, three died in violent confrontations with rural cadres, while the other nine committed suicide. Still, three of the suicides took place after the peasants had been humiliated by rural cadres. Regardless of the reasons for the deaths, when such cases were revealed, the cadres involved were punished. In thirty-eight of the cases reported in Table 4.1, 339 cadres, including provincial-level officials, received party, administrative, or legal punishment. From July 2002 to June 2003, there were fifteen serious incidents that caused fourteen peasant deaths. As a result, 142 officials were disciplined, including three at the city level and thirty at the county level. Six were tried in the courts.[37]

Hence, despite the fact that serious casualties did not disappear in tax collection before the abolition of the agricultural tax starting in 2004, the central government's determined attention to the taxation issue created

TABLE 4.1
Serious Incidents in Tax Collection

Year	Cases	Deaths of Peasants	Cadres Punished
1992	17	17	—
1993	30	—	—
1994	9	9	—
1995	13	12	—
1996	26	26	—
1997	16	—	—
1998	16	—	—
1999	8	8	42
2000	19	—	—
2001	26	—	—
2002	13	13	126
2003	15	14	142
2004	3	3	29

SOURCE: Li Maolan, *Zhongguo nongmin fudan wenti yanjiu* (Research on peasants' financial burdens in China) (Taiyuan: Shanxi jingji chubanshe, 1996), 127; Liang Jun, *Cunmin zizhi* (Villagers' self governance) (Beijing: Zhongguo qingnian chubanshe, 2000), 18; retrieved on March 5, 2004, from: www.china-village.org/bbs/showtopic.asp and on May 22, 2004, from: www.xcagri.gov.cn/ news; *Zhongguo qingnian bao*, December 26, 2005.

tension in the government hierarchy below the central level. As a result, upper-level local governments (at the provincial level, for example) also put pressure on the levels below them to avoid conflicts over taxation.[38] Certainly, this was premised on the condition that peasants were able to stage a powerful action that made both the upper-level government and the public aware that local officials seriously violated government regulations.[39] One county party secretary in Hunan province described this risk from tax collection prior to the tax reform starting in 2002:

> Now the basic issue in rural areas is social stability. If there is confrontation arising from tax collection, the township government must restrain itself, ensuring that nothing serious will happen. This is because such incidents may have serious consequences. If an incident catches the attention of upper-level authorities, especially the central government, it is no longer an issue of whether we are able to collect enough money to pay the employees but an issue of violating party discipline and the law.[40]

For example, in a township in Hunan province, peasants owed 4.2 million yuan in taxes and fees by 1998. Their widespread resistance to paying taxes was beyond the control of the township government. In 1999, the county government required the township to turn over one million yuan in revenue or face the removal of township leaders. This overt pressure left the township government with little choice but to use force on the peasants. The township party secretary held a meeting of township cadres, during which they decided to launch a campaign to fulfill the quota. At the meeting, it was decided that cadres could use force to deal with younger peasants who resisted. Cadres were cautioned, however, not to inflict head injuries or to wound peasants to the extent that they would require hospitalization. On September 10, 1999, over 100 cadres were sent to the villages to collect taxes and fees. In this campaign, more than seventy peasants were beaten, and property was confiscated. In response, angry peasants appealed to authorities at the city and provincial levels. The township government's use of force was viewed by the city and provincial authorities as a blatant violation of the central government's policy, and the county government was pressured to act. As a result, the township party secretary received party discipline and was transferred, the township head was removed, and six other cadres were tried in court.[41]

However, given that the threshold of intervention from above was often determined by the occurrence of serious incidents or large-scale confrontations, some local officials concluded that as long as they could prevent serious incidents, their imposition of fees on peasants and their use of force in fee collection would be tolerated.[42] Consequently, those peasants who staged resistance that was not deemed serious encountered tremendous difficulties. For example, there were many cases where peasants' petitions regarding their financial burdens were ignored by upper-level authorities.[43] Nonetheless, peasants who engaged in smaller-scale resistance over tax and fee collection did not always fail. When some peasants threatened to trigger intervention from above, they applied extra constraints on local officials by linking their cause to other relevant issues.

ISSUE LINKAGE AND DUAL CONSTRAINTS ON LOCAL OFFICIALS

In peasants' resistance to local cadres' tax and fee collection, the central government's policies regarding burden reduction were not the only constraints on local officials. Perhaps more commonly, peasants resisted tax and fee collection by linking payment of fees to other issues concerning cadres.[44] Issue linkage could place pressure on rural cadres, especially at the village level, because certain issues could not be easily addressed without revealing some cadres' misconduct or corruption, putting them in a defensive position. Some rural cadres, for example, abused their power to allocate farmland by retaining an excessive amount of farmland without distributing it to peasant households. In some cases, there was a mismatch between the amount of land farmed and the amount of land taxed. Perhaps the most serious misconduct of village cadres concerned their mismanagement of village finances. Reports of mismanagement abounded in the media. The major problem with the management of village financial affairs was the lack of transparency. In more than 60 percent of the sixty-four villages surveyed in Hubei province, for example, the finances of the villages were not transparent.[45] Similarly, a survey of forty-eight villages in Henan province between 1997 and 1998 found that 80 percent of villages did not publicize financial reports.[46]

The lack of fiscal transparency provided many opportunities for corruption. First, village cadres did not report all income, such as fines collected from those who violated the family planning policy, income from land sales or leases, and fees paid by peasants for housing construction.[47] Second, village cadres fabricated expenditures and created phony receipts to receive reimbursement. Third, although their salaries were determined by the township government, in some cases village cadres increased their income by providing subsidies to themselves under various pretexts. Finally, village cadres took advantage of receiving guests for personal gain because the reception fees were paid by the village. Reception fees were a large— and sometimes the largest—expenditure in many villages.[48] Because the accounting rules in many villages were loose, a reimbursement could be made without any formal receipts. In other cases, receipts were written by the village cadres themselves. In a village in Jiangxi province, village cadres spent nearly 300,000 yuan on receptions between 1997 and 1999, and cadres' self-written notes accounted for 95 percent of the receipts.[49]

Many malfeasant village cadres have been punished for such misconduct. In a city in Anhui province, serious corruption was found after an investigation of the finances of 2,000 villages, and, as a result, 1,000 village cadres were punished. An investigation of the thirty-seven townships making up a city in Jiangsu province found that thirty of them mismanaged village finances. Forty-one cadres were punished, including fifteen village party secretaries, nine village heads, and twelve village accountants.[50] In another example in Shandong province in 2000, a county discipline department punished eighty-six village cadres for their mismanagement of village finances, including forty-four village party secretaries and twenty-four village directors.[51]

As a result of the likelihood of punishment for financial corruption, malfeasant or corrupt cadres were reluctant to reveal their disputes with peasants over issues like the mismanagement of village affairs to upper-level authorities. This reluctance provided a basis for issue linkage, as peasants could threaten not to pay if their other grievances were not addressed.[52] To be sure, not all mismanagement was the fault of incumbent village cadres; some problems were inherited from previous village authorities and were too difficult for current village cadres to address. If cadres did not have a high stake in maintaining their position, they might be reluctant to collect taxes and fees from peasants.[53] Reportedly, some local cadres who were sympathetic to peasants supported or even led peasants' resistance to tax collection.[54] But the post of village cadre remains attractive to some peasants because of the benefits (such as the control over public property) associated with the position. Many village cadres had a strong incentive to fulfill the responsibility of tax and fee collection to keep their positions. As a result, the issue linkage by peasants placed dual constraints on village cadres by highlighting their general misconduct or corruption and their specific abuse of power in matters of tax and fee collection.

ISSUE LINKAGE AND TAX EVASION

Successful tax evasion produces a domino effect: When initiators succeed, others are encouraged to follow. In one township in 2002, the amount of taxes and fees owed by peasants totaled 400,000 yuan. When the township government failed to remedy this situation in a timely manner, the amount increased by 75 percent the following year.[55] Hence, large-scale tax evasion required a critical mass to trigger the process. To be sure, individual peasants or households had always refused to pay taxes and fees in rural China.[56] For example, one peasant in an inland province refused to pay village-retained fees for several years for a number of reasons. He believed that his family had not been treated fairly in the allocation of farmland. In addition, he was responsible for collecting electricity fees in his group in 1997. Because the actual amount he collected was less than what should have been collected, he paid the difference himself. When he went to turn in the fees to the group head, he collapsed and had to spend 200 yuan for medication. His request to deduct the medical expense from his village-retained fees was rejected, though the village had paid for medication when the group head himself got hurt. Further, when the village built a road, the stones that were thrown in his field destroyed his harvest. "For all these reasons," he explained, "I have not paid the village-retained fees these years, but I have paid the agricultural tax, and I never owe the state tax."[57]

The use of issue linkage by individual peasants to avoid paying taxes and fees may fail. The many suicide cases over financial matters indicate the limitations of resistance by individual peasants. According to an investigation of 230 cases in Henan province between 2002 and 2003, where individual peasants had conflicts with rural cadres concerning tax and fee collection, peasant households were assaulted by rural cadres and suffered losses in more than 200 cases. In their conflicts with rural cadres, a majority of these peasants linked tax and fee payment to other issues that needed to be addressed or clarified, such as village or township authorities owing peasants money, failing to allocate land properly, and charging more taxes than peasants actually owed. In most cases, however, the peasants' individual resistance was put down by cadres through the use of force, though without causing deaths.[58]

Rural cadres faced a different situation when groups of peasants (rather than individual peasants) refused to pay by making use of issue linkage. Peasants placed rural cadres in a morally weak position when issues were shown to affect a large number of people. Moreover, their threat to appeal to higher-level authorities was more credible, and their chance of success was greater compared to individual appeals. In some cases, peasants' collective tax evasion was a natural extension of their fights against village cadres on issues like the mismanagement of village affairs or corruption. As a result, the participants in the previous instances of resistance could take further initiative in tax evasion. When a critical mass begins the process of resistance and village cadres fail to stop them, tax evasion spreads.

In a village I visited in an eastern province, many peasants failed to pay taxes and fees at the initiative of a leader.[59] In this village, the cadres had mismanaged the village's finances for years, and peasants strongly suspected that the leaders had embezzled public funds. The village had two collective factories that made some profit, but the village cadres never publicized how the collective income was spent. Although peasants had appealed to the township government and other higher-level authorities, they failed to receive meaningful responses to their letters or their personal visits to these authorities. Then, in 1999, a former village cadre refused to pay the tax, demanding that the village authority publicize information about the village's finances first. Following his lead, about 20 percent of the villagers did not pay their taxes and fees that year, and the number reached about 50 percent in the following year. This resistance forced the village cadres to appeal to the township government for help. The township was unable to use force against the peasants, however, because the local government had a regulation that stipulated that no more than four cadres could go to a peasant household to collect taxes. Given that the peasant who led the tax evasion was a party member, a township leader held a party meeting of cadres and party members in the village and compelled the peasant to stop the tax evasion in the name of the party. The leader had to agree, and tax evasion in the village began to decrease.

Peasants' chances of success were greatly enhanced when they were able to divide the different government levels by undermining the upper-level government's incentive to support lower-level governments. Compared to village cadres, township officials have more resources to deal with disobedient peasants. Without support from the township government, village cadres find it difficult to make disobedient peasants pay. In a village with about 1,240 people I visited in an inland province,[60] tax and fee evasion was very common. More than 93 percent of the 379 households in its thirteen production groups owed fees averaging 327 yuan. Village cadres categorized these peasants into three types: (1) those who were too poor to pay, (2) those who were financially able to pay but reluctant to do so for various reasons, and (3) those who would not pay if others did not. They admitted that a majority of those who refused to pay belonged to the second category.

According to the peasants in this village, their tax evasion was triggered by the cadres' refusal to allow them to see the village's accounts. In 1996, some peasants reached a private consensus and claimed that no tax would be paid until the mismanagement of the village's finances was addressed. Their decision to withhold the payment of taxes was then followed by many other villagers, who believed that they would incur a loss if they paid while others refused. As a result, an overwhelming majority of peasant households in the village participated in the tax evasion.

In this village, as elsewhere, village cadres received "gray" income derived from their positions, and they thus tried very hard to collect township-retained fees to avoid disappointing the township government, which controlled their tenure (despite the introduction of village elections).[61] It is clear that peasants understood the importance of dividing the village and township authorities. They agreed to pay the agricultural tax and the township-retained fees but not the village-retained fees. Because the township government received its share, it had no incentive to help the village cadres collect the village's share. Peasant resistance and the lack of support of the township government demoralized some cadres in the village, especially those who lacked the power to receive gray income, leading some of them to quit.

The Case of Yang Village

Analyzing the case of Yang village effectively reveals peasants' strategies in exploiting the divide between different levels of state authorities, as well as their use of issue linkage. Yang village is a small village that belongs to a large administrative village in Jilin province. It consists of two production groups and more than 100 households.[62] From 1993 to 2000, peasants in Yang village refused to pay all taxes and fees, an amount worth 2.2 million yuan. In 1992, cadres of the administrative village went to Yang village to take back the land of those peasant households that had failed to pay taxes and fees. The village cadres ended up confronting some peasants, causing relations between village cadres and peasants to sour further. A second source of contention occurred in 1993 when, after the township asked villagers to donate 400,000 yuan to build a road, only a limited portion of the money raised was put toward the project. Peasants were not informed about how the remaining funds were used and were thus resentful. In addition, after the administrative village built a factory, it required villagers to pay the taxes and fees on the occupied land. When villagers requested to see the accounts, the village cadres refused, and the peasants in Yang village decided to stop paying taxes and fees. In response, the administrative village successfully sued some of the village peasants. Grain from households involved in the legal tussle was seized as part of the sentence.

The village cadres encountered increasing difficulty in tax and fee collection in subsequent years. To investigate the problem, the township government sent a work team to the village. The peasants cooperated with the team because they hoped that township cadres would be able to address the problems in their village. When the work team failed to resolve their problems, however, the peasants again began to evade taxes and fees. They resisted tax collection in an unprecedented way by preventing cadres from entering their village: Whenever cadres came to the village, villagers would ring a bell, and women, old people, and children would first rush out to surround the cadres and their vehicles. Then, male adults would come out to join them. In 1994, the newly appointed party secretary of the township went to the village to investigate the problems. As he tried to enter the village, the bell rang and the villagers appeared, surrounding his car and driving him out of the village. From that point forward, township cadres were reluctant to go to the village.

Gradually, the village became "a special zone" not managed by the local government. The township government requested that the city government (at the administrative level of a county) address the problem of Yang village, but this request was rejected, and the city government told the township and village governments to solve the problem themselves. The township government lost morale and gave up its fight to collect taxes from Yang village, and the village authority lost all support, making it customary not to pay taxes or fees in the village. A few township cadres tried at a later point to enter the village but failed. In addition to their tactic of surrounding cadres, the villagers also lodged complaints with the city and provincial governments about local cadres' failures to address their problems every time township cadres came to their village. Authorities at the city and provincial levels made phone calls to the township cadres and criticized their work style. A township leader admitted, "We are sandwiched like dry bean curd." Tax and fee collection was entirely given up in Yang village. The villagers' successful tax evasion had a demonstration effect in neighboring areas.

Provincial leaders eventually addressed this case after an internal circulation in 2000 brought it to their attention. The provincial party secretary demanded a swift solution, and the city formed a task force headed by the mayor. A work team consisting of fourteen cadres was sent to the village. Peasants' mistrust of these cadres was deep. With the team's painstaking efforts, the peasants began to cooperate. The city mayor also visited the village to address the peasants' problems. All of these efforts combined to eventually return the village to "normal" after 2001.

In Yang village, peasants' use of issue linkage put rural cadres in a defensive and difficult position simply because the issues peasants linked to tax and fee collection were politically sensitive for the corrupt village cadres to address. Further, the villagers' solidarity and determination in resisting external cadres made the cadres reluctant to go to the village in the first place. More importantly, the split between the different levels of government put serious pressure on the grassroots cadres. In Yang village, the villagers' appeals to city and provincial governments and the phone calls made by provincial and city officials made it possible for them to "sandwich" the local cadres. Without the support of the city government, the township government was reluctant to intervene, much less to use force, and, without support from the township government, the village authority lacked the means to make peasants pay.

The case of Yang village is not isolated. The statistical bureau of Sichuan province states: "Conflict between peasants and cadres has affected tax collection. Some township and village cadres turned a deaf ear to peasants' problems and angered peasants. Some peasants linked tax payment to various problems of the past and refused to pay if those problems were not solved."[63] Similarly, in Hubei province, "Some rural cadres failed to help address peasants' disputes or issues that affected peasants' common interests. Peasants were dissatisfied and were reluctant to pay taxes. . . . Some peasants asked township cadres to solve their disputes with village cadres, and they would refuse to pay if their problems were not addressed."[64] Further, in Henan province, "Rural issues are complex and intertwined. If the interests of some people are affected, it would become another reason for the peasants not to pay taxes and fees."[65] Such villages, which were called "small Taiwan" by some cadres because of their autonomy in matters of tax payment, existed because of the constraints faced by local cadres.[66]

Conclusion

Successful resistance targeting the government is conditional everywhere. In China, where local officials are answerable only to upper-level authorities, the success of resistance is determined by whether citizens are able to apply effective constraints on local officials by getting upper-level authorities involved in addressing their grievances. However, the threshold of intervention from above is often too high for most citizens, either because their grievances are not high on the agenda of upper-level governments or because the complaints are too many for upper-level authorities to handle. While forceful action can pose a serious threat to local officials by disrupting the social order, not all protesting groups are able to stage such resistance. Like weak groups everywhere,[67] these groups need to gain extra leverage to strengthen their position versus local governments. In China, access to extra leverage is often determined by the resisters' ability to exploit the latent opportunities embedded in the political system.

In this chapter, I show that one method employed by Chinese citizens in defending their rights is to link their grievances to other issues for which the local government is also held accountable. This method of issue linkage strengthens the resisters' bargaining power versus the local government because it allows them to reveal local officials' different types of malfeasance to upper-level authorities, thereby increasing the likelihood of intervention from above. Issue linkage may thus limit the choice of local governments or prevent them from choosing certain modes of reaction, such as suppression, because suppression tends to provoke more resistance. The effectiveness of issue linkage depends on the upper-level authorities' degree of tolerance of the linked issues. In the case of peasant resistance to tax payment, issue linkage became a useful weapon because some rural cadres were corrupt or abusive and they were reluctant to see their malfeasance revealed to upper-level authorities. The upper-level governments had limited tolerance of the use of force in tax and fee collection, which made tax payment both a means (to other ends) and an end in peasant resistance to tax collection.

Issue linkage is not unique to peasant resistance; it has also been used by some workers in preventing their firms from being reformed in ways that favored managers at the expense of the workers. Chinese workers may tolerate the corruption of their managers if the corruption does not threaten their livelihood. But, if the reform measures initiated by managers are perceived to pose such a threat, workers tend to resist. Some workers resorted to issue linkage by approaching or threatening to approach upper-level authorities and requesting investigations of corrupt managers, which deterred the managers from adopting certain types of ownership reform.[68]

This method of issue linkage thus provides extra leverage to those weak groups that lack institutionalized power to protect their legitimate rights. On the other hand, the conditions for effective use of issue linkage also imply that this method is not always feasible because not all groups can find linked issues or not all linked issues are serious in the eyes of upper-level authorities. However, the case of peasants' use of issue linkage discussed in this chapter does reveal that it is possible for citizens to exploit the divide between different levels of state authorities to achieve success, although the divide should not be overestimated. As the next chapter will also show, an effective exploitation of the potential opportunity for resistance may significantly strengthen citizens' positions in relation to local state authorities.

FIVE

Social Networks and Effective Resistance

Political opportunities are not necessarily predetermined in popular resistance; they may be created or even perceived rather than real.[1] As existing research suggests, some opportunities arise during interactions between members of movements and their targets or other actors.[2] Goodwin and Jasper argue that "political opportunities and mobilizing structures are also heavily shaped by strategic considerations, by the choices movement leaders and activists make."[3] In some cases, as Banaszak shows, activists may fail to perceive some of the opportunities open to them or to develop potentially useful tactics.[4] Therefore, both the perceptions and efforts of the challenging groups may make an important difference in their ability to exploit or create opportunities for effective resistance. As the previous chapter shows, citizens' use of issue linkage can help expand the opportunities for successful resistance in China.

This chapter demonstrates another important method that Chinese citizens employ to create opportunities for successful resistance—to exploit the political space by disaggregating the state and seeking support or allies from within the state or "among the bureaucratic elite."[5] Such allies can provide crucial resources for participants, make the system more open to them, and alter their perceptions of their opportunities for resistance.[6] O'Brien and Li find that citizens may receive support from "sympathetic and powerful advocates who have a stake in seeing that a policy is held."[7] In this chapter, I show that Chinese citizens may also tap their social networks with the people who have political power or influence to create opportunities for successful action with or without bending state rules.[8]

Social Networks as a Political Resource

Literature on social movements shows that the existence of social networks helps to overcome the problem of free riding and to mobilize participants in collective action.[9] McAdam, for example, suggests that social networks played a key role in determining who was likely to participate in the Freedom Summer campaign during the civil rights movement in the United States.[10] Tarrow explains that connections among participants "affect the likelihood that one actor's action will incite another."[11] But existing research tends to focus on the horizontal dimension of social networks among participants. In China, citizens' social networks affect their resistance both horizontally and vertically. Horizontally, social networks among prospective participants promote group solidarity and encourage participation in collective action. Vertically, the networks between participants and individual officials or people with political influence significantly increase the chance of success of the collective resistance. Networks enable participants to exploit the divide among state authorities and generate support from within the state. By exploiting social networks, participants maximize their opportunities for success.

First, networks with state agents can be an effective way of obtaining support from the agents or a way of moving a complaint onto the agenda of the state authorities. For example, while petitions remain a commonly used mode of action by Chinese citizens, they are often ineffective.[12] A crucial condition for the success of petitions is that pertinent leaders pay serious attention to petitioners' grievances. While some petitioners may be lucky enough to receive help from sympathetic officials, many more are not. Therefore, petitioners may need to find other ways to seek help from state agents. In a society that has traditionally been permeated by personal connections, social networks are a tool.[13] Connections or social networks with state agents create a moral bond that helps state agents to see it as a moral responsibility to help the people with whom they are connected. In this sense, social networks are an important political asset.

Moreover, networks also help citizens gain access to the media, another powerful weapon against state agents or other social actors. Very few people will dispute that the media, including the Internet, have become an influential channel through which citizens seek justice. The proliferation of the media and the emergence of the Internet in China make it more possible for citizens to have access to information and voice their grievances.

For example, according to the 2005 China General Social Survey (the China GSS 2005), among the 10,372 people surveyed, more than 92 percent (95.9 percent among urban residents) watched television several times a week or every day, more than 39 percent (60 percent among urban residents) read newspapers several times a week or every day, and about 10 percent (17.4 percent among urban residents) used the Internet several times a week or every day. Citizens' access to information means that businesses and the government no longer have a monopoly on the discourse on any important issue that is closely linked to their livelihood. Indeed, voicing grievances in the media has become an important mode of political participation in China.[14] In a number of cases, citizens' grievances were addressed after they were exposed by the media. A survey of 661 journalists in 2001 found that more than 7 percent reported that all the problems they had reported were addressed, about 33 percent reported a majority, more than 32 percent reported a small portion, and 13 percent reported none.[15]

Nevertheless, while the media can be a powerful weapon, they are not easily accessible by most citizens who encounter injustice. According to the China GSS 2005 (see Chapter Two), only 4.6 percent of those 261 citizens who had conflicts with state agencies approached the media for help. The reasons for such a low percentage are complex given that the media can be such a powerful weapon. One reason is that the media, including the Internet, still face the serious constraints imposed by the party-state. Some of the complaints or grievances of citizens may be seen as inappropriate to be reported. However, the consequences of the exposure of some cases can only be discerned after they are exposed, and some sensitive cases may still be reported because the media or the state authorities may not anticipate the impact. Connections with media workers can be an important reason for some of such cases to be exposed, which in turn provides significant help to citizens seeking justice.

In the remainder of this chapter, I demonstrate how social networks can help citizens staging successful resistance by analyzing a case in which homeowners in a community in Shanghai staged a nine-year collective action. This case reveals that urban homeowners, despite their greater economic wealth compared to peasants and some workers, are weak in relation to the government and business. They have a strong incentive, however, to protect their interests through almost all acceptable means, including collective action. As in other social groups, homeowners' ability to exploit the cracks within the state crucially affects the outcome of their resistance.

The Case of Homeowners' Resistance

Since the 1990s, homeowners' resistance has occurred in many cities due to changes in housing allocation policies.[16] By the early 2000s, more than 70 percent of urban households in China owned their homes[17] as a result of the privatization of public housing and the development of the real estate market.[18] Housing is perhaps the most important asset of most urban families. Due to the weak rule of law in China, however, violations of homeowners' rights by the government or businesses are common. These violations can be divided into three categories: (1) those concerning housing per se; (2) those arising from housing demolition (see Chapter Eight); and (3) those concerning the environment in a residential community. The problems associated with the first category include, among many others, the poor quality of housing, unilateral changes in construction plans by builders or contractors, and disputes over the calculation of the floor area.[19] Problems with the second category—housing demolition—overwhelmingly stem from limited or unreasonable compensation paid to homeowners.[20] Problems associated with the environment are also complex, as they involve the government and real estate companies. In a typical situation, a company begins to construct new projects that were not included in the original neighborhood plan after buyers have already purchased their homes. Homeowners believe that these new projects threaten to destroy the environment of the neighborhood and directly encroach on their interests. This chapter focuses on homeowners' responses to such situations by examining interactions among citizens, government agencies, and business people.

To be legal, changes in construction plans should be relayed to residents before they are implemented, but businesses often ignore this government stipulation. One reason is that businesses may reap benefits that far exceed the compensation they will have to pay to homeowners if a dispute is settled in court, so it is in their interest to proceed without homeowners' approval rather than risk their veto.[21] Perhaps more important, businesses are able to gain the support of local government agencies to proceed with plans that are disagreeable to homeowners. Urban construction cannot proceed without approval from the relevant government agencies, especially the urban planning bureau and the land management bureau.[22] Local governments benefit from construction projects because these projects may promote local development, enhance local leaders' images, or bring personal gain to officials. For these reasons, homeowners' rights are frequently violated.

In defending their rights, homeowners, like other groups of citizens, have employed a range of techniques.[23] One technique is to file lawsuits, though these are often ineffective, especially when directed at government agencies.[24] More commonly, homeowners turn to nonjuridical channels, writing petitions, making media appeals, and staging noninstitutionalized actions, such as protests and demonstrations. Regardless of the method, the main goal of homeowner resistance is to generate pressure on the government, which has authority over government agencies, businesses, and legal departments. If the government supports the business, homeowners will encounter great and sometimes insurmountable difficulty in defending their rights. The example from Guangzhou discussed below reveals this difficulty when the local government and businesses face little pressure from upper-level authorities.

THE LG CASE IN GUANGZHOU

As a developed city in China, Guangzhou has been experiencing large-scale construction and a housing boom. But, as the following case indicates, construction is sometimes carried out at the expense of residents.[25] In 1991, Company L, which was owned by the provincial government of Guangdong, developed LG as a residential neighborhood. At the onset, the company aimed to attract middle- and high-income residents. Because the neighborhood was beautiful, with rivers, gardens, and trees; a good infrastructure and facilities; and effective management, it soon became a model community in the city, and Company L's reputation grew. By 2001, the community had 12,000 residents, including some foreigners. Most of these homeowners were white-collar employees, and about 55 percent were business managers.

The peaceful life of LG residents was disrupted in December 2002 when a construction project began in the neighborhood. Company X was creating a new neighborhood near LG. Residents soon learned that a 40-meter-wide road would be built through LG, disturbing the quiet atmosphere of the neighborhood. The road, which was to be constructed on LG land, was put in to connect the new neighborhood to an existing road. The original plan for the new neighborhood approved by the city government did not include the road, but the township government, without receiving an approval from the city urban planning bureau, had permitted it to be built.

On learning of the planned road, some residents chose to leave and sold their apartments at discounted prices. Many others chose to stay on and resist the proposed changes. On December 20, an anonymous notice was posted in the neighborhood that urged residents to meet to discuss the issue, and more than 100 residents attended the meeting. After the discussion, LG residents decided to approached Company L, their neighborhood's property management company, the homeowners' committee, and the residents' committee. But none of these organizations offered to help.[26]

When LG residents did not know what to do next, a man named Hong, who was in his thirties, emerged as a key player and coordinator. Hong worked for an insurance company and was articulate, but he lacked experienced in leading collective action. A lawyer living in LG at the time suggested several strategies to Hong and a few other activists: First, they needed to hire a lawyer as a legal advisor to ensure that their activities did not violate the law. Second, they needed to establish a rights protection group that homeowners would trust to gain a legitimate basis for action.[27]

Following the lawyer's suggestions, the home owners organized a rights protection group consisting of fifteen members.[28] The group raised 30,000 yuan from homeowners for its activities. The establishment of the rights group enhanced the organizational basis of the residents' collective action, allowing them to take steps to protect their rights in various ways. Group members went to the construction site to talk directly with builders, approached government agencies together with lawyers to collect information about the road project, contacted the media and used their social connections to garner support, and visited the pertinent authorities at the district, city, and provincial levels.

To prevent the construction, homeowners set up camps at the construction site on December 30, 2002. Two days later, a large group of people, including police officers and government officials, dismantled the camps, provoking a confrontation with LG residents. When residents demanded to see an official approval document for the road construction, the township officials could not provide one. The next morning, the government again sent a large number of people to the construction site so that the construction team could resume work. Arrogant township officials told homeowners not to bother resisting because their efforts were useless, causing another confrontation.

Hong and more than 100 other residents lodged complaints with the city and provincial governments. The city complaints bureau then informed the district government that construction should not start until the conflict with residents was resolved. In addition, the complaints bureau required the district government to hold a meeting at the construction site to resolve the issue. These instructions were ignored, however, and construction was resumed. On January 4, another violent confrontation occurred, and two residents were injured.[29] Under this circumstance, the police suspended the construction.

To maintain momentum, the rights protection group organized a protest. It distributed 6,000 flyers to inform residents of its plans, and about 1,000 residents participated in the neighborhood protest on January 6, 2003. The turnout was not especially good: Many residents did not participate because they lived far enough from the new road that they did not perceive it as a direct threat. Additionally, not all homeowners read the flyer. Further, the protest lacked leadership. Three days before the protest, Hong had received a telephone call from the property management office. He was told not to participate and chose to withdraw because his file had been called up for examination by the police.[30]

In taking action to punish Hong, the protest's organizer, the local government that had jurisdiction over the LG community employed a traditional method of squelching protests.[31] Reflecting on his role, Hong admitted that he did not show up at the protest because he felt it was safer to stay behind the scenes, but he indicated that he had never really withdrawn from the resistance.[32] Another person, Yu, took over the coordinating responsibilities in Hong's absence. Also in his thirties, Yu worked for an advertising company and was considered to be a pragmatic person.

As some homeowners worked in the local media or had connections with media workers, they tried to expose the case in the media. A local newspaper reported the incident in which homeowners were beaten on January 4. More media organizations began investigating the case, and journalists soon learned that the township government planned to obtain all the legal documents for the road construction within fifteen days. Under these circumstances, the rights protection group decided to hold a second demonstration; this time, Hong showed up and led more than 1,000 participants. They demanded that the construction cease, threatening to return their apartments to the real estate company for a refund.[33]

At the time of the protests, the provincial people's congress and the provincial political consultative conference were about to be held in Guangzhou. Therefore, the homeowners tried to appeal for help from the deputies of the congresses and members of the conference. They succeeded in receiving the support of two members of the provincial political consultative conference. The two people submitted a suggestion to the consultative conference that was reported in a local newspaper.[34] They argued that the controversial road should not be built in the community because of the consequences for the natural environment and that the road construction would make people reluctant to buy homes there. This action attracted significant attention to the dispute.

After the conflict on January 4, construction of the new road stopped. Homeowners hired peasants to plant about 100 trees at the construction site. Meanwhile, residents sued the government agencies that had approved the road construction project, demanding that it be cancelled. Just before a court hearing, the township government had obtained all the permissions for the project, making it legal. In April, the newly planted trees were removed within half a day, and in May the road was completed. Company X declared victory by publishing news of the road completion in a local newspaper.

Intervention by the media, assistance from members of the political consultative conference, and the residents' own appeals all failed to thwart the construction. An influential newspaper, *Southern Weekend*, reported in May that the completion of the road marked the failure of the LG residents' five-month resistance. But LG residents did not rest. Instead, Hong and other activists decided to target Company X's market appeal. Because potential buyers would have to pass by residential buildings in LG to reach the new buildings, the activists planned to discourage potential customers from buying the apartments by using a method that accords with local culture.

Like people everywhere in China, local Guangzhou residents are superstitious about living in a place that brings bad luck. To make potential buyers believe that the new buildings constituted such a place, Hong and other leaders asked residents living along the newly constructed road to display elegiac couplets on their own buildings condemning Company X and its new buildings. The company often ferried potential buyers to the new buildings for visits on weekends; in response, LG residents living along the newly built road played recorded funeral music during peak times. The words of the couplets and music were carefully chosen to avoid political risk. For example, one song had originally been written to honor an anti-Japanese hero. Hong also came up with two other options that were ultimately not used. He recalled, "We also planned to hold a memorial ceremony in honor of a nurse who had lost her life in the fight against SARS at a time when buyers were viewing the new buildings or to hold a mock memorial ceremony for myself. If the latter option had been chosen, I would have returned to my hometown in Sichuan for two weeks and then 'come back to life' later."[35]

The methods proved effective at discouraging buyers. Company X published advertisements claiming that the new buildings had attracted a large number of buyers, but both the company and LG residents knew that the sales were in fact quite disappointing. LG residents' resistance finally forced Company X to come to the negotiation table on June 1, 2003, at a local hotel. Participants from the real estate company included the chairperson of the board of directors, the general manager, an assistant general manager, and the general manager of the property management company. Five representatives of the residents, including Hong and Yu, took part in the negotiation. The two parties reached a compromise in which the residents agreed to discontinue their protests in return for the company's promise to beautify the road and manage it to keep the neighborhood as attractive and quiet as possible.[36] Although the residents had failed to prevent the construction of the road, they ultimately managed to win some concessions from the company.[37]

GENERATING SUPPORT FROM WITHIN THE STATE: THE BG CASE IN SHANGHAI

The partial success of residents in the LG case was rather accidental. In the absence of context-contingent factors, homeowners might have failed completely. The homeowners' fundamental difficulty was that the township government supported the real estate business. The homeowners also failed to solicit effective intervention from higher-level authorities. In cases where homeowners receive intervention from above, the chance that the resistance will be successful is significantly improved. The BG case in Shanghai is such a case: Homeowners achieved success by mobilizing their networks with government officials and media workers to generate support from within the state.[38] This example illustrates how the opportunity for successful resistance can be exploited or created in China.

Since the late 1980s, the Shanghai government has made unprecedented efforts to solve its well-known housing shortage by building a large number of new neighborhoods in the countryside. BG is one such neighborhood, built in the early 1990s and designed to house 21,000 residents.[39] It consists of four subneighborhoods, two in the south and two in the north.

The southern half contains dozens of six-story buildings surrounded by bamboo, while in north BG, in addition to some six-story buildings, there are twelve twenty-six-story buildings surrounded by approximately 8,000 square meters of open ground. The open area was designated as a greenbelt by the city urban planning bureau. Because of its beautiful environment, more and more people moved to BG from downtown Shanghai. BG residents were proud of their neighborhood because it was named a "Civil Residential Neighborhood" by the central authority in 1993.[40]

The life of BG residents was disrupted over discussions about the 8,000-square-meter open area. Although BG is far from downtown, the expansion of the city increased the value of the land on which it is situated. As a result, both real estate companies and the district government coveted the open area, and protecting the greenbelt became a constant problem for residents. From 1993 to 2001, residents in BG engaged in a nine-year collective action to protect the open area under the coordination and leadership of two leaders from their community.

Before presenting the BG case, an introduction to the administrative hierarchy in urban Shanghai is required. The hierarchy involves (from top to bottom): the city government, district governments, street offices (an agency of the district government), residents' committees, and residents' groups. The residents' committees are intended to be self-governing organizations with the leaders elected by residents.[41] In reality, however, the government controls residents' committees, which often appoint the heads of the residents' groups.

RESISTING BUSINESS

In September 1993, the real estate company that developed BG was preparing to build a twenty-six-story building on the 8,000 square meters of open ground. Fang, a retired teacher living in one of the two subneighborhoods (Neighborhood A) of north BG, initiated resistance to the plans.[42] The reason for Fang's resistance was simple: If a new building were built, her fifth-floor apartment would see little sunshine. Fang first approached the residents' committee of her subneighborhood, hoping that the committee would report the problem to the X Street Office.[43] Because the real estate company was owned by the city government, however, the office refused to help.

Fang decided to present petitions to the next upper-level district government. As individual petitions may be ignored, Fang planned to mobilize more participants to present a collective petition. She then tried to contact the heads of residents' groups, as they were familiar with the households in their groups and could mobilize participants. She began by visiting the group heads in the two subneighborhoods of north BG. However, those heads and many residents did not know her and were suspicious of her motives.[44] Fang had to convince them that she needed their participation because a collective petition would be more effective. She assured them that she would take the lead in presenting the petition and take the risk.

Fang's insistence and residents' worry about the construction of a new building finally convinced some to participate. One day in September 1993, Fang led about forty residents to present a petition against the proposed construction to the district government, but they were barred from entering the office yard. It was not until Fang happened to see one of her former students, a high-ranking official in the district government, that they were allowed to present the petition. A leader of the district government ordered the estate company to stop construction, but the company ignored the government's order and continued construction. Fang then organized a petition to the city people's congress. A leader in the congress ordered the district government to investigate the issue, claiming that resident resistance might cause social disruption. As a result of the pressure from both the district government and the city people's congress, the real estate company had to address residents' concerns.

The company believed that, because it was a state firm, the district government and the city's people's congress would turn a blind eye to its illegal occupation of the open ground if it could manage to silence the residents. It first presented a fake construction plan to convince the district government that its construction project was legal. It then proceeded to discredit Fang in the BG community. In early 1994, the company conducted discreet negotiations with Fang, promising to provide her with a new apartment elsewhere if she stopped organizing resistance, thereby undermining her determination. The company then leaked news of the negotiations to the community. The residents felt betrayed, and their trust in Fang evaporated. Having discovered the trap, Fang tried to clear her name and organize another collective action but failed.

THE EMERGENCE OF TAN AND SUCCESSFUL RESISTANCE

Frustrated residents believed that having a reliable and able leader was crucial to successful resistance. An activist in the other subneighborhood of north BG, Neighborhood B, recommended Tan.[45] In his fifties at the time,

Tan was a factory cadre with a reputation for helping others. Tan had a much more extensive social network than Fang had and was more familiar with the laws and government regulations regarding city construction. He was also very articulate and had experience leading collective action during the Cultural Revolution.

Tan understood that residents needed to do two things to win the battle. First, only a large-scale collective action would be effective. To this end, Tan convened a meeting in his building to explain to the residents the undesirable consequences of the new construction. Second, in urban China, construction projects need the approval of the urban planning bureau. Tan pointed out that the original plan approved by the planning bureau almost certainly did not include the new building. Tan urged residents to find ways to obtain a copy of the original plan to prove the truth of this assertion. One resident was able to obtain a copy through a relative who worked in the city government. As Tan thought, the original copy showed that the plan did not include the new building.

By June 1994, the company had finished laying the underground framework of the new building and was ready to pour the concrete foundation. Once the foundation was poured, the project would be difficult to derail. To stop the progress, Tan, armed with evidence of the project's illegality, took action. On the evening of June 15, 1994, he and dozens of residents paraded through north BG, informing residents through loudspeakers that they had evidence showing that the construction project was illegal and calling on residents to destroy the underground framework before it was too late. About 1,000 residents responded to Tan's call and destroyed the framework.

Tan also sought the intervention of state agencies. Because the company was engaging in illegal construction, Tan believed that the city urban planning bureau should intervene. With the help of a friend working in the city government, Tan learned the responsibilities of the departments of the bureau and their work schedules. In the ensuing few days, Tan led scores of residents in flooding the bureau's relevant departments with copies of the original construction plan.[46] Paralyzed by these visitors, the bureau agreed to investigate the issue as soon as possible. In the meantime, Tan organized residents to appeal to the media for help and convinced *Wenhuibao*, the newspaper (and mouthpiece) of the city party committee, to investigate and report on the case. Under pressure from both BG residents and the media, the planning bureau revoked the construction license of the estate company, and the construction automatically ceased.

After the estate company's failure, several other organizations tried to oc-cupy the open area. Tan succeeded in leading residents to frustrate all such attempts. But BG residents understood that as long as the ground remained open, there would always be attempts to occupy it. Tan appealed to the media to put pressure on the district government, which was responsible for the greenbelt project. He and the other protesters succeeded in having the case concurrently reported on in four influential newspapers, including *Wenhuibao* and *Xinmin wanbao*, the most widely circulated newspapers in Shanghai.[47] The reports not only warned off potential land users but also urged the district government to finish the greenbelt project. Under pressure from residents and the media, the government planted grass and bamboo on the open area in 1995, turning the space into a beautiful landscape.

BG residents' resistance had an important impact on the community. First, Tan established his reputation as a leader, which facilitated his mo-bilization of participants in collective action. Second, due to increasing interactions, many residents got to know each other, and their solidarity was enhanced. In almost every building in north BG, which housed about 7,000 residents, there were activists from all walks of life, including engi-neers, teachers, other white-collar workers, blue-collar workers, housewives, and retirees.[48] Third, in the process of resisting the various organizations that attempted to occupy the land, Tan established and strengthened his networks with the media and government officials, which proved crucial to the success of his cause.

In the 1990s, due to the numerous conflicts between real estate compa-nies and homeowners, the Chinese government began to encourage home-owners to form self-governing homeowners' committees to protect their interests against real estate developers.[49] The city government in Shanghai promoted this program in 1996. In BG, each committee consisted of three to five members. In his building, Tan was elected head of the committee. This position not only introduced him to relevant laws and stipulations regarding residents' rights but also provided more chances for him to inter-act with other residents. This experience aided in his later resistance to the district government.

RESISTING THE LOCAL GOVERNMENT

The peace did not last long in north BG. In 1997, workers sent by the district government destroyed the eastern part of the greenbelt to build a recreation center for retired senior cadres. The government's construction plan called for the use of one-fourth of the greenbelt area. The project was to be undertaken jointly by the district government and the X Street Office. The district government would provide the funding, and the office would be responsible for the construction. The Street Office had a strong incentive to see the project succeed because it would retain the recreation center after all the senior cadres who started work before 1949 passed away.

Residents in north BG were upset because the center would also be used for commercial purposes, which they predicted would destroy the quiet environment of their neighborhood. Tan was aware that he and the other residents now faced a different and more powerful target, but he also knew that they had legitimate grounds for resistance. First, the district government and the Street Office had violated the city government's regulation that greenbelts could not be destroyed without its permission. Second, the two authorities had departed from the construction plan of the urban planning bureau. Third, it was disputable whether the two authorities had the right to carry out construction within the greenbelt without the permission of residents. By 1996, Shanghai had started to implement housing reform, which required residents to buy the housing allocated to them. Thus, the residents of the BG community believed that the greenbelt was now their common property and that the district government and the Street Office did not own the land.

Tan mobilized the nine homeowners' committees in north BG. All of them agreed to endorse the appeal letter drafted by Tan, who approached *Wenhuibao* to lodge the complaints and deliver the letter. The newspaper sent journalists to investigate the case and then published a report. Believing that the issue might provoke protests, a few leaders of the city government told the district government to suspend the project. The Street Office then met with the nine homeowners' committees. The two parties agreed to the construction of a two-story Senior Citizen Recreation Center for both senior cadres and elderly residents of BG on a parcel of land no larger than 8 percent of the greenbelt area. However, the district government nullified this agreement in December 1998. BG residents did not learn of the change until April 1999, when workers hired by the Street Office resumed construction.

Feeling betrayed, Tan and other residents repeatedly appealed to both higher-level authorities and the media to expose the district government's violations of the agreement. *Wenhuibao* again sent journalists to investigate the case. These efforts were not successful, and construction continued.

Tan realized that if residents did not stop the construction, it would soon become a fait accompli. He consulted with one of his close friends, a police officer, about destroying the structure. The officer advised him that he might get away with destroying the walls but not the construction equipment and other facilities. Following this advice, Tan and more than forty residents pulled down the walls and destroyed the building's foundation in May 1999, thus halting construction.

On learning of this action, the Street Office claimed that the activities of Tan and his supporters were destructive and that the police planned to arrest Tan. Realizing the risk, Tan and other activists decided to make a direct petition to the city government, believing that if the case received more widespread attention, the Street Office and the district government would hesitate before imposing punishment. As has been shown in the previous chapter, making successful petitions to the government is not a simple undertaking in China. The timing of petitions is crucial for success. For this reason, collective actions tend to occur when important meetings convene, such as the people's congress, the political consultative conference, the party's representatives' conference, or the government's work conference. As social stability and social unity are especially emphasized on these occasions, people taking action believe that their chance for success is higher.[50]

After discussing the matter with his friends in government agencies, Tan decided to present the petition to the city government on the evening of June 1, 1999. June 4 has been a sensitive date for the Chinese government since the 1989 Tiananmen incident. Governments are on guard against any event that may cause social instability around this time every year, so taking action at this time is likely to attract the government's attention. It is risky to choose a date too close to June 4, however, due to the possibility of an excessive government response. This explains why Tan chose June 1 for his action. In addition, by approaching the government during the daytime, the protesters hoped to paralyze local traffic. While that strategy might be effective, it could also backfire by prompting the government to take drastic action if it felt that its authority was being seriously challenged.

Based on these considerations, Tan and about fifty residents approached the city government to lodge complaints on the evening of June 1, 1999. As anticipated, their collective petition immediately caught the attention of the complaints bureau of the city government. The bureau telephoned the district government and the X Street Office, informing them of the residents' petition and ordering them to recall the residents and solve the problem lest the bureau be forced to intervene. The district government and the office were very upset because the petition exposed their failure to maintain local stability. Without delay, the office sent a bus to bring back the protesting residents. As a precaution, the office also sent cadres and police officers to the homes of Tan and other activists to warn them against presenting more petitions to the city government and to keep watch over the entrance of the city government's office yard.[51]

Due to the pressure from the city government and the media's repeated coverage, the construction was suspended. Meanwhile, the city garden and forestry bureau named Tan "the Guard of Greeneries" in February 2000. Every year, this official honor is bestowed on ten people who have made an outstanding contribution to the protection of greenery in the city. Tan received the award mainly because a bureau leader knew him well. The bureau leader's nomination of Tan was supported by his colleagues in part because the district government, by violating some of the bureau's regulations, had thereby challenged the bureau's authority. After Tan received the award, the BG case received more coverage in the media, which not only inspired confidence in Tan and other activists but also provided them with a legitimate basis for their resistance.

LOCAL AUTHORITIES' COUNTERMEASURES

The district government and the Street Office realized that Tan was the pillar of the resistance and that the most effective way to repress the resistance was to discredit him. To this end, the local authorities launched a propaganda war. First, they contacted the media and provided false information about the construction project, claiming that they wanted to build recreation facilities in BG only for elderly citizens, not senior cadres, and that Tan and his supporters had unreasonably stopped them from doing so. The Street Office also held public interviews with journalists, claiming that the construction project was part of their effort to improve the welfare of the BG community.

Second, they claimed that Tan and his supporters were a minority in the community and that most residents supported the project. To provide evidence, they asked the residents' committee in Neighborhood A to mobilize residents to sign an appeal letter urging the government to resume construction. After obtaining the signatures of a number of residents, most of whom were older people who hoped to gain a recreation venue from the construction, the residents' committee asked a deputy of the district people's congress to present the letter to the congress. The district government planned to use the letter as proof that their construction plans reflected the residents' will. The Street Office and the residents' committees also spread a rumor that Tan was resisting the new construction because he wanted to blackmail the Street Office and obtain the construction contract for his friends.

In addition to propaganda, the office attempted to divide the community. Its leaders contacted a number of Tan's supporters and tried to build connections with them. Also, because Tan did not consult with the other eight homeowners' committees when he pulled down the walls in May 1999, the residents' committee in Tan's neighborhood claimed that he had violated the law and that the local government would sue him. Through their social networks, the cadres of the residents' committee asked the members of other homeowners' committees to stop participating in the resistance organized by Tan.

Unlike farmers, who have a deep distrust of local officials in rural China,[52] urban citizens in BG, especially older ones, had significant trust in the local government, which gave some credibility to the countermeasures. Also, the local government claimed that it would provide senior residents free access to the recreation center on its completion. As a result of this campaign, some citizens became resentful of Tan and the other activists. The relatives of some activists also opposed their continued participation in the resistance, which had, by this time, dragged on for several years. Many members of the homeowners' committees withdrew their support for Tan, believing that he was too radical. The solidarity of the community was in crisis.

With the appeal letter submitted to the district people's congress, the district government resumed construction. Tan again sought the help of the media: In September 2000, Tan invited two correspondents from Shanghai Television to conduct a discreet investigation of the case. If city television broadcast the case, it would greatly help the cause. Yet no sooner did the correspondents finish their investigation than the city propaganda department issued a notice prohibiting them from reporting on and investigating the BG case. It was an unprecedented setback for Tan, who believed that one of the residents had alerted the Street Office or the district government.[53] In another effort, Tan appealed to the city government in the name of the nine homeowners' committees, but the other eight all refused to endorse his letter of appeal.

Shocked, frustrated, and scared, Tan decided to fight back; both his personal reputation and the community's interests were at stake. If he lost the battle, he might end up socially isolated like Fang. Tan also worried that if he lost the fight, those journalists who had supported his resistance over the years might also suffer. If the district government succeeded in charging him with illegal resistance, it would imply that those journalists had been encouraging illegal acts. In his words, he was facing a war that he could not afford to lose.

Tan understood that residents' trust of the local authorities was the crucial reason for the effectiveness of their propaganda. He decided to discredit the local authorities, especially those from the Street Office. Tan first approached the journalists who had published the reports that supported the claims of the office. He presented to them all the documents regarding the construction project in BG and explained that it was an illegal project. Some of these journalists were convinced, which upset the office. Tan also approached the deputy who delivered the appeal letter to the district people's congress and convinced her of the illegality of the construction project. The deputy apologized to Tan and explained that she had not known the truth of the situation.

Most important, Tan obtained evidence of deceptive documents made by the office. When *Wenhuibao* interviewed cadres from the office, they had provided the journalists with a copy of the description of the construction project that stated that the office's purpose was to build a recreation center for *senior cadres*, not for residents. Because of his connections to journalists, Tan obtained a copy of the statement and was able to convince the residents that the real purpose of the office was to make profits for itself.[54] Tan also pointed out that the residents' committee, which was supposed to represent and defend their interests, had never helped them; instead, it was simply a tool of the Street Office to suppress their resistance.

Tan's countermeasures seriously damaged the office's reputation.[55] Deep distrust of the office became pervasive among BG residents. The residents' disappointment with the residents' committee was also profound, and relations between the two entities grew so tense that the committee could not exercise any influence in BG. There was also a split among the administrative hierarchy. The Street Office blamed the residents' committee in Tan's neighborhood for its failure to prevent collective resistance, whereas the head of the committee complained that the illegal construction had caused the committee to lose residents' trust. She refused to support the office on this issue, and the conflict culminated in her transfer to another job.

After winning back the trust and support of many residents, Tan proceeded to stop the local authorities from resuming construction. In September 2000, he called on 200 residents to sign an appeal letter and led dozens of residents to lodge complaints with the city government. He also wanted to appeal to the media for help, but, as mentioned earlier, the media in Shanghai were restrained from reporting the case. Some journalist friends introduced Tan to the Shanghai branch of the Xinhua News Agency, which investigated the case and informed some city leaders that if the case were not settled appropriately, the agency would report it in its internal circulation for central leaders. The internal circulations of the party's news agencies in China have enormous influence because their contents are referred directly to central leaders for instruction and comment. It is common for officials to lose their positions or even their lives after their reported misconduct captures the attention of high-level leaders in this way.[56] Unable to ignore this pressure, the leaders of the city government urged the urban planning bureau and the garden and forestry bureau to resolve the issue. Leaders from the two bureaus then met with the major leaders of the district government, who officially canceled the construction project in 2001.

Social Networks and Successful Resistance: A Discussion

The case of the BG residents in Shanghai points to the possibilities and difficulties of civil resistance in China. It suggests that when there is a divide between state authorities that creates potential opportunity for civil resistance, the success of the resistance depends on the protesting group's ability to effectively exploit such opportunities. In the BG case, the homeowners' ability is affected by a number of factors, including capable leaders and their social connections with political elites who have authority over the local government in confrontations with citizens.

DISCREPANCIES AND OPPORTUNITIES FOR CIVIL RESISTANCE

The complex process of the BG residents' resistance shows that the state authority is fragmented in China, even at the local level. State power was disaggregated in several ways in this case. First, there are disparate priorities between local state authorities at different levels or between different departments. These disparate priorities created opportunity for citizens' resistance and their success. The municipal government was more concerned with local stability, whereas lower-level governments were more concerned with their own interests (e.g., the building of a recreation center for senior cadres). This discrepancy makes it possible for the higher-level authority to require lower-level authorities (e.g., at the district and street levels) to attend to citizens' interests when the higher-level authority feels the pressure. This is why Tan and his fellow residents were not punished for their collective petition to the government on June 1.

Second, the departmental interests of state agencies may also become a potential source of support for those taking action. In the BG case, there were conflicting interests between the district government and the two municipal government agencies. The municipal planning bureau and the garden and forestry bureau exerted significant pressure on the district government and the Street Office in favor of the residents. The occupation of the open area threatened the planning bureau's authority to determine land use in the city, and the destruction of the greenbelt would undermine the authority of the garden and forestry bureau in charge of the city's landscapes. In theory, these bureaus were motivated to defend their authority.

Third, the media can be a credible threat to local officials. In China, the media, especially those controlled by the central or provincial party organizations, are, to some extent, an extension of state power. As the media controlled by higher-level authorities are not subject to the discipline of lower-level governments, they enjoy a certain degree of freedom in disclosing the misconduct of lower-level local officials. Media exposure of the misconduct of local officials may attract the attention of higher-level authorities who will redress the wrongs because of their concern for legitimacy or for the possible escalation of conflict in the absence of intervention. Hence, the media can have enormous influence over local officials who "do not fear citizen appeals but are afraid of media disclosures."[57] Consequently, appealing to the media has become an important mode that Chinese people have employed when their rights are violated by state agencies, though it is not easy to gain access to the media.[58]

The discrepancies between different levels of government also imply that both the people taking action and the targeted local government must obtain the support of higher-level authorities to prevail. In the BG case, while residents tried hard to obtain the support from various higher-level authorities and the media, the local authorities also sought the sympathy and support of higher-level authorities. For example, the district government achieved significant success when the municipal Propaganda Department accepted its request and prohibited the local media from covering the BG story. In comparison, homeowners in the LG case in Guangzhou failed to generate any significant support from inside the state. No single upper-level state agency seriously intervened in their disputes. Worse, all the pertinent city government agencies supported the township government and helped the latter to obtain all the legal documents needed for the construction of the road.

LEADERS, NETWORKS, AND COLLECTIVE ACTION

The case of the BG residents also points to the important role of leaders in collective action, especially in a regime where formal organizations for mobilizing participants are absent. Activists in BG admitted that the result of their resistance might have been different without Tan's leadership. Current explanations of leaders in collective action tend to stress their sense of moral obligation and altruism (see Chapter Two).[59] Research on collective action in China suggests that these people emerge because of their personalities, self-interests, community pressure, sense of justice, or a combination of these factors.[60] The emergence of Fang was largely driven by her concern over the destruction of her own living environment, whereas Tan's willingness seemed to be a combination of community pressure and his personal stake in the action. In China, it is common for leaders to fail to achieve success or even to be arrested. Tan's success lies in the fact that his social networks and those of other participants enabled him to generate support from within the state.

The BG case shows that because individual officials or media workers value their relationships with relatives and friends, participants' social networks with officials can be a crucial factor contributing to success. First, such networks become an important channel for information. In resisting the government, citizens must act within acceptable boundaries or at least "in the shadow of the law" to preempt the government's use of extralegal forces.[61] The construction plan of the real estate company was a crucial piece of evidence for Tan and his supporters to defeat the company. Similarly, the report on the project provided by the Street Office to the media, obtained by Tan, became a strong basis for him to discredit the office. Both pieces of crucial evidence were obtained through participants' social networks.

Second, networks with individual officials become a source for advice on strategies. As the government possesses the ultimate power to judge whether an action crosses its boundaries, it is crucial for resistance participants to be aware of the zone of government tolerance. But that zone is not easy to understand because laws are vague and their implementation is flexible. While flexibility creates room for "boundary-spanning" action, it also implies risks.[62] Hence, inside information or advice can be of crucial help. Tan's decision to pull down the walls without destroying the construction equipment and the timing of approaching the municipal government reflect the importance of such advice. In addition, collective petitions to the planning bureau, which paralyzed its important departments, were also based on the information provided by his friends working for the municipal government. In the whole process of resistance, Tan sometimes obtained information from his friends in the district government about the moves to be taken by the district government and the Street Office in advance, which greatly aided him in choosing appropriate strategies.

Third, social networks can strengthen the position of the participants and exert pressure on the target of action. Fang's initial success in obtaining the support of the district government in resisting the real estate company was due to a former student who had become a leader in the government. Tan's winning the award from the Garden and Forestry Bureau enhanced the legitimacy of their collective action. His connection with a leader in the bureau was an important factor in his receiving the award. The trust between Tan and that leader also contributed to his being offered the award two more times in 2001 and 2002. Finally, participants' networks with the media were also an important reason for their success.[63] The Shanghai branch of the Xinhua News Agency provided crucial help in the final stage of the residents' resistance. Tan was able to approach the branch because of a liaison with journalists of Shanghai media who became his friends over the course of his resistance.

In fact, BG residents were so successful in obtaining the support from higher-level authorities that local authorities had to win the support of some residents to restart the project. The X Street Office explained to the public that their intention of building the project was to provide welfare to the residents. It promised elderly citizens that they would have free access to the proposed recreation center and won the support of some of them. To justify their action, the office mobilized some residents, mostly older ones, to sign an appeal letter delivered to the district's people's congress. Local cadres also tried to build personal relationships with some activists. Their efforts paid off in that they obtained crucial information about the investigation conducted by the municipal television network. Therefore, in the BG case, the social networks of the participants allowed them to exploit the latent opportunities or create new ones. In comparison, in the LG case in Guangzhou, the participants lacked effective means to create, exploit, or expand the opportunity for resistance.

Conclusion

Literature on social movements shows that favorable political opportunities may arise from "the availability of influential allies and from cleavages within and among elites."[64] This can be true in China. Such opportunities may remain latent, however, if they are not effectively exploited. Kowalewski and Schumaker argue that in the Soviet Union whether protesters made their demands on the incumbents of national or other various subnational offices, their chances of success were equally small. "Protest outcomes," they conclude, were "seemingly unaffected by variation in the characteristics of protest targets."[65] This certainly happens in China, as discussed in Chapter Three. However, some Chinese may exploit the potential opportunities by tapping their access to political resources or securing allies.

This chapter demonstrates a mechanism—participants' social networks—through which Chinese citizens can exploit these opportunities and seek favorable intervention from upper-level authorities based on a case of sustained resistance. This BG case represents an ideal outcome in which citizens obtain almost all possible support from the upper-level government, state agencies, and the media in this nondemocratic system. Precisely because citizens in most cases are unable to receive as much support as the residents of BG, this case points to the significance of social networks in providing aid to citizens. While the networks between action leaders and participants help to cement their solidarity, the networks between action participants and individual officials maximize citizens' abilities to exploit the divide within the state. The BG case also demonstrates that such networks, to some extent, blur the boundary between the state and society in China and make political participation, or the way citizens exercise political influence, more subtle and perhaps more effective.

SIX

The Power of Disruptive Collective Action

In 2003, protesters blocked roads, highways, and railways at least 3,100 times in China.[1] This large number of instances of disruptive collective action is not surprising. Piven and Cloward assert that protest movements have always been the modus operandi of those who lack institutionalized forms of political access and influence.[2] In popular contention, participants stage disruptive action to move their issues onto the agendas of pertinent authorities. As Tarrow suggests, "by blocking traffic or interrupting public business, protestors inconvenience citizens, pose a risk to law and order and draw the state into a conflict."[3] Tilly points out the same rationale for state intervention in disruptive action: "The authorities intervene because they find their interests—or those of their allies—threatened by other actors."[4] In China, many Chinese citizens' grievances and requests are legitimate and lawful, but the threshold of intervention from above is simply too high for most to reach because they are unable to use the nondisruptive tactics described in the previous two chapters. To increase their chances of success, protesters turn to illegal disruptive action, including disruptive collective petitions, protests, demonstrations, traffic blockades, attacks on state agencies, and confrontations.

Nevertheless, the success of disruptive tactics is also conditional. Research on social protests in democracies suggests that there is an issue of legitimacy involved in the use of disruptive tactics.[5] The legitimate use of disruptive tactics may increase the odds of success and reduce the risks involved. In China, disruptive tactics are used for both aggressive and defensive purposes. When used aggressively (in blocking traffic or office compounds or in attacks on state agencies, for example), citizens' actions can be justified on the basis of their legitimate rights, which have been ignored. In defensive resistance (such as protecting farmland or resisting tax collection), citizens' use of disruptive tactics is justified because the local government has violated their rights in the first place. However, in a political system where local officials are not held accountable to the people, the legitimacy of the use of disruptive tactics neither guarantees protesters' success nor necessarily reduces the risks of their actions. Instead, the effectiveness of these tactics, which largely means the likelihood of intervention from above, is determined by whether it has a large number of participants, whether the action is disclosed by the media, and/or whether it involves serious casualties or deaths of the participants.

Disruptive Action and the Politics of Intervention from Above

The China GSS 2005 discussed in Chapter Two suggests that most citizens are willing to use permitted channels, including the legal system, to address their grievances. But disruptive tactics are certainly an option when such channels fail. It is also true that disruptive (but not necessarily destructive) action has brought success to participants by causing social disorder and/or triggering intervention from above or posing a threat of such intervention. Among the 261 cases I collected (see Appendix B), the central government intervened in thirteen cases, and ten of them succeeded; while the provincial authority intervened in seventeen cases, and thirteen of them succeeded (Table 6.1). This does not mean that a lack of intervention from above always implies failure. Among the 231 cases in which upper-level authorities did not intervene, fifty-five succeeded. However, the chance of success in this circumstance (i.e., 23.8 percent) is rather small as compared to the chance of success when intervention from the central and provincial governments is possible (i.e., twenty-three out of thirty, or 76.6 percent).

Intervention from above is highly conditional, however. As discussed in earlier chapters, the central government's intervention results from its concerns for legitimacy and social stability. An action is likely to be perceived as a threat to regime legitimacy if the citizens' resistance is disclosed by the media or if it involves casualties. Media exposure of citizens' resistance with legitimate claims makes it common knowledge to both the government and the public that citizens' rights have been violated. Protests that involve

TABLE 6.1

Intervention from Central and Provincial Authorities

	Cases (*A*)	Successful Cases (*a*)	*a*/*A* (percent)
Intervention from the center	13	10	76.9
Intervention from the provincial authority only	17	13	76.5
No intervention from above	231	55	23.8
Total number of cases	261	78	29.9

SOURCE: Author's collection.

serious casualties of participants not only damage regime legitimacy but also embolden local officials if upper-level authorities fail to intervene. Needless to say, media exposure of protests involving casualties will generate even more pressure on upper-level authorities.

Kowalewski and Schumaker's research on protest outcomes in the former Soviet Union suggests that "militant groups can increase the probability of favorable outcomes regardless of size."[6] In contrast, in China, size does matter because large-scale resistance poses a more serious threat to social stability, while small-scale disruptive action may be suppressed. The Chinese police department has complained that some citizens have the "incorrect thought" that "a big disturbance leads to a big solution, a small disturbance leads to a small solution, and no disturbance, no solution."[7] But the policies of state authorities have confirmed citizens' belief in the effectiveness of large-scale resistance. For example, the government agency in charge of the construction sector, together with the trade union and the association of construction enterprises, has been urged to form a three-party group to address labor conflicts in this sector. In Guangdong, the criterion for the three-party body's intervention in labor disputes is based on the number of workers involved. It occurs if an instance of social unrest involves more than 1,000 participants, if a drastic or violent action involves 100 to 1,000 participants, if 500 to 1,000 people make five or more consecutive petitions on the same issue, or if the rights of a large number of employees in the sector are violated.[8]

Given that the number of cases involving serious casualties is rather limited and the media in China still face serious constraints in reporting ongoing protests, the size of the protesting group is often the most important factor that affects participants' chance of success. Table 6.2 reports on the scenarios under which intervention from above occurred in the thirty of the 261 cases with information on the outcome (intervention also occurred in another three of the five riots without specific demands). Certainly, the small sample size does not allow for a conclusive assessment of the proportion of cases in which the central government has intervened. The collected cases seem to suggest that central authorities more frequently intervened in citizens' disputes when they were directly approached by the citizens (i.e., six cases) or when citizen resistance was large scale (i.e., six cases). As discussed below, directly approaching central authorities also requires a reasonably large number of participants to be effective. Provincial authorities intervened most frequently in large-scale confrontations and disruptive actions (i.e., eleven of seventeen). The two levels of government intervened in another five cases that involved the deaths of participants or received media coverage.

Not surprisingly, the central and provincial authorities generally do not intervene in relatively small-scale collective resistance. Among the 261 cases, participants succeeded in twenty-three cases where the central or provincial authorities intervened and in fifty-five cases without intervention from the two levels of authority. Most of the remaining 183 cases were small scale, with fewer than 200 participants. These incidents of small-scale resistance were likely to be beyond the notice of the central or provincial authorities. Nevertheless, even though upper-level authorities knew about some of these incidents, they might still have not intervened simply because the pressure for intervention was very limited.

My collection also reveals that the likelihood of intervention from above is affected by the cost associated with addressing citizens' grievances. Of the 261 cases, thirty-one large-scale instances of resistance failed to attract

TABLE 6.2
Scenarios of Intervention from Above

	Center	Provincial Authorities	Total	Success
Large-scale confrontations	4	6	10	9
Large-scale deadly confrontations	2		2	1
Petitions	6	4	10	7
Disruptive action or strikes		5	5	3
Deadly confrontations, media exposure		1	1	1
Media exposure	1	1	2	2
Total number of cases	13	17	30	23

SOURCE: Author's collection.

intervention from above. In twenty-six of the thirty-one suppressed or toler-ated cases, the number of participants exceeded 1,000, which suggests that they were relatively forceful. An examination of the level of state authorities involved in these cases points to the rationale behind upper-level authori-ties' reluctance to intervene. Table 6.3 presents the large-scale cases that attracted and did not attract intervention from above in light of the ad-ministrative level of the state's authority involved in each of the cases. Most of the cases that attracted intervention from the central and provincial au-thorities involved authorities at the county or lower level. Only two cases involved city-level authorities (one was not addressed). In contrast, of the thirty-one cases that did not attract intervention from above, sixteen (or 51.6 percent) involved state authorities at the city or provincial level. It takes a great deal of political determination for the central authorities to discipline city-level governments or their leaders, not to mention provincial governments. In at least eight cases in my collection, the central govern-ment knew about the citizens' serious grievances but refused to intervene. This occurred either because of the high cost of making concessions or because of the less serious pressure faced by the central government.

Moreover, intervention from the central or provincial authorities does not always mean success for the participants. In three of the twelve cases in which the central government intervened, the participants did not achieve success. In two of these three cases, local governments resorted to false compliance. In the third one, which occurred in Shanwei in Guangdong province and which involved the city government, the central government did not take serious measures, as discussed below. In four of the seventeen cases that had

TABLE 6.3
Intervention and Nonintervention in Large-Scale Resistance

Level of government involved	Cases	Intervention	Nonintervention[a]
Province/Ministry	5		4
City	31	2	12
County	78	11	4
Township	53	4	4
Village/Street	34	5	2
Others	60[b]	8	5
Total number of cases	261	30	31

SOURCE: Author's collection.
NOTE: Intervention is from the central or provincial government.
[a]Includes only large-scale protests.
[b]It mainly includes disputes between employees and their firms in urban areas.

intervention from provincial authorities, the participants did not succeed. In three of the four cases involving disruptive tactics, the provincial authorities tolerated the lower-level governments' use of suppression partly because the participants' demands were seen as unreasonable. In the fourth case, the lower-level local governments did not address the peasants' complaints about land use despite instructions from the provincial party secretary.

The cases I collected show that the central and provincial governments do not intervene in most instances of citizens' resistance in China, which is understandable given the magnitude of the incidents of resistance in the country. However, selective intervention still creates uncertainties for abusive local officials. In my collection of the 261 cases, seventy-one government officials were punished in twenty-one cases because of their abuse of power or their mishandling of citizens' resistance. As the cases below show, intervention from above or the threat of intervention makes successful resistance possible.

Intervention by the Central Authorities

Intervention from the central government is not frequent, but once the central government has decided to intervene, it has to make concessions to citizens and sometimes punish malfeasant agents to show "how your sins have provoked the wrath of the fanatics and have brought this punishment upon yourselves."[9] The central government tends to intervene when the pressure on regime legitimacy mounts, especially after media exposure. In Jiahe county in Hunan province, for example, local government agents carried out housing demolition in 2003 without providing reasonable compensation to the home owners and arrested three people who resisted. After the case was disclosed by Chinese Central Television, the central government sent a team to the county to investigate. In the end, the homeowners received greater compensation, and the three people arrested were released. Four officials, including the county party secretary and the county magistrate, were removed from office, and a fifth was disciplined by the party.[10]

However, the media are rarely allowed to cover ongoing resistance. More often, the central government will intervene in cases that are not reported by the media if the actions are large in scale. For example, in October 2004, about 100,000 peasants in Hanyuan, a county in Sichuan province, protested about the poor compensation they received for their farmland and homes due to the construction of a dam. After making repeated but fruit-less petitions to higher-level authorities, tens of thousands of peasants ap-proached the construction site on the night of October 27, 2004 to halt work on the project. The government sent about 1,500 police officers to maintain order. Violent confrontations broke out between the participants and police officers, resulting in the deaths of both citizens and police of-ficers. Given the vast number of peasants involved in the collective protest, the local government then sent more than 10,000 militia to help reestablish order. The provincial party secretary went to the site to address the problem but was reportedly surrounded by peasants for hours. When the central government learned of the disturbance, it sent a work team headed by a leader of the State Council to the county. The team announced the central government's view that the event was a "large-scale gathering of migrants who did not know the truth about the cause of the confrontation." Most of the participants were thus exempted from punishment. Meanwhile, the provincial government promised to have the protesters' homes relocated and to increase compensation for their lost property. At least eight local officials were detained on charges of corruption, and the county's party secretary was removed from his post.[11]

The scale of resistance is relative to the location where the action takes place. A few hundred participants may not be able to put serious pressure on the state authorities if their action takes place in a remote or politically unimportant area, but they will have a more immediate impact if they stage their protest in front of central government agencies. Therefore, the combi-nation of a relatively large number of participants and innovative tactics can put serious pressure on local and central governments. One such tactic is to directly approach the central government. In a county in Hebei province, a village sold a large amount of land to external land users, but the village party secretary refused to distribute the money to the peasant households. After fruitless petitions to local authorities, the villagers decided to appeal to the central authorities in 2003. When the county authority learned of this plan, it ordered the police department to prevent peasants from en-tering the railway station or the bus station. Peasant leaders held a secret meeting to discuss what should be done. The next day, about 800 peasants made their way to Beijing on bicycles. The county government immedi-ately reported the case to higher-level authorities and asked for help from a county government in the suburbs of Beijing, which managed to stop the peasants. Officials from provincial and central government agencies came to investigate the case. As a result of the protest, the county party secretary faced the "most serious crisis in his career." Meanwhile, the county authority sent buses to bring the peasants back, and the village was ordered to pay the peasants immediately.[12]

The use of certain traditional methods by a relatively large number of participants also puts pressure on the legitimacy of the central government. For instance, kneeling down in front of government officials is a traditional way of showing respect and obedience, but it also places moral pressure on officials if they fail to respond. A former minister of the Ministry of Labor and Social Security recalled such an instance. On a winter morning in 2003, more than seventy mine workers from a city in the northeast knelt down in front of the ministry, blocking the office compound. These workers had been laid off. Too poor to pay for heating, their families had been forced to live without it despite the cold weather. As a result of their action, the minister immediately called the provincial governor, and their case was addressed.[13]

This method is perhaps most frequently employed by peasants.[14] In one case in Lingquan county in Anhui province, the government imposed heavy taxes and fees on peasants.[15] In 1992, several peasants' representatives from one village approached the township and county authorities to complain about these burdens, but to no effect. Three peasants' representatives then appealed to the central authorities in Beijing. The central government agencies mandated that local authorities address the peasants' problems, but their instructions were ignored by local officials. Worse, local police arrested the peasants' leaders. Three of the peasants' representatives managed to flee to Beijing to make further appeals, only to be arrested by police sent to Beijing by the county government. Two of the representatives were put in jail. In October 1995, the peasants mounted their last appeal. Under the leadership of one peasant who had been released from prison, seventy-four protesters went to Beijing. On Sunday October 29, 1995, they gathered in Tiananmen Square, departing for the square one after another to avoid being identified as a group. After all of them had arrived, they suddenly knelt down. Their action attracted attention from the central government, which required that the local officials from Anhui travel to Beijing that night. The peasants' problems were addressed, and the county party secretary was transferred.

Intervention by the central government can both enhance regime legitimacy and warn local officials about abusing power. But such concessions are conditional. In the above cases, the highest-level officials to be disciplined were county-level officials, who are in the lower rungs of the political hierarchy. As mentioned earlier, when high-ranking local officials are involved in a dispute or its settlement, the central government is less willing to intervene.[16] In these circumstances, the central government will prevent media exposure to reduce damage to its legitimacy. This reluctance to intervene has been well reflected in the case of rural land use, as discussed in Chapter Three. One high-profile case occurred in Guangdong province in 2005.

In December 2005, a bloody confrontation occurred in Dongzhou, a village in Shanwei city in Guangdong province. The city government built a power plant in this village. The villagers complained about the possible pollution of their water as well as the inadequate compensation for the land on which the plant was constructed. A deadly confrontation between villagers and police officers took place on December 6 in which, according to the official account, three peasants were killed and eight others wounded.[17] The shooting of unarmed citizens has been very rare in China since 1989, but in this case only the deputy head of the city's public security bureau was detained and accused of mishandling the event. The central government managed to keep the case very quiet. It was not until December 10 that the Xinhua News Agency released a short news report on the event, accusing a few peasants of inciting the riot. Reportedly, the central government sent a team to the province (but not to the village), where the team members apparently accepted the explanation of the local government, which blamed a few peasants for the confrontation. Although a few local officials were given party discipline, no officials, including the deputy head of the public security bureau, were held legally liable for the incident.[18]

It is not clear why the central government chose not to intervene significantly in this case, but it seems likely that its decision was because provincial leaders in Guangdong had already directly intervened in its settlement. The shooting occurred on December 6, and the provincial party secretary visited the village the next day. The party secretary was a member of the Politburo, the paramount party body in China, and his views had to be respected even by the central authorities. The brief news account of the incident released by the Xinhua News Agency was provided by the local government. Hence, even if the central government found that the released report was flawed, it would have been almost impossible for it to change the statement later.

The central government's intervention is not only conditional but also limited in that it does not intervene in local governments' punishment of some participants, especially in drastic actions, after concessions are made. This is understandable because unconditional concessions will make the local government vulnerable. Tarrow writes, "[O]ne of the most remarkable characteristics of collective action is that it expands the opportunities of others. Protesting groups put issues on the agenda with which other people identify and demonstrate the utility of collective action that others can copy or innovate upon."[19] By punishing certain participants, the local government shows that a victory can be very costly, thereby reducing the encouraging effect. In the Hanyuan case, the county and city governments imposed serious punishment on some participants *ex post*. In 2005, twenty-eight participants were tried in local courts and were ruled guilty. One of the participants was even executed on the charge of killing a police officer.[20] In the Linquan and Jiahe cases, the participants were jailed before intervention from the central government occurred. In the Shanwei case, the local government put thirteen villagers in jail for up to seven years for their part in the confrontation in 2006.

Intervention by the Provincial Authority

The tragic incident in Shanwei indicates the degree to which the central government may tolerate the local government's repression of protests. Bloody repression, however, is not an ideal choice for local governments simply because its agents cannot be certain that they will be exempted from punishment. After the incident in Shanwei, the provincial party secretary warned local officials that those who failed to follow proper land use procedures and thereby caused collective resistance would be removed.[21] Hence, local government concerns about central government intervention can lead to concessions. As discussed in earlier chapters, most conflicts between the state and citizens in China have been caused by grassroots governments or their agencies, especially at the county level.[22] The highest level local authority is the provincial-level authority, and intervention by the provincial government is the most important way for citizens to have their voices heard in the absence of attention from the central government.[23]

When a serious confrontation occurs, the provincial government will naturally react because the central government will interpret its response as indicative of the local leaders' ability to govern. In addition, regulations require that serious confrontations should be reported to the pertinent central authorities within two hours.[24] If such cases are disclosed in the media or are reported to the central government, provincial leaders are put under pressure to resolve them as soon as possible, and they may thus punish those officials deemed responsible for the confrontations so as not to disappoint the central government.

In one case in Dingzhou city (a county-level city) in Hebei province, the local government constructed a power plant, and the plant needed a piece of land on which to store its coal ashes.[25] The construction of the ash-storage facility was contracted to a businessman who received strong support from the local government. In March 2004, when villagers from whom the land was appropriated learned that the local government retained more than half of the compensation funds paid by the land user, they began to make petitions to authorities at different levels, but their appeals were ignored. A few villagers were sentenced to jail for protesting. To prevent the construction, the peasants then erected dozens of tents on the land where the facility was to be built and placed 100 to 200 villagers on duty each night. Between March and July, the city government and the contracted business made more than ten attempts to construct the ash-storage facility by sending police officers to forcibly vacate the site, but they met strong peasant resistance each time. Such resistance was becoming increasingly unacceptable to the local government and the contractor. In the early morning of June 11, 2005, more than 300 thugs suddenly attacked the peasants who were sleeping in the tents, killing six and wounding another forty-eight. One peasant managed to videotape the fighting at the cost of a broken arm. The five-minute footage became an important piece of evidence that was later shown on the Internet as well as by foreign television networks.

The casualties and media coverage generated serious pressure on the local authorities, including the provincial government. The provincial public security bureau immediately formed a task force to deal with the case. It found that the thugs were hired by the contractor. The police department detained 106 people. Two days after the event, the provincial authority in Hebei removed the city party secretary and the mayor. In December, twenty-seven of the people who had persecuted the protesters were tried. Four suspects who organized the attack were sentenced to death, three were sentenced to the death penalty with a reprieve, and another six, including the party secretary and the contractor, were sentenced to life imprisonment. The party secretary was accused of participating in the planning of the attack. In the end, the provincial government decided not to use the village's land for the project.[26]

Local officials have been punished even when their handling of collective resistance did not cause deaths. In a high-profile case in Zhejiang province, peasants succeeded in forcing the local government to accept their demands. The government in Dongyang city (a county-level city) set up an industrial park in one of its townships in 2001.[27] The chemical factories in the park produced pollutants that threatened the villagers' health and damaged their farmland. The villagers appealed to the local and central authorities repeatedly, but their appeals were ignored. In 2001, the local government arrested more than ten villagers for attacking factories in the park. After four years of fruitless protest efforts, the villagers put up tents at the industrial park's entrance in 2005. About 200 elderly villagers lived in the tents to maintain a twenty-four-hour vigil, blocking the industrial park's entrance for two weeks in April 2005. In the early morning of April 10, the city government organized about 3,500 police officers and government officials to disperse the villagers and dismantle the tents. A rumor circulated that two elderly women were killed in the confrontation with the police, which seems ultimately to have been false, and thousands of angry villagers clashed with the police and government officials, beating them, overturning police cars, and smashing dozens of buses that had ferried the police officers and officials. The local officials and police did not dare to use further force; after failing to defeat the peasants, they retreated. In the end, more than 140 people were sent to hospitals, the majority of whom were police officers and government officials, including a deputy city mayor.

After the confrontation, the local government was eager to put an end to the situation. Six of the thirteen factories were ordered to move out of the industrial park permanently. The provincial authority also imposed serious punishment on the local officials deemed responsible for the event. The former city party secretary, who had been promoted as head of the propaganda department of the higher-level city party committee, was removed from his position. The deputy city party secretary, who was also the mayor, was removed from both positions. The township party secretary was also removed. Another five officials, including a deputy mayor, the head and two deputy heads of the environmental protection bureau, and the township head, were also disciplined.[28] The peasants, however, also paid a high price. Eight peasants were sentenced to eight months to five years in jail. One official said to them, "If you're not guilty, then the government is. And the government cannot be guilty." As a result, the Huaxi case illustrates that "even when farmers win, they lose."[29]

Provincial authorities are not different from lower-level governments in their attitude toward those who are seen as disrupting the social order or damaging the image of local governments. In addition to tolerating local governments' punishment of activists, provincial authorities may require local governments to punish participants in certain types of collective action. For example, in Zhejiang province in 2000, because of a dispute over the naming of a railway station, some villages blocked the railway, resulting in the stoppage of traffic for fifteen minutes. Both the provincial party secretary and the governor required the local government to ensure the flow of traffic and punish the activists. As a result, thirteen people were put in jail for up to four years.[30]

Not surprisingly, the provincial government also tolerates local governments' use of suppression when the provincial government itself is involved in a dispute and the cost of concessions is high. In 2003, fifteen county governments in Shaaxi province decided to take back the rights on the use of oil wells that had been legally contracted to private businesses before the contracts expired. This move met strong resistance from more than 1,000 contractors and over 60,000 investors because they were offered compensation of only 1.3 billion yuan, while the actual loss was estimated to be 7 billion yuan. County and city governments claimed that what they did was simply to follow the orders of upper-level authorities. The contractors then decided to sue the governments at the county, city, and provincial levels, turning the provincial governor and the city mayor into the defendants. Local governments were upset by the peoples' resistance, including petitions to the central authorities. In 2005, more than 300 investors gathered in front of the provincial party committee and requested a dialogue. The peaceful gathering became the pretext for suppression. Six activists were arrested by the police from their counties under the charge of disrupting the social order, while another two fled. One of their lawyers who did not even participate in the gathering was also arrested for "disrupting the social order" and "illegal gathering." Their lawsuit against the three levels of government was unsurprisingly rejected by the provincial court.[31]

At other times, the provincial authority itself may use force to deal with popular resistance when the cost of concessions is too high. In July 2005, a steel factory in Chongqing that had 18,000 employees was declared bankrupt. Workers could not accept the bankruptcy plan because the compensation was perceived to be unreasonably low. They required higher compensation and protested for about two months, mainly by blocking the traffic. It was estimated that the city government needed to pay 2 billion yuan to meet the workers' demands, which was apparently a heavy financial burden for the government. In addition, making concessions to this factory could trigger resistance by workers from other factories. After the negotiations between the government and the workers broke down, the government lost patience and resorted to suppression.[32]

Concessions without Intervention

My collection of 261 cases also reveals that participants succeeded in fifty-five cases without receiving intervention from the central or provincial authorities. As discussed in earlier chapters and the earlier section of this chapter, the type of demands and the forcefulness of the action significantly affect the chance of success. Figure 6.1 reports the outcomes of 231 cases, excluding the thirty cases that attracted intervention from above. Among the sixty-one cases with low-cost demands, 46 percent succeeded, as opposed to 16 percent of the 170 cases with high-cost demands. Compared with the outcomes reported in Figure 3.1 in Chapter Three, it is clear that in resistance with high-cost demands, citizens' chances of success are smaller in the absence of intervention from above. On the other hand, the cost of concessions is relative to the forcefulness of the action. Of the seventy-two cases with forceful action, 57 percent succeeded, as opposed to 8.8 percent of the 159 with less forceful action. As discussed in Chapter Three, citizens are most likely to succeed when their demands are not costly and their action is forceful (i.e., 85.7 percent), and they are least likely to succeed when their demands are costly and their action is not forceful (i.e., 3.4 percent).

Among the fifty-five successful cases without intervention from above, forceful action was used in 74.5 percent of them (i.e., forty-one cases), which implies that state authorities are generally under more serious pressure in such cases. Some modes of forceful action can easily cause social disruptions that local governments cannot ignore. It is not uncommon for participants

Forcefulness of Action

		Forceful			Not Forceful	
Cost of Concessions	Low	a. Concessions	16	a. Concessions	8
		b. *a* + discipline	2	b. *a* + discipline	2
		c. Suppression	2	c. Suppression	17
		d. Tolerance	1	d. Tolerance	13
	High	a. Concessions	14	a. Concessions	3
		b. *a* + discipline	9	b. *a* + discipline	1
		c. Suppression	22	c. Suppression	109
		d. Tolerance	6	d. Tolerance	6

FIGURE 6.1 Concessions without Intervention from Above (N = 231). SOURCE: Author's collection, excluding the thirty cases that received intervention from above.

to block traffic, including roads, highways, railways, and bridges; they also block the office compounds of state authorities. For example, in Xi'an, the capital city of Shaanxi province, there were 337 instances of disruptive action between 1995 and early 1999. In 103 of these cases (31 percent), participants blocked traffic, and in 141 of them (42 percent), participants blocked the office compounds of state authorities, with the number of participants ranging from dozens to over 10,000.[33]

Therefore, many instances of forceful action place a dual pressure on local governments by paralyzing the social order and posing threats of intervention from above. Local governments make concessions to protestors in forceful action when repression is risky, insufficient, or infeasible. For example, some protestors, like the old people, cannot simply be suppressed, but a lack of concessions may lead to the recurrence of such protests. In one case, thousands of retired workers from several factories of a textile company in a city in Anhui province took to the streets for three days in October 2004 to protest their low pensions. Thousands of sympathizers joined them in the streets, forming a kilometer-long demonstration that blocked a major road into the city. Riot police were initially deployed but were then withdrawn because the government worried that any repression of the protest would trigger a riot. After three days of the traffic blockade, the local government agreed to increase the workers' pensions. In this case, the government exercised tolerance and caution because many of the participants were elderly, and repression might have put the government in a morally weak position and triggered intervention from above. The participants also tried to avoid giving the government excuses to use force.[34]

A second scenario of successful forceful action without intervention from above is that suppression is not feasible. Piven and Cloward suggest that the power of the poor lies in their ability to create institutional disruptions that threaten social or economic operations. A protest is more likely to be effective if it produces political repercussions. In other words, when challengers are crucial to institutions and when powerful allies or power holders have a stake in those institutions, disrupting such institutions is effective.[35] In China, this rationale has been reflected in taxi drivers' strikes.

In recent years, taxi drivers have held strikes in a number of cities in China because of their disputes with the government or their companies. Given their role in public transportation, it is common for them to achieve success. For example, in Yanji city in Jilin province, the number of taxi stands was so limited that many taxi drivers often had difficulty finding a place to park to take on passengers or allow them to disembark, yet they were heavily fined by the police for violating parking regulations. On July 12, 2004, more than 2,500 taxies in the city held an anonymously initiated strike, partly paralyzing traffic in the city. The local government was shocked, and it acted by reimbursing the taxi drivers for their parking fines. Additionally, the head of the local police department apologized to the drivers.[36] In another case, in 2004 in Yinchuan, the capital city of Ningxia Hui Autonomous Region, taxi drivers had a dispute with the city government over how many years business licenses were valid. Thousands of taxi drivers held a strike, some of them blocking traffic with their cars. The traffic in the city was at a standstill, thereby forcing the government to "surrender" by revoking the policy that disfavored the taxi drivers.[37]

These cases reveal that unorganized collective actions can be powerful because they are difficult for the government to handle. Research on social movements suggests that organized action can be less effective than unorganized action because the former tends to use acceptable modes of action to receive support from elites.[38] For example, Kriesi argues that when a social movement organization is integrated into established systems, the integration may impose limits on the mobilization capacity of the organization and thus alienate important parts of its constituency.[39] In China, where resistance usually takes place without discernable organizational bases or leaders, disorganization, while making sustained resistance difficult, provides the advantage of unpredictability, which makes citizens' acts of resistance difficult to prevent and to negotiate. As a result, the government may face a situation where "there is no organization to be banned" or "no conspiratorial leaders to round up or buy off."[40]

Certainly, a precondition for the success of such disruptive actions is the large number of participants. My collection of 261 cases shows that actions involving more than 4,000 participants rarely failed. This does not mean that all actions require this many participants to succeed, but it does prove the logic of the idea that "a big disturbance leads to a big solution." The fundamental reason for the effectiveness of large-scale or forceful resistance in China is that the occurrence of such incidents indicates local officials' failure in maintaining social stability, thereby forcing them to use all possible means to end the resistance quickly. Given that repressing a large number of participants is politically risky, concessions or concessions with discipline are a common option. The following section elaborates on this rationale with the case of worker protests in Liaoyang in Liaoning province in 2002.

THE POWER OF LARGE-SCALE RESISTANCE: WORKER PROTESTS IN LIAOYANG

In March 2002, about 10,000 workers from more than ten factories in Liaoyang city in Liaoning province took to the streets.[41] Workers demanded the punishment of corrupt cadres and the protection of their economic rights.[42] The protests turned into a high-profile case because it was one of the few cases in which workers from different factories acted together, although their joint action was not consciously orchestrated by the workers.[43] The major participants of those protests were workers from a local state-owned enterprise, the Liaoyang Ferroalloy Factory. This case not only reveals why some workers are able to stage powerful action but also shows the pressure Chinese local governments often face in dealing with large-scale protests and some strategies they use to stop popular contention.

Background of Worker Protests

The Liaoyang Ferroalloy Factory was established in 1956, and it had 7,100 workers in its state-owned units and 1,200 workers in its collective units by the early 1990s. The factory was successful in the 1980s but began to lose money in the 1990s. Workers blamed Fan, who was the manager between 1993 and 1998 for the poor performance of the factory. During Fan's term, the factory retrenched fifty cadres and 1,500 workers. In 1994, the factory owed workers salaries for two months. The situation became worse between 1996 and 2000 when workers were not paid for ten to twenty-two months. By November 2001, when the factory was declared bankrupt, the assets of the factory amounted to 100 million yuan, but its debts totaled 668 million yuan. The total amount of salaries owed to the workers reached 16 million yuan, and the amount of overdue medical insurance premiums reached 27 million yuan.

Workers complained bitterly about the manager and other managerial personnel, believing that these cadres stripped state assets, mismanaged the factory, and raised salaries for themselves. After Fan resigned in 1998, the local government appointed a previous deputy manager of the factory to be the general manager in 1999. One year later, in 2000, the government considered declaring the factory bankrupt, and it sent a new manager to the factory to start the procedure. In 2001, the provincial governor came to the factory and confirmed the bankruptcy plan; the procedure started in September 2001, but the workers resisted the plan. In October, the government organized workers' representatives to vote on the proposal for bankruptcy by sending police officers to the site. Before that, the government detained four activists to prevent them from stirring up resistance. Without publicizing the result of the vote, the government declared the passage of the bankruptcy plan.

Worker Resistance

The problems at the factory not only caused grievances among the workers but also triggered their resistance. From 1998 to 2002, workers staged actions to demand salary, pension, and medical reimbursement; protect factory assets; demand punishment of corrupt factory cadres; and prevent irregularities in the bankruptcy of their factory.[44] Worker resistance evolved from peaceful actions, such as petitions, to more drastic protests not only because of their repeated failures but also because of their increased solidarity and mobilization capacity.

Between 1999 and 2000, the workers' major mode of resistance was presenting petitions. From the beginning of 1999, the workers began to present petitions to city government agencies, including the complaint bureau, the procuracy, the court, the economic and trade bureau, the party discipline committee, the city government, and the city party committee, but they did not receive any meaningful replies. After repeated failures in appealing to local authorities, including the provincial authorities, the workers appealed to the central government. Starting in June 2000, workers' representatives made five trips to Beijing and lodged complaints with a number of central agencies. The funds needed for the trips were donated by workers. During their first trip, the Central Discipline Inspection Commission gave the representatives two letters, one for the provincial discipline inspection committee and the other for the anticorruption bureau of the provincial procuracy. But the workers received no responses after submitting the two letters to the two agencies.

Despite their failures, the workers' ability to organize collective resistance was strengthened because of the emergence of activists in the process of resistance. To mobilize workers and build consensus and solidarity among workers, some activists began to repeatedly discuss the corruption in the factory and the stoppage of salary payments with other workers. An informal group of activists emerged in May 1999 when some workers were elected to be representatives to negotiate with the factory. After the negotiation failed, the workers organized a protest and blocked traffic on a major road near the factory on May 15, 1999. The government sent police officers, but the workers refused to leave. The next day, when the police tried to arrest three representatives who were delivering public speeches (they had been elected the previous day), there was a confrontation. When the police eventually arrested the three, about 3,000 workers marched to the city government for the release of the workers. In the evening, the government promised to release the three people and pay the workers their retirement pensions.

After this incident, this informal group of activists began to organize. The workers took some measures to protect themselves and their cause of resistance. There were two types of representatives or activists among the workers. One group consisted of those so-called public activists who were known to the workers in their respective neighborhoods. Each neighborhood had two such public representatives who were elected. The other group consisted of the so-called secret activists, who worked behind the scenes. For example, they prepared handbills or posters for the public activists. The secret activists might also replace the public activists if the latter quit for various reasons. The secret activists normally did not take the lead in resistance publicly, but the public activists would consult with them when they decided to take certain action.

These representatives or activists also respected the views of ordinary workers to gain both support and legitimacy. Each representative was responsible for keeping contact with dozens of workers. Each time activists planned to approach the city government or present petitions, they would distribute handbills that listed the proposed demands to the workers for comments. Activists would take action if most workers believed that there was a need for action; otherwise, no action would be taken. The activists might also revise their demands based on the suggestions of the other workers. The number of such activists reached more than 100 at the peak. It was believed that the government was less tolerant of younger people and might accuse them of assembling the masses to disrupt the social order or of stirring up trouble with "special motives" (*bie you yong xin*), so many of the activists were older people.[45]

The networks not only enhanced the solidarity of the workers but also strengthened their mobilization capacity, making subsequent large-scale collective action possible. As a matter of fact, before the 2002 protests, workers had organized a series of large-scale protests. On February 12, 2000, workers made a petition to the city government with more than 1,000 participants. In April 2001, workers held their first demonstration, blocking the traffic for salaries. In May 2001, more than 4,000 workers approached the city government, complaining about the loss of state assets due to the bankruptcy. Despite these actions, the workers did not achieve success until they organized the 2002 protests.

On February 28, 2002, or three months after the bankruptcy was declared, the workers failed to receive their monthly allowance of 180 yuan. Their frustration arising from repeated failures was intensified by a major local leader's lie. At that time, the National People's Congress was soon to be held in Beijing. A local official from Liaoyang, Gong Shangwu, who was attending the Congress, said to a correspondent from Liaoning television, "Liaoyang has laid-off workers, but there is nobody who is unemployed. Each laid-off worker receives 280 yuan per month."[46] Workers were angered by his words. In early March 2002, about 100 worker representatives held meetings and decided to hold a protest on March 11. They disseminated and posted four public letters addressed to the people in Liaoyang, Jiang Zemin, the provincial governor, and the city authorities, including the party committee and the government. On March 11 and 12, the workers from this ferroalloy factory took to the streets and were joined by workers from more than ten other factories, holding a picture of Chairman Mao and a banner with the slogan, "Fire Gong Shangwu, Liberate Liaoyang City." The total number of participants was estimated to exceed 10,000, and a nine-day protest ensued.

Government Response

The resistance of the workers from this ferroalloy factory had been a serious problem for the local government. Given the limited financial resources and the many money-losing factories in the city, the city government was neither able to pay the workers of this factory nor to keep the factory operating. As a result, the government had not responded positively to workers' demands despite their repeated petitions and protests in the past. Both the central and provincial governments also seemed to understand the difficulties faced by the city government, so they did not seriously intervene in the workers' grievances, which explains the fruitless petitions made by the workers.

Nevertheless, the city government felt tremendous pressure after the large-scale protests in March 2002. This was one of the largest protests by Chinese workers at that time, and this incident received attention, or in local officials' words, "too much (overseas) media exposure," because workers from other factories joined. This incident was thus perceived as a serious failure by local officials in maintaining local stability, so the city government reacted quickly. The city government used concessions with discipline to end the workers' protests. It was said that the police had a list of more than forty activists, but because of worker resistance and the exposure of overseas media, the police eventually targeted only a few major activists. On March 17, 2002, one activist was detained, and another three were arrested three days later. Two of the four were released in the end of 2002, and another two were put in jail for seven and four years, respectively, on the charge of subverting the government.[47]

Meanwhile, the government adopted two measures to appease the workers. One was to punish some factory cadres. Three factory cadres, including Fan, were put in jail, and another nine were given party discipline. Fan was sentenced to thirteen years in jail on the charge of smuggling and other crimes. The other measure was that the city government mobilized almost all possible financial resources to address workers' needs. By May 4, 2002, the city government paid workers of this factory half of the overdue salaries; by June 2003, all the overdue salaries were paid, and all the medical expenses were reimbursed. In addition, the city government allocated 20 million yuan to pay workers their housing fund, children's medical care, labor insurance, heat fees, and other expenses.

The city government also adopted other measures to help the workers to stop their resistance and complaints. In an official statement, it was reported:

> In order to address the problems arising from the bankruptcy, the city party committee and the city government expended many efforts. The city party committee formed seven teams consisting of more than 200 cadres from forty-five party or government agencies. These teams went to visit worker households, listening to and addressing their problems. The work teams provided special aid to the 162 especially poor households, paid pension premium for the employees, and provided a lump-sum unemployment relief fund. The work teams also adopted measures to solve workers' problems regarding their livelihood and created conditions for reemployment. With the coordinated efforts made to protect workers' rights, social stability was maintained.[48]

As some workers reported, "As long as workers did not ask about the bankruptcy of the factory or the corruption of local officials, if their problems could be addressed with money, they would be solved." As the local government was desperate to silence the workers, it depleted its financial resources. But, apparently, it was impossible for the workers to have most of their economic demands met without the large-scale protests.

SUCCESS IN SMALL-SCALE RESISTANCE

In my collection, some participants also succeeded in small-scale resistance in the absence of intervention from above. One reason is that some small-scale resistance can be forceful because it involves serious casualties and forces the local governments to make concessions to avoid punishment from upper-level authorities. In one case that occurred in a county in Hubei province in 1995, because of a dispute over the compensation for the loss of land, the local government sent more than 100 police officers to a village to arrest two peasant leaders. A violent confrontation between villagers and police officers resulted in the death of a peasant (who was shot by the police) and injuries to ten police officers and six peasants. After the confrontation, the local government exempted the victim's family from agricultural taxes and fees, gave them compensation, and took on the responsibility of raising the victim's three children until they were eighteen years old. In addition, all the detained peasant activists were released. The local government also compensated the village by, among other things, giving the village a factory.[49] Certainly, the number of cases involving serious casualties or deaths of participants is very limited.

A second reason that participants succeed in small-scale resistance is that the cost of concessions incurred by the government is relatively small. In the 261 cases I collected, participants succeeded in fourteen cases with less forceful action in the absence of intervention from above. Ten of the fourteen cases belong to the low-cost category and largely concern disputes between workers in the public or private sector and their employers. In addressing these disputes, local governments did not need to provide financial aid. In 2006, for example, more than 100 migrant workers in a factory in Hongzhou in Zhejiang did not receive their salaries. They blocked the traffic of a highway, which triggered intervention by the city authorities. The workers eventually received their overdue salaries. In several cases, workers in state-owned enterprises (SOEs) succeeded in receiving their demanded compensation or even in choosing the mode of the ownership reform in their firms. But not all labor disputes belong to the category of low-cost cases. When local governments were directly involved in the reform plan as in the Chongqing case, it was difficult for the workers to change it.[50]

Finally, some participants in small-scale resistance succeed because of their use of certain tactics. For instance, persistence was the crucial reason for peasants' success in one of the few cases of high-cost demands in my collection. In 1986, about 190 peasants in a village were granted urban household registrations and allocated jobs as a result of their farmland being taken away by the provincial bureau of tourism. The land conversion was carried out by the city government. These peasants were subsequently laid off in 1993 because of the poor performance of their firms. They started their petitions in 1993 and intensified their efforts for seeking compensation in 2000. Because the compounds of both the provincial and city governments were guarded, peasants mainly targeted the unguarded bureau of tourism. From 2000 to 2004, dozens of peasants approached the bureau continually. They blocked the office compound, locked the door of the bureau, had meals in the corridors of the bureau during the daytime, and slept in the corridors at night. The bureau called the police, but the peasants' behavior did not seriously violate the law, so the police could not simply arrest all of them.

The bureau approached the provincial government and city government for help. The provincial government then told the city government to solve the issue, but the latter did not take action because it thought that the issue was too complex. Unable to stand the peasants' persistent disruption any longer, the leader of the provincial bureau of tourism and several of his subordinates went to the city government in May 2004, but the city leaders tried to find excuses not to meet with these officials for a discussion on the issue. Like average petitioners, the officials of the provincial bureau said that they had brought food with them and would not leave the city government if they did not get a reply, thereby greatly embarrassing the city leaders. The next day, the city government convened a meeting and decided to grant compensation to the peasants.[51]

Conclusion

This chapter discusses an important method used by Chinese citizens—disruptive tactics—to move their issues onto the agendas of state authorities. As elsewhere, disruptive actions are "'outside of normal politics' and 'against normal politics' in the sense that people break the rules defining permissible modes of political action."[52] Disruptive tactics have been used by protesters in both democracies and nondemocracies, and a common factor that affects protesters' chances for success is the size of the protest: "There always seems to be power in numbers."[53] In democracies, a large-scale action may signal the preference of a large number of people, which then places pressure on politicians.[54] Authoritarian governments are even more sensitive to unauthorized large-scale action because such actions not only threaten social or political stability but also signal the weakness of the state and may escalate into crises if mishandled.

In China, disruptive tactics are generally illegal, but they have helped citizens achieve success. Large-scale disruptive actions are effective because they pose a direct threat to local officials' images. As mentioned earlier, lower-level local governments are required to report large-scale protests to upper-level governments, including the central government, within a regulated period of time. Given that local officials are not allowed to cover up such incidents,[55] the threat of intervention from above becomes a serious constraint for local officials. Central or provincial authorities do intervene when the pressure for maintaining social stability or regime legitimacy mounts. In these circumstances, local governments feel the necessity of concessions. This is why Chinese citizens believe in the rationale of "no appeals without enough participants" (*ren shao bu shangfang*) or "no action without enough power" (*li bo bu dengchang*).[56] Understandably, when a case involves serious casualties and/or receives media coverage, local governments that are responsible for dealing with such incidents face even more pressure. Concessions tend to be the only option if protesters' demands are legitimate. However, the forcefulness of resistance is weighed against the cost of concessions. A number of cases of forceful resistance have been ignored or even suppressed by local governments. Cases that involve higher-level local governments may deter intervention from the central or provincial authorities.

The cases presented in this chapter suggest that disruptive resistance involving only a small number of participants tends to be suppressed by local governments when the cost of concessions is high. To be sure, such cases may create a false impression of the extent of repression by the Chinese government, leaving out as they do the many cases in which citizens' resistance is ignored and therefore tolerated. For example, local governments rarely use force to deal with elderly protesters, such as retired workers. One method used by local governments in dealing with retirees' protests is to ferry these elder protesters to suburbs and leave them there.[57] The cases I collected do point to a common rationale behind local governments' response: The suppression of weak groups is more likely because it is more feasible and less costly. As Tilly suggests, "The more powerful the group, on average, the less repression it receives."[58] As discussed in the next chapter, this rationale is also reflected in local governments' response to protestors' use of violence.

SEVEN

The Limits of Disruptive Tactics: The Use of Violence

In China, protesters' disruptive tactics take a number of forms, including the use of violence. As Perry has found, violence has been possible in protests in communist China.[1] The frequency of the use of violence seems to have been rather high in recent years. In 2003, protesters attacked state agencies 3,900 times in China, up from 2,700 incidents in 2000.[2] If violence is defined as a deliberate physical injury to property or persons,[3] then it is illegal in most societies and more so in China, where disruptive modes of action are normally considered illegal. The issue becomes why people engage in this mode of action despite the high risk. Is it because violence increases protestors' chances of success or because violent protestors are irrational risk-takers? Given the frequent use of violence in Chinese citizens' protests, it is important to analyze its occurrence to understand why citizens choose this mode of resistance.

This chapter shows that violence does not necessarily increase the participants' odds of success or strengthen their intervention-seeking ability. On the contrary, the use of violence tends to be counterproductive, especially in small-scale resistance, because violence is largely unacceptable to local governments. However, violent protests have continued to occur in China. Chinese protestors are risk conscious. Their use of violence is significantly affected by the structure of their protesting group that shapes their perception of risk. More specifically, in certain protesting groups, violence is more likely to occur because the composition of the group weakens the members' sense of risk and/or places fewer constraints on the members. It can also be that violence is a defensive reaction when participants face state agencies or businesses that use violence offensively.

The case of violent protests reveals that while Chinese citizens' use of disruptive tactics may help trigger intervention from upper-level authorities (Chapter Six), not all disruptive tactics are acceptable to the party-state. On the other hand, however, although the use of violence carries serious risks and does not increase the odds of success, it signals widespread popular resentment in society. The large number of violent protests, including failed ones, places serious pressure on the party-state to address the sources of social conflicts.

The Effectiveness of Violent Collective Action

Gamson's research on social movements in the United States suggests that protesters who use violence "have a higher-than-average success rate."[4] But other studies on the effectiveness of violence have yielded mixed results.[5] Consider research on strikes: Snyder and Kelly show that violent strikes by Italian workers were much more likely to fail than were peaceful stoppages.[6] This contradicts the findings of Shorter and Tilly, who concluded from their study of strikes in France that workers' use of violence tended to have a positive effect on strike outcomes.[7] In their research on protest outcomes in the Soviet Union, Kowalewski and Schumaker find that militant groups increase the probability of favorable outcomes.[8] Shin's research on protests in South Korea also suggests that violent tactics tend to have more impact on the responsiveness of the government in terms of policy making than do peaceful tactics.[9] Others suggest that violence has no independent effect on the outcome of protests.[10]

In my collection of 261 cases (see Appendix B), violence occurred in 107 cases (i.e., 41 percent). This small sample size cannot provide an accurate estimate of the proportion of violent protests that have occurred in China. However, these cases can provide important indications regarding the government's attitude toward the use of violence and thereby predict the participants' chances of success when they use this mode of action. My collection suggests that the use of violence does not increase the odds of success. As presented in Table 7.1, 70 percent (or 183) of the 261 cases failed. Of the 107 cases that involved violence, 73.8 percent failed, as opposed to 67.5 percent of the 154 cases that did not involve violence.

TABLE 7.1
The Effectiveness of the Use of Violence ($N = 261$)

Resistance	Violent		Nonviolent	
	Successful	Failed	Successful	Failed
Large scale	24	17	27	14
Small scale	4	62	23	90
Total	28	79	50	104

SOURCE: Author's collection

Given that the size of the protesting group is an important or even the most important factor affecting the success of protests as discussed in earlier chapters, I divide the instances of collective action into two categories, one with 500 or more participants and the other with fewer than 500 participants. Of the eighty-two cases with 500 or more participants, 62.2 percent succeeded. Among the 179 cases with fewer than 500 participants, only 15.1 percent succeeded. As a matter of fact, participants had a rather high chance of success in large-scale resistance regardless of whether or not violence was used. While 58.5 percent of the forty-one large-scale protests involving violence succeeded, 65.9 percent of the forty-one large-scale protests not involving violence succeeded. However, the use of violence is counterproductive in small-scale resistance. Of the sixty-six small-scale acts involving violence, only four cases (or 6.1 percent) succeeded, whereas of the 113 small-scale acts that did not involve violence, twenty-three cases (or 20.4 percent) succeeded.[11]

Why does violence seem to be counterproductive in citizens' resistance, especially in small-scale resistance? An important reason is the cost of making concessions incurred by the local government (see Chapter Three). In my collection, violence occurred in eight of the sixty-four cases with low-cost claims (or 12.5 percent), whereas it occurred in ninety-nine of the 197 cases with high-cost claims (or 50.3 percent). Except for riots, the occurrence of violence implies that both the participants and the government or other actors (e.g., businesses) are reluctant to compromise because both parties have a high stake in achieving success. The violence can be seen as the result of the lack of compromise. On the other hand, local governments must protect their authority and reputation. Given that most protests are handled by local governments, they are under direct pressure to maintain local stability. Tolerating violence is likely to be seen as undermining the government's authority and encouraging more (violent) resistance.

In China, local governments have great discretion in interpreting citizens' actions. When the government feels that it is costly to make concessions, the use of violence by protesters provides an excuse or justification for the government's suppression. This explains the large number of participants being arrested or jailed in many cases regardless of the scale of the resistance. Local governments' low-level tolerance of the use of violence has affected citizens' choice of the modes of resistance. It is not rare that Chinese citizens avoid violence in their protests.[12] But if the use of violence involves serious consequence for the protesters, why do people use it at all?

The Use of Violence in Social Protests

Literature on disruptive actions has provided two strikingly different explanations for the use of violence in protests. One sees violence as the result of frustration, desperation, and weakness.[13] From this approach, violence is a mode of action that is emotionally driven or initiated by those who see no other means of achieving their goals. The other approach maintains that violence is an instrumental act, aimed at furthering the purposes of the group. Protesting groups use violence when they have some reason to believe that it will help their causes. This approach thus sees the use of violence as a strategic choice. Tilly asserts that "collective violence is not, by and large, the result of a single group's possession of an emotion, sentiment, attitude, or idea." He explains that "it grows, for the most part, out of strategic *interaction* among groups."[14] Tarrow suggests that violence is an easy kind of collective action for small groups to initiate without encountering major costs of coordination and control. However, larger movements also use violence deliberately to weld supporters together, dehumanize opponents, and demonstrate a movement's prowess.[15]

The primary issue that protesters face is the potential risk or cost of violence. In the approach that sees violence as an act of desperation, the costs or risks are not a serious consideration for the protesters. As Eisinger writes, "violent actors . . . have essentially thrown cost considerations to the winds."[16] Nevertheless, Tarrow points out that a limitation of using violence is that it damages legitimacy and allows the authorities to use repression: "Where violence occurs or is even likely, this gives authorities a mandate for repression and turns non-violent sympathizers away."[17] Gamson also notes that under certain circumstances, violence "merely hastens and insures its failure because its actions increase the hostility around it and invite the legitimate action of authorities against it."[18] Therefore, the use of violence can be self-defeating.[19]

The strategic-choice approach treats violence users as risk conscious. They choose to use violence in the right situations to avoid risk and increase the chance of success. More specifically, violence users escape misfortune because they are clever enough to use it primarily in situations when public sentiment neutralizes the normal deviance of the action, thereby reducing the likelihood and effectiveness of counterattack. In other words, protesters use violence when it will not trigger a negative reaction by the public or "when the normal condemnation which accompanies its use is muted or neutralized in the surrounding community."[20] In nondemocratic systems, governments are generally less tolerant of protests, including violent ones, because tolerance may signal the state's weakness and trigger more protests.[21] Therefore, according to the strategic-choice approach, violent protests should be rare in such political contexts because the "right situations" for using violence are rare. But this is not true in China, where violent protests do occur.

GROUP STRUCTURE AND THE USE OF VIOLENCE

An important assumption of the strategic-choice approach is that the protesting group is a unitary actor. This is not an inaccurate assumption about protests that are organized by independent and lawful organizations (e.g., trade unions) that assume the decision-making power for participants. Such organizations have been highlighted in the literature on social movements, and the existence of organizations is a precondition for the rise and development of movements.[22] As a result, research on individual participants in movements is largely focused on how to recruit participants,[23] as opposed to their role in the choice of movement strategies.

In nondemocratic countries, however, most instances of collective action may not be classified as social movements because these actions are not organized or sustained. Independent organizations that can orchestrate activities against the will of the government are normally not allowed. While there are also spontaneous protests in democracies, protesting groups in nondemocracies are generally loosely organized. A significant implication of this loose structure is that the decision-making power is diffused or decentralized, and this gives individual participants more freedom in choosing the mode of action.

The loose structure directly bears on participants' behaviors. If we see a protesting group consisting of participants and organizers or activists, the choice of the mode of action is affected not only by the interaction between the participants and leaders but also by the interaction among the participants themselves. An important factor that affects the participants' behaviors is their awareness of the risk involved. In a community of participants who have a high awareness of risk, violence is less likely to occur because risk-averse participants influence one another's behaviors. By the same token, in a community of participants who have a low awareness of risk, violence is more common because the participants are less constrained by themselves or their community. Different groups of participants may have different levels of awareness of risk, and violence is more likely to be used by those groups with a low awareness of risk.

The leaders in a collective action also affect the group's propensity for violence. Piven and Cloward find that organized action tends to be less effective than unorganized action: "In large part, organizers tended to work against disruption because in their search for resources to maintain their organizations, they were driven inexorably to elites, and to the tangible and symbolic supports that elites could provide."[24] In a political context in which noninstitutionalized actions are discouraged or even prohibited by the government, organizers or leaders are less prone to violence not primarily because of their worry over the loss of elite support but because of the potential punishment. Leaders of a collective action are therefore risk averse. As a result, in a protesting group with leaders, violence is less likely to occur. The converse is also true: The absence of leaders or strong leaders or the presence of risk-taking leaders increases the possibility of violence.

This group-structure approach provides an explanation for violent protests in authoritarian regimes by pointing out the importance of the microlevel group structure. It sees the occurrence of violence largely as a result of the participants' perception of the risk involved. This approach shares the assumption of the strategic-choice approach: individual participants tend to be risk averse. However, it is also different from the strategic-choice approach. For one, this approach suggests that the use of violence may not be the group's intentional strategic choice but the risk-conscious move of certain individual participants. For another, this approach does not see emotional factors or frustration as entirely irrelevant.[25] In certain protesting groups, frustration or anger is more likely to translate into violent action when the group structure imposes few constraints on participants.

EVIDENCE FROM THE DATA

In this section, I elaborate on this group-structure argument with my collection of 266 cases, including five riots in which participants did not have clear goals. In my analysis, the structure of a protesting group includes the following components: (1) the type of participants, (2) the presence or absence of leaders, and (3) the type of protesting communities. The police department in China has found that, compared with urban residents, rural residents are more ignorant of the law and are more prone to violence.[26] In this study, I divide the participants into peasants and urban residents to examine whether the former are more likely to use violence than the latter. Given the risk of leading collective action in China, it is assumed that the presence of leaders in a protest reduces the likelihood of the occurrence of violence. The absence of leaders or strong leaders or the presence of risk-taking leaders will increase the likelihood of the use of violence. Regarding the type of protesting communities, my hypothesis is that if the participants are from a single community (e.g., a village or a work unit), they have a high awareness of risk (because it is easy for the government to identify the participants) and they make it easy for their leaders to control their activities. The converse is also true for participants who come from different communities.

My collection of 266 cases provides evidence that supports the above hypotheses (Table 7.2). First, violence is less likely to occur in leader-led actions. Among the 120 leader-led instances, 30 percent involved violence, as opposed to 52.1 percent of the 146 leaderless actions. The difference is rather large between these two types of action (i.e., about 22 percent). This is understandable because, as detailed below, many of these incidents of resistance were directed against the government or other state agencies, and violence is not acceptable by state authorities. Therefore, the organizers or leaders of a collective action have a strong incentive to prevent violence to avoid punishment.

Second, violence is less likely to occur in actions based in single communities. Among the 184 cases based in single communities, 35.3 percent (or sixty-five) involved violence, as opposed to 57.3 percent of the eighty-two cases (or forty-seven) based in multiple communities. The difference is again 22 percent. Violence is least likely to occur in leader-led actions based in a single community (i.e., twenty-nine out of 101 cases, or 28.7 percent), and it is most likely to occur in leaderless actions based in multiple communities (i.e., forty out of the sixty-three cases, or 63.5 percent).

TABLE 7.2
The Use of Violence in Protests in China (*N* = 266)

	Leader-Led		Leaderless	
	Violence	Nonviolence	Violence	Nonviolence
Rural				
Single community	22	52	27	16
Multiple communities	5	7	20	6
Urban				
Single community	7	20	8	31
Multiple communities	2	5	20	17

SOURCE: Author's collection, including the five cases without specific demands.

Nevertheless, violence also occurred in a significant number of leader-led actions based in single communities (i.e., twenty-nine cases). Does this imply that these leaders are irrational or fearless? An examination of these cases reveals that violence occurs in this circumstance mainly because of serious injustices or citizens' perceptions of serious injustices. This is particularly true for conflicts between citizens and law enforcement agencies, such as the police department. It is not rare for these agencies to abuse power and seriously violate citizens' rights or even cause deaths.

For example, in several cases, the suspects died in the police stations where they were detained, but the police were unable to provide convincing or acceptable explanations for why they died. When the victims' families demanded clarification or investigation, they were denied their request. As a result, frustrated family members might resort to force. In one example, a villager in Guangxi autonomous region was detained by the police and died in the detention house. The police claimed that the person committed suicide by drinking poison. This explanation was dubious for a simple reason: How was the person able to get poison in the detention house? This explanation was not acceptable also because of one basic fact: The police in China have a reputation for abusing power in dealing with suspects. Dozens of the victim's family members, relatives, and friends protested in the county seat. When several of the protesters were detained in the compound of the county government, others broke into the compound. Their protest was repressed, with eight people being sued by the county government for attacking state agencies and staging illegal demonstration.[27] In such cases, by suppressing citizens' resistance, local authorities can deal with the cases in a way that allows them to avoid responsibility even if they are responsible for the outcome (e.g., the deaths).

In six cases, participants used violence because they were not satisfied with the ways state agencies dealt with the cases in which their family members died in conflicts with other people other than the police. In another ten cases, violence occurred when the law enforcement departments detained some people for questioning, which triggered confrontation or attacks organized by family members, colleagues, or fellow villagers. There is no reason to believe that all these protesters had legitimate grounds for using violence. But the participants in many of these cases did not intend to use violence initially. Instead, violence was used often when they failed to receive meaningful responses through permitted channels. In this sense, violence is a tactical escalation.[28]

The collected cases show that there are both similarities and differences between urban and rural residents in their use of violence. As Table 7.2 shows, the presence of leaders reduces the likelihood of the use of violence among both groups. Of the eighty-six leader-led acts that occurred in the countryside, 31.4 percent involved violence, as opposed to 68.6 percent of the seventy leaderless acts. In urban areas, violence occurred in 26.5 percent of the thirty-four leader-led cases, as opposed to 36.8 percent of the seventy-six leaderless cases. Second, violence is less likely to occur in actions based in single communities among both rural and urban residents. In rural areas, violence occurred in 42.3 percent of the 118 cases based in single communities, whereas it occurred in 65.7 percent of the thirty-eight cases based in multiple communities. In urban areas, violence occurred in 22.7 percent of the sixty-six cases based in single communities, as opposed to 50 percent of the forty-four cases based in multiple communities.

However, there are also differences in the use of violence between these two groups of people. First, proportionally more violent actions occurred among rural residents. Among the 156 instances that occurred in rural areas, 48 percent involved violence, as opposed to 33.6 percent of the 110 incidents that occurred in urban areas. Second, there is a significant difference between these two groups of participants in terms of the use of violence in leaderless protests based on single communities. In rural areas, 63.6 percent of the forty-four such cases involved violence, whereas it was 20.5 percent of the thirty-nine cases in urban areas.

Do these differences mean that rural residents are less risk averse than urban residents? In the next section, I show that there are several reasons for peasants' more frequent use of violence, and it cannot be simply attributed to their ignorance of the law or their low awareness of risk. Instead, they used violence more frequently for reasons that have much to do with the structure of their protesting group as well as the circumstances under which the confrontations between peasants and their targets occur.

Violent Protests in China: The Scenarios

In this section, I present cases of violent protests to show the circumstances under which violence occurs or does not occur in China. These cases reveal how those factors analyzed above affect protesters' behaviors in reality. I elaborate on the use of violence by mostly, but not exclusively, using large-scale protests. One reason is that the most serious violence has occurred in large-scale protests. Another reason is that my collection of large-scale protests may be relatively more complete, based on the assumption that such cases are more likely to be disclosed by the media, especially outside China, which makes a systematic comparison across different protesting groups more valid. Of the forty-four large-scale protests (i.e., with about 5,000 or more participants in each), sixteen were staged by workers; seventeen were undertaken by peasants, including two riots; and another eleven were staged by urban residents other than workers (see Appendix C).[29]

A COMPARISON BETWEEN WORKERS AND PEASANTS

From the late 1990s to the early 2000s, workers' collective actions were the most important source of social conflicts in China largely because of the reform of public enterprises.[30] In 2001, for example, instances of social unrest arising from conflicts related to workers' welfare or the reform of public enterprises accounted for 38 percent of the total number of instances of collective action in China.[31] Another major source of conflicts was in the countryside, where peasants took action mainly because of the conflicts over tax or fee payments, the loss of farmland, or the mismanagement of village affairs.[32] However, there seems to be an important difference between the two groups of people in terms of their propensity for using violence. Among the forty-four large cases I collected, workers used violence in three of the sixteen protests, whereas fifteen of the seventeen protests by peasants involved violence. There are several reasons for the difference.

One is the level of awareness of risk that these two groups have. There is no direct measurement of the awareness of risk. However, if a group's propensity for using the law is, to some extent, indicative of its awareness of the law and thereby likewise the risk of violating it, available surveys may provide some clues about this propensity among different groups. As the 2005 China General Social Survey shows (see Chapter Two), urban residents are more likely to use the legal system than rural residents. Other research has presented similar findings. For example, a national survey conducted in the late 1990s asked respondents the question, "What would you do if you were injured by other citizens?" There was a clear difference between the answers of urban and rural residents. About 42 percent of 1,490 urban residents replied that they would use the law (it was 50 percent in large cities), as opposed to only 16 percent of 4,000 rural respondents. More specifically, 18 percent of 2,650 peasants reported that they would use the law, whereas 32 percent of 940 workers responded in this way.[33]

Existing research on workers' collective actions suggests that workers tend to be cautious in staging collective action. For example, some workers do not wish to draw outsiders or participants from other firms or communities into their collective action to reduce the government's suspicion or negative response. Some workers therefore wear their uniforms to prevent others from joining their action and causing chaos or violence. Other workers stick to the practice of holding "civilized demonstrations."[34] It is largely because of this caution that intentionally organized joint actions by workers from different factories have been uncommon, though such cases do occasionally occur.[35]

The sixteen large-scale workers' protests in my collection were all based in single factories. In one of the three cases involving violence, more than 1,000 police officers tried to rescue factory managers detained by 5,000 workers who did not agree with the privatization plan in a factory in Sichuan province in 2006. In a second case, violence occurred because the participants included other people, mainly family members of the workers. In 2000, 20,000 mine workers, joined by their family members, staged a violent protest in a town in Liaoning province. The protesters smashed windows, blocked traffic, burned cars, and fought with armed police for several days. The cause of the protest was the bankruptcy of the mine, which affected the workers and their families in this industrial town because of the low severance pay. The participation of thousands of workers' family members was an important reason that the protest turned into a riot. The third case, which involved much less serious violence, also happened in Liaoning province. In one factory, more than 10,000 workers failed to receive their salaries, so they held the factory leaders as hostages for hours. The local police department sent police to disperse the crowd but failed, and the situation was put under control only after the provincial authority dispatched riot police from nearby cities. In spite of the violence, no one was seriously injured in this protest.[36]

By comparison, violence seems to be more common in peasants' large-scale protests not merely because of their low awareness of the law but mainly because of the structure of the protesting group. Unlike large-scale protests by workers, large-scale protests by peasants often involve participants from different villages. The average population size of an administrative village was 1,260 people in 2000.[37] Excluding children and old people, the number of adults in a village is limited, more so in those villages that have residents working as migrants elsewhere. This by no means implies that peasants from a single village cannot stage powerful resistance, but it suggests that large-scale protests are normally possible when peasants from different villages act together. However, large-scale protests by peasants are often less controllable and prone to violence because of the lack of (strong) leaders. Fifteen of the seventeen incidents of large-scale protests by peasants eventually turned into riots.

In protests that have participants from different villages, even the presence of leaders may fail to prevent violence because the participants are not effectively controlled. For example, in one case in a district in Guangdong province, a few villagers who had conflicts with the township government, together with students who were resentful about the high tuition fees, organized a demonstration in February 2001. Their demonstration attracted some bystanders who also participated in the action. As they marched to the township government, the demonstration attracted more participants and then turned into a riot. The participants attacked the township government, burned down 107 rooms, and took more than twenty motorcycles and other property belonging to government employees.[38]

In addition, when the number of participants is large, violence may also occur as a result of tactical escalation.[39] This happens when the participants fail to receive any meaningful response from the target at which their action is directed. For example, in one case, a few thousand peasants in a city in Guangxi autonomous region approached the city authority to present a petition in 2002. Failing to receive a response, the large number of people lost control. They assaulted the office compounds of the city government and the city party committee, damaging twenty-two cars. They blocked not only the traffic at the center of the city but also a railway for eight hours.[40] In another case in Zhejiang province, a construction project resulted in more than 1,000 peasants being required to move elsewhere. These migrants were dissatisfied with their compensation, and, for years, they presented petitions to the central and local authorities to no effect. In 2002, more than 600 migrants approached the city government for a solution. Failing to receive a meaningful response, dozens of the participants made their way into the office compound, took a government official as hostage, and brought him to a railway to block the traffic. When the local police arrested a few activists, other participants attacked the city government compound again, smashing equipment and destroying documents.[41]

Distrust and the Use of Violence

Another important reason for the more frequent use of violence by peasants is that they face predatory governments or businesses more often than workers do. Dispute-related violence usually begins with the expression of a grievance. The sequence of events in the development of a grievance begins with some negative event. The victim tries to discern whether the action was intentional or malevolent. Intentional actions that are perceived as malevolent are seen as particularly blameworthy.[42] The worsened relationship between peasants and local officials has been an important reason for the former to distrust the latter. Violence is very likely to occur when peasants from different villages are strongly resentful against local officials and act together. This has been reflected in peasant resistance to tax and fee collection before the tax reform and in their resistance to land seizure.

For example, in a county in Hunan province, peasants resorted to violence in resisting fee collection because of their distrust of and resentment against local officials.[43] On July 5, 1996, when several township cadres went to a village to check on the progress of fee collections, the village party secretary replied that the village was unable to collect the fees because some previous village cadres, including the former village party secretary, refused to pay. Just as the township officials began to talk to the former village party secretary, villagers struck gongs, and 700 villagers came to surround the township cadres, smashing the windows of their car and throwing their motorcycles into the river. The township and county governments began to investigate the case the next day.

On July 18, 1996, the county police department decided to punish five peasant activists. A township police officer went to the village to deliver the subpoena. However, right after the policeman left his car, he was surrounded by more than 300 villagers, and the subpoena was torn up. The county government then decided to detain the five activists. In the early morning of August 21, 1996, guided by a township official, more than 100 police officers went to the village and arrested the five activists. However, on his way to the township government, that township official was taken hostage by the villagers. About 300 villagers attacked the township government, smashing the signboards and beating township officials. Villagers then broke into the homes of the major township leaders. In this circumstance, the city and county leaders had to handle the case directly and promised to return the extra fees previously collected from peasants.

Significantly, news of the successful resistance effort encouraged peasants in other villages. In the ensuing months, villagers from another five townships in the county staged actions against their respective township governments to demand the return of fees. The number of participants in each action ranged from 100 to 700. In the course of the demonstrations, villagers marched to their township government offices with banners, drums, and fireworks. They broke into the offices, smashed widows and signboards, and broke into the homes of major township leaders. The number of participants in these actions reached almost 10,000, and forty-eight homes of township cadres and seventy-nine cadres were attacked. As it was in the first village, this chain of resistance placed tremendous pressure on local officials, who ultimately decided to return the fees to peasants to prevent further resistance. Within two weeks, 21.7 million yuan was repaid.

It is not rare for local governments or businesses to directly encroach upon the peasants' interests, and they may use force first. In these circumstances, the peasants' use of violence is defensive.[44] This is particularly obvious in disputes over pollution and land use in rural areas (Chapter Three). In my collection of 266 cases, confrontation occurred in twenty-three of the sixty-six cases (or 35 percent) of land use, whereas it occurred in eight of the thirteen disputes over pollution. The most salient characteristic of defensive confrontations is that they are leaderless or they are not intentionally organized by particular persons. Rather, the strong resentment among peasants, together with the offense of the government or the business, is sufficient to drive people to action. This is an important reason why violence occurs much more frequently in leaderless action based on single communities in rural areas than in urban areas, and violence is even more likely when a large number of peasants from different villages act together.

High-profile cases involving violence include the Hanyuan case and the Dongyang case presented in Chapter Six. In another case in Guangdong, the police reported how they dealt with peasant resistance to the occupation of their land for the construction of the so-called city of universities in 2003. On April 15, 2003, four police officers went to a village to ask peasants to follow the government decision that required them to give up their land. The villagers, who were frustrated by the unreasonable compensation, refused and took the four police officers as hostages. When hundreds of police officers arrived to rescue the four police officers, more villagers came, until the number exceeded 1,000. There was a stalemate. The police reported: "The police officers in charge took into account various factors and decided to take action early next morning. The several hundred police officers formed a circle and swiftly entered the site when the number of villagers declined, and those who stayed became tired in the early morning. By segregating the villagers, the police rescued the four officers."[45]

SPONTANEOUS VIOLENT PROTESTS AS A SIGNAL

Violent protests that involve leaderless participants from different communities have also occurred in urban areas. Violent protests in China today suggest that resentment or frustration is not an irrelevant factor. Although such factors are not sufficient to give rise to protests, they can trigger large-scale participation when the right opportunities come. Such actions may be provoked by government policies, businesses, or moral shocks. Like large-scale protests in the countryside, such protests in urban areas often involve violence because they are spontaneous and leaderless. The eleven of the forty-four large-scale protests in my collection show that this type of spontaneous protest often causes the most serious violence in cities, and they signal citizens' strong resentment against a number of different issues.

In one case in Hunan province, a small city was merged into a large neighboring county in 1997. The residents of the original small city felt that the county government was biased against them. In 1999, when the county government decided to further redraw the administrative boundary of the previous small city, a riot occurred. From February 9 to April 12, 1999, people from the former small city engaged in various modes of resistance, including demonstrations, protests, blocking office compounds and traffic, destroying state property, attacking government employees and police officers, damaging police cars, and breaking into the residential buildings of the investigation team sent by the provincial authority. The participants included rebel leaders of the Cultural Revolution, ex-prisoners, laid-off workers, retirees, disabled people, and common citizens.

According to the police department, the residents' resistance was a "very rare case" in terms of the degree to which violence was involved. In one instance, when the police fired teargas, the crowd did not back down; instead, they rode motorcycles to attack the police nine times with sticks and bricks. Nonetheless, the authorities also found that the citizens' resistance was not planned by any of the participants. In the whole process, there were no planners or core organizations; instead, the action was based on a strong consensus among the residents. Confrontation was often a result of improvised action. The authorities did not find any organizational connections between a series of large-scale protests and their participants.[46]

In another similar case in Huangshi city in Hubei province, residents in Daye, a county-level city in Huangshi, learned that their city would be turned into a district of Huangshi city in August 2005. This measure would affect some officials in Daye but not the average citizens. Yet residents were easily mobilized. Someone posted the news of a demonstration on the Internet. The next day, about 20,000 people participated in the demonstration, assaulting the offices of the Huangshi city government, destroying property, and wounding police officers. The plan to turn Daye into a district was consequently given up.[47]

In both cases, local officials were puzzled by the fact that although these reform measures would not affect average citizens, they still triggered strong resistance. As a matter of fact, spontaneous violent protests in China reflect the broad social mood. During the transitional period, many of the reform measures (e.g., the reform of public firms) caused harm to a large number of people. Socioeconomic changes and problems (e.g., rising inequality, rampant corruption) have also fomented strong resentment among many citizens.[48] This implies that the motivations for participation in such incidents are complex, and violence (e.g., attacking the government) per se may be the reason for some people to participate when they believe that the risk of doing so is low.

Against this background, some incidents that create moral shocks can trigger spontaneous violent protests if the government fails to respond in a timely and appropriate manner. Moral shocks are seen as an important factor that draws participants into social movements. Such shocks occur when an unexpected event or piece of information raises such a sense of outrage in a person that he or she becomes inclined toward action, whether or not that person has acquaintances in the movement.[49] In these situations, some people play the role of providing anger-provoking accounts of the incidents or even spreading rumors. By framing the problem in certain ways, a moral judgment is suggested: Humans are being abused by greedy businesspeople or unfeeling bureaucrats. As Vanderford suggests, activists tend to "identify concrete and specific adversaries, characterize enemy action in an entirely negative light, attribute corrupt motives to the foe, and magnify the opponents' power."[50] Once such action starts, people may participate for other reasons in addition to seeking justice for the victims.

In the eleven of the forty-four large-scale protests that I collected, seven occurred because citizens could not accept the injustice encountered by other individuals. For example, in Chizhou city in Anhui province in 2005, a car carrying the owner of a private hospital crashed into a high-school student riding a bike. Instead of taking the student to the hospital for a check, the businessman and his men beat the student and demanded compensation for the damage to his car. Reportedly, the businessman told his men, "300,000 yuan is enough for a life." The people present were angered. After the police came, the student was sent to the hospital. The several people were taken to a police station, and bystanders gathered in front of the police station and refused to leave despite local officials' persuasion. Later, with a rumor that the student had been mortally injured, the gathering turned into a riot. The participants burned a police van and looted a nearby department store when they found that the store sent drinking water to the police station. To a large extent, the case reflects the deep public resentment against rising inequality in society.[51]

In another similar case in Chongqing, a conflict between a self-proclaimed official and a migrant worker also led to a riot. In October 2004, Yu, a peasant working as a porter, had a conflict with a woman after he accidentally hit her with a pole. The woman slapped Yu in the face after he refused to apologize, and her husband struck Yu in the legs and back repeatedly with the pole until Yu crumpled to the ground. The husband added that Yu would be in big trouble. "I am a public official. If this guy causes me more problems, I will pay 20,000 yuan and have him knocked off." He did not expect that his words would trigger a riot in which more than 30,000 people not only burned a police van and destroyed a fire truck but also ransacked the local government building, smashing windows, computers, and office furniture.[52]

In this Chongqing case, journalists later found that residents took action not only for the sake of Yu; some people participated to vent their resentment against the government, which had been growing over the years. A businessman told a journalist, "In our daily lives, we do not have a place to voice our grievances, and it is also useless to speak about the grievances. This is the time we feel joyful."[53] The police department also found that some people were hired to transport bricks to the square, which could have been used as weapons to attack the government and police officers. In the Huangshi case in Hubei province, it was also found that some businessmen paid 30 to 100 yuan to some participants to encourage more participation.[54]

There are several other similar cases in my collection, although they did not have as many 5,000 or more participants. One case happened in Henan province in 2007, in which a riot with thousands of participants was triggered by city management officials who beat a female college student. In another case, a riot of thousands of participants occurred in Sichuan in 2007 because the local government failed to investigate the death of a female employee in a local hotel in a timely manner. Still in Sichuan, a riot happened because of a rumor that the hospital failed to save a boy who accidentally drank insecticide because his grandfather could not afford to pay his medical fees. In Guizhou in 2007, a riot occurred simply because three peasants lied that they were beaten by government officials.

The government has also realized this problem. In 2007, the secretary of the central Political-Legal Affairs Committee admitted that some people participate in instances of collective action without direct interest in the action; instead, they participate just to vent their resentment. He urged that serious attention should be paid to this phenomenon.[55] An investigation by Xinhua News Agency journalists in Guangdong, Shanghai, Jiangsu, and Zhejiang also found such instances.[56] The report states: "Many people who participated in the incidents had no demands or direct interests. They participated because they had been unfairly treated and had strong resentment. The incidents provided a chance for them to vent their resentment, and the risk of doing this was small." These cases reflect the serious popular resentment held by many in Chinese society during the transitional period. The consequences of the prevalence of such resentment suggest that Gurr's statement is also true in China: "Low levels of legitimacy, or by inference feelings of illegitimacy, apparently motivate men to collective violence."[57]

Conclusion

Gamson suggests that violence is a common consort of social protests in the Unites States and "is not a matter of serious contention."[58] Similarly, violence is also common in Chinese citizens' protests. This chapter finds that the use of violence in China is often a risk-conscious move instead of a strategic choice that aims to increase the chances of success. As a result, while violence has repeatedly occurred during protests, its effectiveness is discouraging. The cases I collected suggest that violence tends to reduce the odds of success. Protesters are likely to succeed in large-scale protests regardless of whether violence is used. In contrast, small-scale resistance that involves violence is much less tolerable by local governments and is very likely to be suppressed. Despite local governments' negative attitudes toward violence, violent protests have never disappeared in socialist China, and they seem to be occurring more frequently in the recent period.

Tarrow suggests that violence "is better understood as a function of the interaction between protesters' tactics and policing."[59] Violence may thus occur as a result of the "tactical adaptations" between participants and their targets.[60] Existing research based on collective action in democracies tends to view the protesting group as a unitary actor and provides "a voluntaristic interpretation of violence as a strategic choice carried out by single groups or organizations."[61] This strategic-choice approach does not explain violent protests in authoritarian regimes because the use of violence is much more risky.

This chapter uses a group-structure approach by assigning a significant role to participants in the choice of the mode of action, including violence. It highlights the participants' perceptions of the risk associated with the use of violence and the factors that affect their perceptions. I show that violence occurs under different scenarios in China, but the occurrence has to do with the composition of the group of participants. The composition affects the participants' perceptions of risk. I assess the participants' awareness of risk by looking at the type of participants, the type of protesting communities, and the presence or absence of leaders.

This group-structure approach does not view the use of violence as irrational in terms of the participants' awareness of risk, nor does it negate the influence of emotional factors such as moral shock and frustration. Violence in some circumstances can be the result of "momentary passion."[62] While emotions do not automatically translate into participation in collective action or the use of violence, they do facilitate mobilization. It is not rare for emotional factors, such as frustration, fear, and indignation, to trigger protests or riots.[63] In leaderless protesting groups, or those groups whose participants come from different communities, moral shocks increase the odds of violent protests. Therefore, the structure of the protesting group significantly affects the behavior of its participants.

The group-structure approach also suggests that it is simply impossible for the Chinese party-state to prevent violent protests as long as the sources of popular resentment remain. Protesters in China have used violence both to defend their group-specific interests (e.g., protecting land) and to help others seek justice (e.g., riots). Spontaneous violent protests reflect the broad social mood. Different groups of people are resentful of various issues. The recurrence of such incidents has indisputably placed pressure on the government, and it has become important for the central government to adjust certain policies to dispel popular resentment, as will be discussed in the next chapter.

EIGHT

Popular Resistance and Policy Adjustment

Earlier chapters demonstrated that many instances of citizen resistance in China are directed at local state authorities, often for their failure to implement the central authorities' policies faithfully.[1] Nonetheless, not all the problems that Chinese citizens face are created by local officials: Their grievances may also be caused by, or tied to, the central or high-level government's policies. Sometimes, the central government's policies have significant loopholes that allow local governments to abuse power and lead to unanticipated negative consequences. As a result, citizens' resistance is likely to persist as long as the source of conflict remains, and it may become an important factor that forces the government to adjust pertinent policies or make new more favorable policies.[2]

In democracies, social movements or protests exercise influence on the government and force the latter to adjust policies mainly through electoral pressure. In other words, citizens' access to democratic electoral institutions forces politicians to pay attention to citizens' grievances and reactions.[3] Most of the time, however, the relationship between protests and policy response is not linear,[4] and it is thus not easy to assess the direct impact of protests on policy making. In the Chinese context, O'Brien and Li suggest that "collective action is typically but one factor in a long chain of events— a factor that at times can play a crucial role."[5] The difficulty of isolating the effect of movements has led some scholars to propose cross-national comparisons to "formulate the link between movement actions and those consequences."[6] A comparative approach can shed even more light on cases that occur in the same country because of the shared social, cultural, and political contexts.[7]

This chapter examines the relationship between popular resistance and policy adjustment in China by comparing five cases. It shows that social groups differ in their ability to generate pressure on the central-party state in making policy adjustments because the forcefulness of their resistance and the cost incurred by the government in adjusting the policies are different. The forcefulness of the resistance determines the salience of an issue and thereby the pressure on the government, whereas the cost determines the pace and degree of policy adjustment. A social group that is able to stage powerful resistance has a higher chance of achieving positive policy responses than other groups that are unable to do so. But weak groups may also receive positive policy responses with the assistance of extra forces.

Popular Resistance and Policy Adjustment: The Rationale

In policy adjustment, the cost incurred by the government is weighed against the forcefulness of the popular resistance. Burstein, Einwohner, and Hollander argue that social movement organizations gain power over their targets in proportion to such targets' dependence on the organizations.[8] In China, the degree of government dependence on resisting groups depends in part on the groups' disruptive power and the strength of their challenge to regime legitimacy. Forceful resistance highlights the problems regarding a policy, and it also provides information to upper-level governments about the local situation.[9] When resistance becomes widespread and persistent, it not only threatens social stability but also shows that the grievances in question have made a large number of people have "a great deal in common" and that their resistance is likely to continue or even escalate.[10] Moreover, forceful resistance prevents the central government from pretending that it does not know about the problem because it makes the problem common knowledge to both the central government and the public. Hence, those groups that are able to stage powerful resistance are better able to move their issues onto the agenda of the government than groups that cannot stage powerful resistance.

Nevertheless, this does not mean that less powerful groups are unable to obtain favorable policy responses because weak groups may gain access to extra leverage, such as alliances. Political alliances are crucial to the effectiveness of social movements, especially when they are staged by the less powerful, because alliances, among other things, provide resources or other forms of political assistance to such groups.[11] As Lipsky suggests, what is crucial to political protests is activating third parties to participate in the controversy in ways favorable to the protest goals.[12] Less powerful groups that need extra leverage to have their voices heard may gain such leverage in several ways.

In their study of protest outcomes in the former Soviet Union, Kowalewski and Schumaker report that "there is little indication that external support by third parties substantially affects the outcomes of specific protest incidents in the Soviet Union. . . . [P]rotest in the USSR is best characterized as a 2-player game in which outsiders play a minimal role."[13] In China, popular resistance is not always a two-player game between citizens and their targets. An important third player is the media. Unlike most other former socialist countries, the media enjoy a certain degree of freedom in China while the communist party is still in power. As previous chapters have repeatedly shown, the media have become perhaps the most important third party in popular resistance in China today. They not only help individual citizens seek justice but also contribute to policy adjustment by covering a group's grievances and thereby enhancing the salience of its issues.

Another extra leverage that may help less powerful groups to achieve policy adjustment is issue linkage. Some issues are linked in a mutually beneficial way in the sense that the resolution of one issue may lead to the resolution of other linked issues. When different issues are caused by the same source, it is certainly more likely for the central party-state to address the source. But issues may also be connected in a mutually exclusively way, in the sense that the addressing of a particular issue makes it more difficult to address other issues due to reasons such as the limited resources of the government.

In the remainder of this chapter, I analyze the Chinese central government's responses toward five social groups who complained about their respective problems. These five groups are workers laid off from state-owned enterprises, workers laid off from urban collective enterprises, homeowners dealing with housing demolition, peasants struggling with financial burdens, and peasants facing nonagricultural use of farmland. The popular resistance staged by these five groups is the most important source of social unrest in China. The central government has adjusted its policies on almost

TABLE 8.1
Important Policy Changes in China

Issues	Initial Policy	Significant Adjustments
Nonagricultural use of farmland	1998 The enactment of the revised Land Law	2004, 2005, 2006 Limiting local governments' power; revising the criteria for compensation
Peasants' financial burdens	1990 The regulation of the 5 percent limit	2000 to 2002 The tax-for-fee reform 2004: The abolition of the agricultural tax
Retrenchment of SOE workers	1997 Nationwide ownership reform	1998 The establishment of reemployment service centers
Retrenchment of urban CE workers	1997 Nationwide privatization	No specific policies were made; included in poverty-stricken population
Housing demolition	2001 Allowing the use of compulsory demolition	2003 Increasing the amount of compensation; regulating compulsory demolition

SOURCE: Author's summary.

all these issues, though to varying degrees (Table 8.1). However, it is important to note that the factors that contributed to the policy adjustment are not the same in these cases.

The Effect of Powerful Action: Worker Resistance

In recent years, the reform of publicly owned enterprises in China has affected a vast number of employees. Public enterprises in China consist of state-owned enterprises and collective enterprises. SOEs are owned by the government at each level, and they used to be included in the state budget of the planned economy. Collective enterprises, whether urban or rural, were not included in the state budget. Rural enterprises, which are not discussed in this chapter, are owned by rural governments. Urban collective enterprises are established by state agencies and SOEs mainly for the purpose of creating employment for urban citizens.[14] A comparison of the welfare of workers laid off from SOEs and that of those retrenched from collective enterprises reveals that a group's ability to stage persistent and disruptive resistance is crucial to receiving a positive policy response. This comparison also shows that the salience of a group's issue is relative to those pursued by other groups. Hence, a group's issue, even if serious, may be overshadowed by the problems highlighted by more powerful groups.

INDUSTRIAL RESTRUCTURING AND PRESSURE ON THE GOVERNMENT

Since the mid-1990s, the Chinese government has launched an unprecedented effort to address the inefficiency of public enterprises through a series of reform measures, chief among them being privatization, bankruptcy, and closure, which have led to massive layoffs. Between 1995 and 2000, the number of employees declined by 28 percent in the state sector and by 53 percent in the urban collective sector.[15] The drop was most obvious during the period between 1997 and 2000, when the number of laid-off workers in the population was between 10 and 13 million people. The massive retrenchment affected millions of employees and their families because of the inadequate welfare system and the harsh reemployment environment.[16] When the reform of public enterprises started, many workers, including retired workers, failed to receive living allowances or pensions if their firms were unable to pay. In 1997, half of the 12.7 million laid-off workers did not find new jobs, and half of the unemployed did not receive living allowances.[17] Meanwhile, the simultaneous layoffs of such a large number of workers created a difficult reemployment environment. The reemployment rate among laid-off workers declined from 50 percent in 1998 to 30 percent in 2001.[18]

The impact of industrial reforms was most serious in the three northeastern provinces (Jilin, Liaoning, and Heilongjiang), which used to form the industrial base of China and have contributed significantly to the economic and industrial development of the country. Between 1998 and 2002, laid-off workers from state-owned enterprises in these three provinces accounted for more than 25 percent of the total number of laid-off workers in China, whereas the provinces' combined populations accounted for only 8.4 percent of the national population.[19] Therefore, more laid-off workers in these three provinces suffered from the economic restructuring than anywhere else in China. Among the 1.96 million pensionless retired workers across the country in 1997, those from the three northeastern provinces accounted for 43 percent. The poverty-stricken portion of the three provinces' combined population was double that of China as a whole (8 percent versus 4 percent).[20]

These reform measures have unsurprisingly provoked worker resistance. From the mid-1990s to the early 2000s, worker resistance, including that staged by unpaid retired workers, was the most important source of social conflict in China,[21] as can be seen by the numbers of collective petitions presented to local governments. The data I collected on collective petitions in twenty-six cities in 1995, forty cities in 1998, and twenty-eight cities in

2002 reveal that the number of collective petitions per 10,000 citizens is positively and strongly correlated with the size of the urban population in a city (see Appendices D through F). Many of these petitions were taken by workers. Nationwide, about half of the instances of social unrest in 1996 occurred because workers or retired workers failed to receive salaries, pensions, allowances, or medical care.[22] In 2001, instances of social unrest arising from conflicts related to workers' welfare or the reform of public enterprises accounted for 37.6 percent of the total number of instances of collective action in the country.[23] This is true in both industrial and agricultural provinces.[24]

The three northeastern provinces saw more resistance than other provinces.[25] According to the statistics I collected from nine provinces, the average number of collective petitions directed at the county-level authorities and above per 10,000 citizens was 1.8 in 1998, whereas it was 4.7 in Jilin that year.[26] The other two provinces, Liaoning and Heilongjiang, did not report on collective petitions in their yearbooks in 1998. But the 2000 yearbook of Heilongjiang province shows that the number of petitions in the province reached 264 for every 10,000 citizens, as opposed to 154 in Jilin in 1999. This may imply that there were more instances of resistance in Heilongjiang.[27] Reportedly, more people in Liaoning approached central authorities with petitions in 2002 than anywhere else in the country.[28] Some research suggests that instances of collective action by workers in Jilin and Liaoning—mainly from the oil, coal, mining, forestry, and textile industries—accounted for 40 percent of the total number of instances by workers in the country in 1999.[29] The data that I was able to collect on the petitions in 1995, 1998, and 2002 also show that the number of petitions was particularly high in northeastern cities (see Appendices D through F).

The central government paid serious attention to the many problems faced by laid-off and retired workers, as well as to their resistance. In 1999, Jiang Zemin inspected a number of provinces and held five meetings attended by provincial party secretaries regarding the reform of state-owned enterprises. He chaired the fifth in Liaoning in August 1999, and eight provincial party secretaries, including the three from the northeast, attended. Jiang declared that the working class was the main force determining social stability in China. The government must correctly handle the relationship among reform, development, and stability, thereby preventing the reform and the speed of development from exceeding the tolerance of society. "The party committee and the government at each level must take great care of laid-off workers' lives and employment. This is a serious political task that must be accomplished by any possible means."[30] From 1997 to 2002, Premier Zhu Rongji inspected the northeast almost yearly.[31] Zhu conducted a nine-day visit to Liaoning in April 2000, during which he acknowledged: "Some laid-off workers could not receive the regulated amount of subsistence allowance, and others failed to receive subsistence allowance. Collective petitions and instances of social unrest have occurred repeatedly." Hence, the party committee and government at each level must see it as "an unshakable duty to establish an adequate welfare system and a stable social environment."[32]

POLICY RESPONSE: ONE CLASS, TWO GROUPS

Beginning in 1998, the central government formulated a number of policies to deal with the situation.[33] In June, the State Council issued the most important document to that point that addressed laid-off workers' welfare. The directive stated: "In recent years, the issue of laid-off workers has become increasingly salient and attracted the attention of society." The most important part of this directive concerned the establishment of reemployment service centers in SOEs as a transitional arrangement to provide living allowances and pay pension, unemployment, and medical insurance premiums for laid-off workers. These centers were also tasked to train and assist workers in securing new jobs.[34] In addition, the central government created favorable policies, such as tax breaks, to encourage laid-off workers to seek reemployment.

In 2000, the State Council issued further directives to ensure payments to laid-off and retired workers from SOEs. In February, in addition to urging local governments and SOEs to pay laid-off workers, it tackled the issue of retired workers by promising to pay a large portion of the overdue pension premiums. Moreover, the central government set the goal that by the end of 2000, 80 percent of the retired workers would receive their pensions from insurance organizations instead of individual firms, thus guaranteeing pension payments. Although these measures did not entirely solve the problems of workers laid off from SOEs, they did help to alleviate their economic plight and contributed to the continuation of industrial reforms in China.[35]

The reforms also affected a large number of workers from urban collective enterprises. From 1995 to 2000, the number of employees in the state sector declined by 30.8 million, while collective sector employment declined by 16.3 million.[36] In the northeast, many SOEs had established collective enterprises to create employment for local people, so the number of employees in the collective sector was large even in places where SOEs were dominant. In Liaoning, laid-off workers from collective enterprises accounted for between 38 percent and 47 percent of the total number of laid-off employees between 1998 and 2003 in the province.[37]

However, the welfare of workers laid off from collective enterprises was largely ignored by both the central and local governments in the initial years of the reform. They were either excluded from the central government's policies or urged to solve their problems with their former employers. In the 1998 directive mentioned above, the central government refused to make any commitment to the former employees of urban collective enterprises. The last paragraph of the directive mentioned laid-off workers from urban collective enterprises: "As to the basic living allowance and reemployment of laid-off workers from urban collective enterprises, the provincial-level party committees and the provincial governments can make policies based on their own local situations." This implied that local governments were not required to make any new policies. Hence, the matter of whether or not collective enterprises would establish reemployment service centers was left to the firms themselves.

In a directive promulgated in February 2000, the central government urged local governments and SOEs to guarantee payments to laid-off workers and retired workers from SOEs, but it did not mention unpaid retired workers from urban collective units. Unpaid retired workers and laid-off workers from collective enterprises were mentioned in a May directive, which stipulated: "If retired workers and laid-off workers from urban collective enterprises have not participated in the insurance programs, they will be covered by the minimum subsistence program." This program was established in the early 1990s to help the poverty-stricken population in urban areas, but it had been seriously plagued by a lack of funding in a number of cities.[38] Hence, although urban collective workers were mentioned, the government's commitment to them remained largely symbolic.

As late as 2002, the Ministry of Finance and the National Tax Bureau jointly issued a directive that allowed laid-off workers to enjoy tax reductions or exemptions in securing reemployment but excluded workers laid off from collective enterprises.[39] In the early 2000s, the central government decided to stop the establishment of new reemployment service centers. The relationship between firms and their newly laid-off workers, as well as their former employees who had stayed in the reemployment service centers for three years, would be terminated. But these workers would be paid severance generally based on the number of years they had been employed by their firms. Again, laid-off workers from urban collective units were not included in this severance plan.[40]

The economic plight of workers from urban collective firms was anything but a surprise. In 1998, 8 percent of the laid-off workers from SOEs who were unable to find jobs failed to receive living allowances, whereas 41 percent of laid-off workers from collective enterprises did not receive their allowances.[41] In 1999, 17.4 percent of workers laid off from SOEs were not paid (6.3 percent) or were underpaid (11.1 percent), and the number was 46 percent (25.7 percent unpaid) for former collective enterprise workers.[42] Even though workers laid off from collective enterprises were able to receive a basic living allowance, the amount was so insignificant that it was often negligible. Table 8.2 reports the monthly allowances provided to laid-off employees in the state and collective sectors. The pattern remained the same at the national and provincial levels. In the three northeastern provinces, the amount of allowance received by laid-off workers from collective enterprises remained unchanged or even decreased between 1998 and 2004. The gap between the benefits received by the two groups of workers remained strikingly large.[43]

WORKERS' POWER AND ISSUE SALIENCE

The challenges facing laid-off workers from SOEs and collective enterprises were comparable in the sense that both groups of workers had to generate moral pressure on the government and cause social disruption to receive

TABLE 8.2
Monthly Allowance of Laid-Off Employees in the State and Collective Sectors (yuan)

	National		The Northeast		Liaoning	
	State	Collective	State	Collective	State	Collective
1998	121	57	71	18	84	29
1999	150	61	99	18	111	28
2000	178	68	124	22	139	31
2001	208	67	139	23	148	34
2002	258	69	178	24	198	29
2003	299	73	209	23	264	27
2004	350	74	245	22	338	27

SOURCES: *China Labor Statistical Yearbooks* (1999–2005); *Liaoning Yearbook* (1999–2005).

government support. However, laid-off workers from SOEs, on the whole, were better able to make their issue salient than were their counterparts from collective enterprises. There are several important factors that overshadowed the problems faced by laid-off workers from collective enterprises in favor of similar issues that their counterparts from SOEs had to face.[44]

First, the Chinese government had traditionally made limited commitments to urban collective enterprises and their workers. Urban collective enterprises in China were established for two major reasons. One was the collectivization of (individual) family businesses in cities in the 1950s, and the other was the creation of jobs for urban residents.[45] What distinguished collective enterprises from state-owned ones was that collective enterprises were not included in the state budget. In the planned economy, the survival of collective enterprises was not a problem because their production was often included in the planning. But with the market-oriented reforms as well as the declining profitability of public firms, public firms began to face the pressure of survival, especially after the government imposed serious restrictions on state banks regarding loans. Like many small SOEs, collective enterprises had to become self-reliant. Budget constraints forced many collective enterprises to stop production and thereby to stop paying their employees. Compared with workers from SOEs, workers from collective enterprises were more likely to be laid off because these enterprises were less likely to receive aid from banks or the government, at least in the initial years of the reforms.[46]

Second and more importantly, workers from SOEs were better able to stage powerful or large-scale resistance. Nationwide, industrial SOEs accounted for 73 percent of large industrial enterprises in the country by 1995, whereas collective enterprises accounted for just 8.3 percent, though they made up 74 percent of all small enterprises. Among medium-sized enterprises, SOEs accounted for 65 percent and collective enterprises for 21 percent.[47] Still, collective enterprises were important. As shown in Table 8.3, collectively owned industrial enterprises hired more people than did state enterprises, but individual firms had an average of forty-one employees versus an average of 504 employees in SOEs. The difference was particularly large in those enterprises owned by the government at the city level and above. In the northeast, the average number of employees in SOEs was much larger than the number of employees in collective enterprises: 704 versus only eighty in 1997. In Liaoning province, the numbers were 747 and eighty-one, respectively.[48]

TABLE 8.3
Description of Industrial Enterprises in China (1995)

	SOEs	Collective Enterprises[a]
Number of firms (10,000)	11.8	147.5
Total number of employees (million)	59.5	60.5
Average number of employees	504	41
In central-level firms	1,490	—
In provincial-level firms	583	150
In city-level firms	476	180
In county-level firms	166	106

SOURCE: Compiled from the National Statistical Bureau, *Da toushi* (A comprehensive perspective) (Beijing: Zhongguo fazhan chubanshe, 1998), 30–33.

[a]Including enterprises established by governments below the county level.

Existing research shows that the pace of reform, such as privatization, tended to be slow in those provinces where there were a large number of laid-off workers from large and medium-sized SOEs who did not receive subsistence allowances.[49] This is because the large number of workers from these firms were better able to stage large-scale resistance. In China, although there have been cross-firm collective actions, such actions remain uncommon. Most instances of large-scale action are taken by workers from large firms.[50] In Liaoning province, more than 863,000 people took part in over 9,000 protests in 1999, with an average of more than ninety participants in each action.[51] This average number is apparently within the reach of workers in many collective enterprises (especially at the county level and above). But workers from collective enterprises were less capable of staging large-scale resistance. The media in and outside China reported at least sixteen large-scale worker protests (those with at least 5,000 participants) (see Appendix C), all of them staged by workers from SOEs. Six of the protests took place in the northeast, with 10,000 participants or more in each. Four of the six occurred in Liaoning.

Collective petitions provide a good example of the difference in scale and frequency of the resistance between SOE and collective enterprise workers. My survey of more than 720 laid-off workers in eight provinces in 1999 showed that, although laid-off workers from both SOEs and collective enterprises had presented collective petitions, those from SOEs were more able to stage large-scale resistance (that is, resistance with more than 100 participants) (Table 8.4).[52] While large-scale actions accounted for 17 percent of the total number of petitions made by laid-off workers from SOEs, in collective units they only accounted for 5 percent. According to

TABLE 8.4
Workers' Collective Petitions by Ownership Type

	Workers	
	SOEs	Collective Enterprises
Number of workers	130	594
Participation in collective petitions (%)	15	26
Petitions with more than 100 participants (%)	5	17
Petitions with more than 500 participants (%)	0	6
Petitions being helpful (%)	16	35

SOURCE: Author's survey, 1999.

the survey, none of the collective petitions by workers from collective units included more than 500 participants. In addition, laid-off workers from SOEs tended to have more confidence in their action because they were statistically more likely to achieve success.

Third, laid-off workers from collective enterprises were disadvantaged in terms of media coverage. In the late 1990s, layoffs and reemployment were among the issues that the general public in China was most concerned with.[53] To a large extent, "laid-off workers" were equated with the poor. Although there were criticisms about laid-off workers being picky in their job searches, the media generally portrayed laid-off workers as victims of the reforms. This image was accurate in the sense that a large number of laid-off workers were in unprecedented economic plight and, as a result, were under tremendous psychological pressure.[54] Together with worker resistance, media reports placed serious pressure on the government at various levels.

Though the policies made by the central and local governments clearly distinguished between the two groups of workers, the identity of the workers from collective enterprises was largely blurred in the media. The media (and even academics) did not specifically point out the problems faced by workers laid off from collective enterprises. In numerous reports, workers retrenched from SOEs and collective enterprises were both referred to as "laid-off workers." Some referred to workers who were laid off from SOEs without mentioning those from collective enterprises. Some reports included the proportion of workers laid off from collective enterprises but did not distinguish between the divergent welfare provisions received by the two groups of workers. An influential early survey of 1,300 laid-off workers in fifty-five cities in 1997, for example, focused mostly on workers from SOEs, as did another survey of 2,870 workers in Hunan province in the same year.[55] A survey of about 6,780 laid-off workers in 1999 by the All China Federation of Trade Unions focused exclusively on workers from SOEs.[56] After the lay-offs reached their peak, the welfare of laid-off workers from SOEs improved due to government policy adjustment. As such, the issue of laid-off workers no longer dominated media reports. Public awareness of the plight of laid-off workers from collective enterprises was thus limited, and moral pressure on the government to help these workers was also limited.

A direct effect of the differing resistance power of workers from SOEs and collective enterprises was that the governments at both the central and local level had to allocate their limited financial resources to workers from SOEs first, especially those from large SOEs who were most able to stage powerful resistance.[57] For example, coping with the closure or bankruptcy of large SOEs was often beyond the financial ability of the local government, which triggered a number of large-scale protests.[58] As a result of the local government's inability to pay, the central government had to allocate funds to cover these costs, especially for the large SOEs in the three northeastern provinces.[59] Other measures that were aimed at accommodating laid-off SOE workers' demands also consumed the limited financial resources of the central and local governments.[60]

Consequently, workers from collective enterprises were at a constant disadvantage compared with their counterparts from SOEs in seeking help from the government. This explains why the gap between the living allowances received by laid-off workers from the state sector and those from the collective sector remained strikingly large over the years. In those places where the number of laid-off workers was large (i.e., the northeast), the gap of welfare provisions between the two groups of workers could be even greater because those from collective enterprises could be entirely ignored while their counterparts from SOEs might receive aid from the government (Table 8.2).[61] In recent years, some workers who were laid off from collective enterprises have been included in the minimum subsistence scheme, under which they can receive subsidies from the government if their income fails to reach a certain level.

Media as External Support: Homeowners' Resistance

Fewer social groups in China have been able to stage action as powerful as workers from SOEs. In this section, I show how less powerful groups can receive policy responses because of external support by examining the case of homeowners' resistance to housing demolition.[62] In Chinese cities,

urban renewal and city construction have affected a large number of urban residents. For example, 820,000 people from 260,000 households in
Beijing were reallocated homes between 1991 and 2000. In Shanghai, 2.5
million people from 850,000 households have been reallocated since the
early 1990s.[63] But urban renewal and city construction frequently provoked
homeowners' resistance because they were undercompensated by the government or government-supported developers for their demolished homes.[64]

The violation of homeowners' rights persisted partly because of the policy issued by the central government in 2001. This policy aimed at preventing citizen resistance from threatening the construction of public projects.
It denied citizens the right to bargain with the government because the
dispute over compensation would be judged by the government or its designated agency. The directive also denied citizens the legal right to protect their homes because it allowed the government to pull down residents'
homes before the court made a judgment, which largely made the lawsuit
meaningless.[65]

Based on the directive of the State Council, local governments also made
regulations to grant themselves the power of compulsory demolition for
commercial projects (e.g., real estate development). As a result, violation of
homeowners' rights frequently occurred, and resistance arising from housing demolition, including petitions, protests, and demonstrations, took
place in most cities across the country. The Ministry of Construction revealed that conflicts arising from housing demolitions resulted in twenty-six
deaths between January and July 2002. Between January and August 2002,
the Ministry of Construction received 4,820 complaint letters, and 28 percent concerned housing demolition. Among the 1,730 petitions presented
in person to the ministry, about 70 percent focused on housing demolition.[66] In the early 2000s, petitions regarding housing demolition directed
to the national complaints bureau continued to rise (Table 8.5)

Despite homeowners' widespread complaints and resistance, the central
government did not adopt serious measures, partly because such resistance
was not forceful enough. One reason is that the solidarity was not very
strong among homeowners. Owing to factors such as differences in the
location of apartments, floor areas, access to sunshine, and expenditures
on housing renovations and decoration, homeowners received different
amounts of compensation, and their incentive to resist varied, although

TABLE 8.5
Petitions to the National Complaints Bureau Regarding Housing Demolition

Year	Letters	Petitions	People Making Petitions
2001	8,516	1,763	5,189
2002	13,513	2,081	6,998
2003[a]	11,641	1,473	5,360

SOURCE: Compiled from Wang Hongliang, "Kaishi bei guifan de chaiqian xingwei" (Regulated housing demolition), *Sanlian shenghuo zhoukan* (Sanlian life weekly), January 19, 2004.

[a]By August 2003.

many homeowners were dissatisfied with their compensation.[67] As a result, homeowners' resistance was often small in scale. For example, in Jilin province in 2001, there were 996 instances of disruptive action due to housing demolition. The average number of participants was only twenty-four.[68] On the other hand, local governments have a high stake in city construction because it improves the local infrastructure and promotes the local image, in addition to bringing other personal gains (e.g., kickbacks) to local officials. For these reasons, homeowners' resistance often failed.

The homeowners' position was not improved until two high-profile suicide cases occurred. In August 2003, a resident in Nanjing, the capital city of Jiangsu province, doused himself with gasoline, set himself on fire, and died because a local government agency pulled down his home without offering satisfactory compensation. About two weeks later, a resident from a county of Anhui province attempted to burn himself to death in Tiananmen Square beneath the portrait of Mao Zedong as a protest against the local government's forcible resettlement of his family, but he was saved by the police. Both cases were widely covered in the media and on the Internet and aroused tremendous sympathy from society. Because the issue of housing demolition affected a large number of urban residents across locations and economic status, public grievances over the practices of local governments and businesses were understandable. It was not surprising that this issue received extensive media coverage during that period of time. For example, my collection from eight newspapers and two magazines published in Beijing, Shanghai, and Nanjing shows that sixty-seven reports were published on housing demolition between January and July 2003, whereas the number doubled to 134 between August and December 2003.[69]

In democracies, public opinion shapes politicians' choice of policies. For example, Page and Shapiro find considerable evidence that "public opinion is often a proximate cause of policy."[70] In China, public opinion may also generate serious pressure on regime legitimacy and lead to policy changes. In the case of housing demolition, popular resentment put serious pressure on the central government. Right after the media exposed the suicide case in Nanjing, the central government sent investigative teams to a number of cities to investigate housing demolition and issued an urgent directive to warn local officials against violating citizen interests. Housing demolition was then largely halted for a few months across the country.[71] At the end of 2003, the central authority issued new policies that not only revised the criteria for compensation and thereby raised this amount for homeowners; the authority also regulated the procedures for compulsory demolition. It stipulated that compulsory demolition needs to go through public hearings. There is no doubt that the new policy has not solved all the disputes arising from housing demolitions. While complaints and petitions about housing demolition remain, many of these complaints are due to legacies of the past practices. In recent years, both local governments and businesses have felt more pressure in carrying out housing demolition if they ignore homeowners' demands. A number of "stubborn" households (*ding zi hu*) that were able to sustain their fight against businesses or local governments also reveal the improved position of homeowners.[72]

Linked Issues as Extra Leverage: Peasant Resistance

In discussing state–peasant relations in African countries, Robert Bates finds that peasants are generally weak versus the governments despite the availability of elections. This is because the governments can adopt an effective strategy of divide and rule.[73] In China, peasants are weak versus the government because they have little institutionalized leverage over the government. By examining peasant resistance to tax and fee collection and to the nonagricultural use of farmland, this section shows that Chinese peasants were able to seek positive policy responses not only because they staged persistent resistance but also because their complaints were closely tied to other important issues that the government could not afford to ignore. Therefore, similar to individual groups' resistance as discussed in Chapter Four, linked issues give peasants extra leverage in seeking policy adjustments.

THE ABOLITION OF THE AGRICULTURAL TAX

As discussed in Chapter Four, tax and fee collection caused numerous incidents of resistance in rural China before the tax reform. O'Brien and Li have shown that peasant resistance is an important reason for improved tax policies in rural China.[74] If the number of serious incidents indicates the intensity of peasant resistance to tax collection, available data presented in Figure 8.1 also suggest that peasant resistance contributed to policy implementation. Before 2000, peasant resistance affected the efforts made by the central government to enforce policies aimed at containing peasants' burdens. In 1993, serious incidents numbered as many as thirty, the highest number recorded. That year, the central government first issued an urgent directive to investigate serious incidents of peasant tax resistance across the country. The central government then held a telephone meeting to cancel forty-three types of projects and thirty-seven programs often funded by peasants. As a result, the tax burden was reduced in 1993, and the number of serious incidents drastically decreased in 1994.

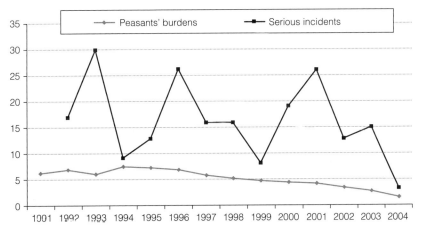

FIGURE 8.1 The Rural Situation in China (1990–2004) SOURCE: The National Statistical Bureau, *Zhongguo nongcun zhuhu diaocha nianjian 2005* (2005 yearbook of Chinese rural households) (Beijing Zhongguo tongji chubanshe, 2005), 35–39; Li Maolan, *Zhongguo nongmin fudan wenti yanjiu* (Research on peasants' financial burdens in China) (Taiyuan: Shanxi jingji chubanshe, 1996), 127; Liang Jun, *Cunmin zizhi* (Villagers' self governance) (Beijing: Zhongguo qingnian chubanshe, 2000), 18; Retrieved on March 5, 2004, from: www.china-village.org/bbs/ showtopic.asp; *Zhongguo qingnian bao,* December 26, 2005.

Nevertheless, peasants' burdens increased again in 1994 and remained at a relatively high level until 1996. The number of serious incidents numbered twenty-six in 1996, the year with the second highest number. That year, the central government again expended serious effort to combat the rise of resistance by issuing two directives to urge local governments to reduce peasants' financial burdens. The directives claimed that "peasants' financial burdens have become an especially preeminent issue that has affected rural reform, development, and stability."[75] The number of serious incidents then declined until 1999 and began to rebound again in 2000. After the sharp increase of incidents in 2001, the central government issued another directive stipulating that responsible officials, including those at the city and provincial levels, would be punished. The rise of serious incidents between July 2002 and June 2003 can be partly explained by rural cadres' efforts to collect overdue taxes and fees owed by peasants when they carried out the tax-for-fee reform. Finally, in 2003, the central government issued a document exempting payment of any overdue taxes and fees owed by peasants before the tax-for-fee reform.

Therefore, peasants' various modes of resistance generated serious pressure on both local and central government officials. Bernstein and Lu suggest that peasants' violent resistance was an important reason for the government's decision to address the issue of peasants' financial burdens.[76] Michelson also argues that the political legitimacy costs of rural taxation were decisive factors in the state's policy adjustment.[77] However, throughout the 1990s, the central government's measures were focused on reducing local officials' discretion in tax and fee collection; it did not take serious efforts to tackle the financial plight faced by local governments in agricultural areas, although this was the root of the peasants' grievances.

The reasons for the prolonged nature of the tax reform process are complex. One was the difficulty of gaining the central government's attention: From the late 1990s, central leaders spent much of their time on the issue of industrial restructuring, as mentioned earlier.[78] A more important factor was the financial resources required. In theory, revenue from agricultural taxes accounted for only a small portion of the total amount of taxes collected. In 1996, it reached its highest level since 1991 at 5.35 percent of the total tax revenue, and in 2000 it accounted for only 3.7 percent of the total revenue.[79] Therefore, the abolition of agricultural taxes should not have significantly affected the tax revenue of the government. But this was only part of the story: If all taxes and fees were abolished, many grassroots governments that relied on legal or illegal fees collected from peasants would not be able to sustain operations. Without subsidies, the economic foundation of rural governments would be destroyed. This consideration was an important reason for the central government's hesitation to reform the tax structure in rural China.[80]

Against this background, although some local governments initiated a tax-for-fee reform trial in 1992, this reform did not receive support from the central government. On the contrary, some policies of the State Council even forced local governments to stop the reform that had been adopted in dozens of counties in seven provinces.[81] It was not until 2000 that the central government decided to try the tax-for-fee reform in Anhui province by combining the state tax, the township fee, and village fee into one tax and thereby reducing local cadres' discretion.[82] However, because of its anxiety about the financial aid that it had to provide to local governments to carry out the reform, the central government became hesitant as to whether the reform should be extended to the whole country. It then issued a directive in 2001 compelling local governments to slow down the pace of the tax-for-fee reform.[83] However, the hesitation did not last long, and the reform was extended to the whole country in 2002 after a consensus was reached among the central leaders.

An official of the State Council reported in an interview that a prominent research officer of the State Council proposed abolishing rural taxes in the late 1990s to central leaders.[84] But it was not until 2004 that the Chinese central government decided to abolish the agricultural tax within five years. The adoption of this fundamental measure was due to several factors that combined to overcome the cost of the policy adjustment. Figure 8.1 shows that, while peasants' financial burdens kept declining after 1995, the number of serious incidents did not decrease correspondingly.[85] Certainly, as mentioned above, the rise of serious incidents in 2003 had to do with local cadres' intensified efforts to collect the taxes and fees owed by peasants in the past, but the peasants' persistent resistance pointed to the need for further reform or the abolition of the agricultural tax.

A close look at the places where serious incidents occurred reveals the limitations of the tax-for-fee reform that was introduced between 2000 and 2002. Table 8.6 reports the number of serious incidents in six provinces in selected years before and after the tax-for-fee reform. These six provinces

TABLE 8.6

Serious Incidents in Selected Provinces

Province	1995	1999	2001–2002	2002–2003
Sichuan	2	2	2	3
Hunan	1	3	2	1
Hubei	2	1	1	2
Henan	2	1	2	
Jiangsu	1		2	1
Anhui	1		1	1
Total number (A)	9	7	10	8
National number (B)	13	8	13	15
Proportion (A/B) (%)	69.2	87.5	76.9	53.3

SOURCE: Liang Jun, *Cunmin zizhi* (Villagers' self governance) (Beijing: Zhongguo qingnian chubanshe, 2000), 18; Retrieved on March 5, 2004, from: www.china-village.org/bbs/showtopic.asp; Retrieved on May 22, 2004, from: www.xcagri.gov.cn/news; *Zhongguo qingnian bao*, December 26, 2005.

accounted for the majority of the total number of incidents in the country in those years when data were reported—about 70 percent in 1995 and 53 percent between July 2002 and June 2003. These six provinces are agriculturally oriented, with Jiangsu being a partial exception: While the southern part of Jiangsu is industrialized, the northern part is primarily agricultural.

The tax-for-fee reform disadvantaged those families that relied on farming for most of their income, at least in a relative sense. Under the tax-for-fee system, tax was collected on the basis of the amount of farmland a peasant household had contracted, as opposed to its family size. Therefore, peasant households with more land had to pay more than those with less. As income from farming is meager in China, the more land a household had, the poorer it could be if the grain price was low and if the household did not have extra sources of income. For this reason, peasants in some agricultural areas felt that they did not benefit much from the reform. According to a 2003 survey of about 2,100 peasant households in six provinces (Anhui, Hunan, Sichuan, Heilongjiang, Fujian, and Zhejiang), those households with more farmland tended to report that the tension between peasants and rural cadres had not been reduced and, in some cases, was even heightened after the tax-for-fee reform. Indeed, the average amount of taxes paid by peasant households in Anhui (i.e., 312 yuan), Heilongjiang (i.e., 483 yuan), Hunan (i.e., 261 yuan), and Sichuan (i.e., 237 yuan) after the tax-for-fee reform was still larger than that paid by their counterparts in Zhejiang province (i.e., 130 *yuan*) or Fujian province (210 *yuan*) where the reform had not been introduced.[86] As a result, in 2004, there were still serious incidents concerning tax collection that involved the deaths of peasants in a few agricultural provinces (i.e., Jiangxi, Shaanxi, and Henan).

The limitations of the tax-for-fee reform underlined several other central government concerns. That farming households benefited less from the reform highlighted the increasingly large urban-rural income gap. In 1997, the income per capita of urban residents was 2.47 times that of rural residents, with the gap increasing to 3.23 times higher in 2003.[87] As agricultural income was already limited, more taxes in agricultural places would further reduce peasants' income. The rural-urban income disparity was connected to the issue of peasants' incentives to farm. From 1999, grain output in China declined despite the tax-for-fee reform. To strengthen peasants' incentives to farm, the central government began to subsidize peasant households, especially in those areas that produced the most grain. A document issued by the central party committee and the government in 2004 expended efforts to help and subsidize farming households, especially in agricultural areas. This marked the first time in the history of communist China that the party-state issued a document with the goal of increasing peasant income in the name of the central party committee and the State Council. In 2004, the decline of grain output was halted. A member of the central party committee's Financial and Economic Leadership Group admitted that that directive was "crucial to the increase in grain output and peasant income." Once the central government was willing to subsidize farming households that were most heavily taxed under the new tax-for-fee system, the abolition of the agricultural tax became both politically and economically rewarding.[88]

POLICY ADJUSTMENT IN RURAL LAND USE

The importance of linked issues in helping weak groups to seek a policy response is more obvious in the nonagricultural use of farmland. Chapter Three shows that the outcome of peasant resistance to land use is bleak. But even the anticipation of repression may fail to deter protests when potential participants are ignorant of the true risks or define risks differently.[89] O'Brien and Li find that "defeat does not . . . cause all rightful resisters to lapse into despair and passivity."[90] According to a survey of 632 peasants presenting petitions in Beijing, 55.4 percent reported that their homes were searched and some property was confiscated; about 54 percent reported that local officials hired local thugs to harass or hurt them. But only 5.8

percent of the peasants reported that they would give up if their actions were repressed.[91] This is partly due to the peasants' high stake in the land. Therefore, despite the credible threat of repression, resistance to the occupation of farmland continues in varying manifestations. The aggregate impact of peasant resistance is not negligible. It is no exaggeration to state that social disruptions arising from peasant resistance to land use have increased the central government's concern over social stability, especially after the rural tax reform.[92] Moreover, as discussed earlier, petitioners' disappointment with the central authorities undermines their confidence in the political system and damages regime legitimacy.

What has significantly strengthened the peasants' position is the central government's concern over the preservation of enough farmland for grain production. To a large extent, peasants' failure to resist local governments' land encroachment is also the central government's failure to achieve its goal of preserving enough farmland. The amount of farmland per capita in China was 1.6 *mu* (one *mu* is equal to one-sixth of an acre) in 1999, or 43 percent of the world average. By 2004, this figure had declined to 1.43 *mu*, or 40 percent of the world average.[93] The United Nations defines the minimum amount of farmland per capita for subsistence-level grain production as 0.8 *mu*. In southeastern China, there is not enough farmland to provide grain for the local population.[94] Thus, preserving farmland has become a national priority, and many regulations have been issued by the central authorities for that purpose.[95]

In theory, only the central or provincial government can grant permission for the conversion of substantial amounts of farmland. But violations of the land law and the central government's regulations are common.[96] By 2003, there were more than 6,000 "economic development zones" in China, of which only about 30 percent had been approved by the State Council or provincial governments. These unauthorized zones consumed a huge amount of farmland.[97]

Figure 8.2 shows a clear association between the number of land law violations and the amount of land lost. Protecting peasants' interests can increase the cost that local governments must pay to occupy farmland, thereby serving the multiple interests of the central government. As the National People's Congress claimed, the goals of protecting farmland, maintaining agricultural production, and protecting peasant interests are interrelated.[98] Premier Wen Jiabo also stressed: "Strictly preserving farmland

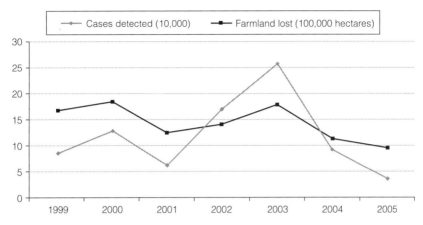

FIGURE 8.2 Law Violations in Land Use and the Farmland Lost (1999–2005). SOURCES: *Renmin ribao*, May 18, 2000; April 12, 2003; *Jingji ribao*, April 27, 2002; *Beijing chenbao*, March 24, 2004; *Fazhi ribao*, April 17, 2005; *Xinjing bao*, May 16, 2006.

is directly tied to the security of grain production, sustainable social and economic development, and social stability. It is not a temporary measure, but a long-term policy."[99]

In 2003, the central government began to intensify its efforts to protect both the peasants' interests and farmland. The timing was not accidental. Figure 8.2 shows that the number of violations of the law and regulations began to rise in 2002 and reached a peak in 2003. Meanwhile, the number of complaints received by the Ministry of Land and Resources increased by 85 percent between 2002 and 2003, and the number of petitioners increased by 52 percent. Nationwide, complaints regarding land conversion accounted for 8.1 percent of the total number of petitions in 2003, the fourth largest category.[100] That year, the National Complaints Bureau sent a report on peasants' petitions on rural land use to central leaders, including Premier Wen. Wen's instructions on the report were forwarded to the Ministry of Land and Resources, which decided to send six teams to eleven provinces to investigate the reported problems. Another reason for the government's new efforts was that China was facing a seriously overheated economy in 2003. As Premier Wen admitted, to slow down economic growth, the central party committee and the State Council made "an important and timely decision" to strengthen and improve the macrolevel adjustment of economic development by imposing especially tight control over land use.[101] Against this background, the central government also required local governments to accommodate peasant interests by, among other things, paying peasants overdue compensation for lost land.[102]

Since 2004, more efforts have been expended to adjust the existing policies or make new ones partly because the central government faces increasing pressure to preserve land. The central government's bottom line is that China must keep at least 1.8 billion *mu* of farmland. But the amount of farmland declined from 1.945 billion *mu* in 1998 to 1.837 billion *mu* in 2004, approaching the bottom line. As a result, the State Council issued a directive on improving the management of land in addition to abolishing 70 percent of the 6,740 economic development zones in 2004.[103] The directive stressed that the conversion of farmland can be approved only by the central and provincial governments. It tried to protect peasants' interests in several ways. First, given the limited amount of compensation required by the land law, the new directive stated that if the mandated level of compensation is insufficient for peasants to maintain their current living standards or, for landless peasants, if it is insufficient to cover the cost of their social security welfare benefits, local governments should increase the amount of compensation. The directive also emphasized the extension of the social security system and job allocation for landless peasants.

Second, regarding farmland conversion, the directive stressed that relevant information, including the purpose of conversion, the criteria for compensation, and the plans for allocation, should be reported to peasants before an application for farmland conversion would be approved. Thus, farmland cannot be taken away if a compensation plan has not been implemented. Applications for farmland conversion must include documents indicating that peasants know about and have approved the land conversion plan. This regulation can serve as a check for the provincial and central governments to monitor local governments' farmland use. It may also be a powerful weapon in the peasants' fight against local governments that occupy land at will. For the first time, the directive urges the establishment of mechanisms that can mediate and arbitrate disagreements over compensation.

More significantly, the central government began to tackle the problem of limited compensation in 2005. It decided to revise the criteria for compensation, basing them not solely on the agricultural output of the farmland but also on other factors, including land quality, location, the local amount of land per capita, demand-supply relations, the level of local economic development, and the local minimum subsistence level, among others.[104] Previously, local governments generated a large amount of revenue from land leases, and this amount of money was included in the extrabudgetary funds entirely controlled by local governments. Thus, this revenue gave local governments a strong incentive to take land from peasants. In 2006, the central government regulated that the rent collected from land leases would be included in the within-budgetary revenue of local governments, which can be monitored by the provincial and central governments. This new measure was also aimed at weakening local governments' incentives to take land.[105] In 2007, the central government further announced that land use applications would not be approved if land users had not addressed the issue of peasants' social security. Finally, more local officials who abused power in land use have been punished in recent years.[106]

Citizen Resistance and Policy Adjustment: A Discussion

The central government's response to these five social groups' grievances varied in terms of the pace and degree of policy adjustment. The central government reacted more quickly to workers' retrenchment in state-owned enterprises and housing demolition than to peasants' financial burdens and the nonagricultural use of farmland (Table 8.1). It took the central government ten years to address the tax issue nationwide and fourteen years to abolish the agricultural tax. Until today, peasants' rights to their farmland have not been adequately protected. The central government almost completely ignored workers from urban collective enterprises, at least in the initial years of the industrial restructuring.

In this section, I examine the central government's policy adjustment in these five cases by comparing the forcefulness of resistance and the cost of adjustment. In all five cases, people's grievances concern economic benefits. For analytical convenience, policy adjustment is defined as costly if it requires the government to provide financial aid or if it makes the government incur a loss of revenue. Certainly, the cost of policy adjustment can be different for the central and local governments.

In looking at the civil rights movement in the United States, McAdam identifies several components of an organizationally strong group, including the ability to recruit members, solidarity, a communication network, leaders, and resources.[107] These components may be present in strong groups in most societies, but they are not easily found in the Chinese context, where most groups that stage resistance do not have an organizational base but instead function as temporary communities. In China, the forcefulness of resistance by a social group is influenced by: (1) the scope and frequency of the resistance; (2) the number of large-scale confrontations, which may involve casualties; and (3) the number of sensational events associated with the resistance (such as suicides), which may be disclosed by the media. What strengthens a group's position is also its access to external assistance or extra leverage.

In light of these criteria, a summary of the cost of adjustment and the forcefulness of citizens' resistance is presented in Table 8.7. The cost of adjustment is high for both the central and local governments in three of the five cases: peasants' financial burdens, the retrenchment of workers from SOEs, and the retrenchment of workers from collective enterprises. This is because both levels of government need to allocate financial resources to address these issues. In comparison, the cost of policy adjustment in the nonagricultural use of farmland is not as high as in the other three cases for the central government. This is because, unlike local governments, the central government does not rely so much on the revenues reaped from land conversion. But it is also true that the central government may also need to use farmland to construct certain public projects (e.g., highways), in which case it will also need to pay the peasants. In the case of housing

TABLE 8.7
Costs, Forcefulness of Resistance, and Policy Adjustment

	Cost of Adjustment to Governments			Resistance
	Central	Local	Action	Extra Leverage
Retrenchment of SOE workers	High	High	a. widespread b. large scale c. most frequent	a. media exposure
Retrenchment of urban CE workers	High	High	a. less widespread b. small scale	a. limited media coverage
Housing demolition	Relatively High	High	a. widespread b. violence/death c. small scale	a. media exposure
Peasants' financial burdens	High	High	a. widespread b. violence/death	a. media exposure b. incentive to farm
Nonagricultural use of farmland	Relatively High	High	a. widespread b. violence/death	a. media exposure b. land reservation

SOURCE: Author's summary. CE: collective enterprise.

demolition, the central government incurs an even lower cost of policy adjustment because most of the housing demolition has been carried out by local governments for commercial purposes.[108]

As far as the forcefulness of resistance is concerned, the resistance of workers from SOEs was the strongest among the five cases. First, their resistance was widespread and most frequent. Second, their actions also accounted for the largest portion of incidents of large-scale resistance in the late 1990s and early 2000s. Third, the problems faced by these workers were also widely reported in the media. Finally, their actions took place in cities and placed a more direct pressure on the government. In comparison, the resistance of workers from collective enterprises was the weakest. Their resistance was less widespread, less frequent, and small in scale. In addition, they received limited coverage from the media.

Peasant resistance to tax and fee collection and to the nonagricultural use of farmland was relatively strong. In both cases, peasant resistance was widespread; it also involved violent or deadly confrontation. Both cases also received media coverage. However, much of their collective resistance occurred in the countryside. Compared with workers from SOEs, peasants staged fewer large-scale resistance events. Homeowners' resistance was weak in terms of the portion of large-scale resistance, but they received significant help from the media, which offset their weakness. It was the media's intensive coverage of the deaths of the two homeowners that placed great pressure on the legitimacy of the central government. There have also been deaths in tax or fee collection and the nonagricultural use of farmland, but such cases have not been covered as intensively as the two suicides resulting from housing demolition, especially the Nanjing case.

If the above analysis of the cost and forcefulness of resistance is plausible, the rationale behind the central government's varied policy response can be illustrated by Table 8.8. The government reacted most quickly in the case of layoffs of SOE workers because the workers were able to stage the most powerful action despite the high cost of policy response. The fast policy response in housing demolition can be seen as resulting from a combination of the relatively forceful resistance and a relatively low cost of adjustment. Peasants' resistance to tax and fee collection and their resistance to the occupation of farmland were similarly strong. The slower policy change in peasants' tax payment is likely due to the higher cost involved in abolishing taxes than the cost of increasing land compensation. As for the laid-off workers from collective enterprises, there were no specific policies made for them.

TABLE 8.8
Policy Adjustments by the Central Government

Resistance	Cost		
	High	Relatively High	Relatively Low
Forceful	Fast adjustment: SOE workers		
Relatively forceful	Slow adjustment: Peasants' burdens	Relatively slow adjustment: Rural land use	Fast adjustment: Housing demolition
Weak	Little adjustment: CE workers		

SOURCE: Author's summary.

What is common in these cases is that the high cost incurred by local governments can significantly undermine the effectiveness of the new policies if those polices fail to eliminate loopholes that can be exploited by local governments. This is particularly apparent in the cases of peasants' financial burdens and the nonagricultural use of farmland. Despite the central government's repeated warnings against local officials, violations of peasants' rights recurred in both cases. The issue of peasants' financial burdens began to be more effectively addressed after 2002 because local officials' discretion was largely eliminated as a result of the reform measures. In comparison, local officials have continued to abuse power in land use not only because they are reluctant to give up their benefits but also because it is technically difficult for the central government to eliminate local officials' discretion in land use.

Conclusion

Popular resistance may contribute to policy adjustment regardless of the political system in which the resistance occurs. However, the relationship between popular resistance and public policy is often difficult to assess. As Linders puts it, outcomes are the result of the "interplay of protest, targets, institutions, and other environmental constraints in distinct historical locations."[109] This chapter examines popular resistance and policy adjustment in China by comparing five cases of citizens' resistance. It finds that two factors figure preeminently in popular resistance leading to policy adjustment. One is the cost incurred by the government in making new policies. The other is the forcefulness of resistance, which is determined not only by a social group's ability to stage disruptive action but also by its access to external support or extra leverage. Those groups that are less able to stage powerful resistance (e.g., large in scale) may thus still be able to achieve favorable policy adjustments if they are able to receive extra support. As in the resistance by individual groups discussed in earlier chapters, the rationale behind the government's policy adjustment reflects both the possibility of and the difficulty in staging effective popular resistance in China.

NINE

Conclusion

During the reform period in China, collective resistance has become an important mode of political participation used by Chinese citizens from all walks of life. This book examines the factors that shape the outcome or impact of their resistance. Research on the outcome of popular contention must address two important issues: (1) how to define the outcome and (2) how to assess or isolate the effect of collective action. But it is not easy to address these issues, as repeatedly suggested by students of social movements.[1] If social movements are defined as "sustained collective challenges to power holders in the name of a disadvantaged population living under the jurisdiction or influence of those power holders" or as a "continuous interaction between challengers and power holders,"[2] then the many instances of collective action in contemporary China do not qualify as social movements because they are, with few exceptions, short lived and are not sustained challenges against state authority.[3] Compared to social movements in democratic settings, instances of popular resistance in China are, in Tarrow's words, "somewhat special" in that they have clear goals and occur over a relatively short time span. Consequently, these factors make it easier to identify their outcomes than it is to isolate the outcomes of social movements.[4]

On the other hand, for understandable reasons, research on collective action in China has to deal with the problem of how to collect data that are systematical or comprehensive enough to allow the examination of the effect of collective resistance. Despite the numerous reports on popular contention in China, information about the outcome and the process of mobilization is generally unsystematic. Based on both firsthand data and secondary sources, this book explores the conditions for effective resistance in China by looking at both individual incidents of resistance and the aggregate impact of these individual incidents. It shows that the outcome of collective resistance is jointly determined by the forcefulness of citizens' resistance and by the cost of concessions incurred by the government in accommodating citizens' demands. In this conclusion, I first review the factors that affect the effectiveness of citizens' resistance and then discuss the less direct effects of this resistance on state–citizen relations in China.

Staging Successful Resistance in China

More than thirty years ago, Piven and Cloward asserted that "a placid poor get nothing, but a turbulent poor sometimes get something."[5] This is also true in China, where various groups of citizens, including homeowners, peasants, and workers, have staged legal and illegal modes of collective resistance to pursue or defend their rights. Participants in these collective actions "sometimes get something." But, as everywhere else, their success is highly conditional. This book examines the factors that shape the conditions for successful resistance by employing the cost–benefit approach and demonstrates that the government's perception of costs and benefits plays a crucial role in shaping the outcome of popular resistance.

It is not new to use the cost–benefit approach to analyze a state's response to popular contention.[6] But there are two points that merit notice. One is that the costs and benefits incurred by the government targeted by protesters have to be specified and operationalized to avoid a tautological explanation. Existing research assesses the costs by differentiating the types of demands made by protesters. Those demands that are aimed to displace power holders are believed to be self-defeating, as are other ambitious and ambiguous demands. For example, Button found that urban riots in the United States during the 1960s were most successful when the protesters' demands were limited, specific, and clear to the authorities.[7] Shin has argued that "under authoritarian regimes . . . protesters tend to have more impact when the scope of [their] demands is narrow and specific rather than broad."[8]

In China during the transitional period, the demands raised by protesters in most cases are nonpolitical or non-regime-threatening; they are often limited, specific, and clear to state authorities. Therefore, the difference between political and nonpolitical demands or the difference between broad and narrow demands is less applicable in the Chinese case. This book uses a different criterion to assess the costs of concession incurred by the government in dealing with nonpolitical protests in China. It shows that whether the government faces a direct economic loss in addressing citizens' grievances significantly shapes local governments' responses. In addition, the level of state authority involved in disputes also affects the chance of success because it determines the political cost of addressing citizens' grievances.

Second, the cost–benefit analysis should not be seen as a static approach; instead, collective resistance should be seen as a dynamic process in which the cost–benefit calculations of both the government and participants may change. Research on social movements has shown that opportunities for collective action can be created in the interaction between participants and other actors, including the state.[9] Goodwin and Jasper point out that "perceptions are not only necessary for potential protesters to recognize opportunities, but in many cases perceptions can create opportunities."[10] In the case of the 1979 Iranian Revolution, Kurzman shows that rather than calculate opportunities solely on the basis of changes in the state, the Iranian people appear to have calculated opportunities on the basis of changes in the power of the opposition. This presents the possibility that protesters will act on the basis of misperceptions of opportunities that do not in fact exist.[11]

Nevertheless, that a favorable opportunity for resistance may be created in the interaction between protest participants and the state or other targets is also conditional on protesters' abilities to tap resources and to adopt proper strategies. In the case of China, despite the nondemocratic system, local governments, which are most commonly targeted by protesters, face constraints in dealing with popular resistance, which creates the possibility for protesters to achieve successful resistance.

CHINESE LOCAL GOVERNMENTS: CONSTRAINTS AND POWER

In China, participants in collective resistance may overestimate the opportunity for resistance,[12] but political space for popular contention does exist. Compared with democractic governments, authoritarian governments are more sensitive to citizens' popular resistance even with nonpolitical demands, so they become deeply involved in the settlement of popular resistance. In China, decentralization gives both responsibility and autonomy to local governments. Governments at the county and city levels deal with most instances of popular resistance not only because they have more direct interaction with citizens but also because they are expected to monitor state agents at the township and village levels. The political hierarchy determines that the settlement of incidents of popular resistance explicitly or implicitly involves more than one level of government. Therefore, a fundamental way of achieving successful resistance is to generate pressure on local officials by gaining favorable intervention from upper-level authorities.

Chinese local officials need to pay attention to citizens' resistance because they are assigned the responsibility of maintaining local stability; their performance or even their political careers are closely linked to their fulfillment of this responsibility.[13] Top leaders (i.e., the party secretary and the head of the government) at each local level assume the most power, and they also assume the most responsibility in maintaining social stability.[14] Top local leaders are thus expected to handle large-scale resistance in person, and failing to do so may mean the end of their political careers. For example, in the Chizhou case in Anhui province in 2005, the city party secretary, who had also been promoted to hold another important position of vice provincial governor, was removed from office because he was absent without justifiable reasons when the riot involving 10,000 people occurred (see Chapter Seven).[15]

Nevertheless, while local officials are assigned the responsibility of maintaining social stability, they do not have to rely on concessions to silence protesters. As governments elsewhere, Chinese local governments may resort to several different modes of response, including concessions, concessions with discipline, tolerance, and suppression. There are several reasons why local governments may ignore or suppress popular resistance with non-regime-threatening claims. One reason has to do with the cost of concessions. If concessions mean that local governments would incur economic losses or would have to discipline their agents, then the price is high for such concessions (e.g., in land use). The cost of concessions is relatively low if local governments do not face a zero-sum game with protesters (e.g., in mediating labor disputes).

Second, local governments or their officials refuse to make concessions because they believe that the risk from not making concessions is limited. Disciplining local officials, especially those holding important positions, is a complex political problem in China. Various factors, such as personal connections, faction politics, and corruption, may undermine upper-level officials' willingness to discipline lower-level agents, creating the so-called political umbrella or protective buffers (see Chapter Three).[16] Chinese local officials are rarely punished if they ignore or violate citizens' interests in the name of so-called local development or public interest. As a matter of fact, local governments and/or their officials themselves are an important source of complaints among the citizens because it is common for them to directly violate citizens' rights. Hence, while the potential differences between different levels of state authorities may create constraints on local officials and therefore opportunities for resistance, it requires great effort to translate such opportunities into success.

GENERATING PRESSURE ON LOCAL AUTHORITIES

In dealing with popular resistance with high-cost demands, reluctance by local governments to make concessions is a natural response. But local governments' perception of the cost of concessions is weighed against the forcefulness of citizen resistance. Forceful resistance places pressure on local governments by disrupting the social order and/or threatening to trigger intervention from the central or provincial authority. Intervention from above is possible mainly because the central government is concerned with regime legitimacy. Chen's surveys in Beijing in 1995 and 1999 revealed considerable support for the political system among urban residents in the city.[17] Li found that peasants in China still have faith in the central party-state.[18] If a government enjoys a significant degree of legitimacy, it certainly has the incentive to protect it, which can be true for both the central and local governments. But this concern for legitimacy does not mean that upper-level authorities will always intervene to help citizens because of the potential costs. Citizens thus need to take actions that would help them to attract intervention from above.

That the Chinese state is not a monolith means that local governments or their officials are unable to monopolize political power and political resources. This implies that citizens may also have access to some political power and resources by employing certain modes of resistance. Broadly speaking, Chinese citizens' modes of action can be divided into two categories. One includes less drastic, peaceful, or even permitted modes, and the other includes noninstitutionalized or even illegal actions, such as strikes, protests, and demonstrations. Both types of action may achieve success but for different reasons.

In employing permitted or less drastic modes of action, participants can strengthen their intervention-seeking ability by applying multiple constraints on targeted local officials. One way of doing this is to blame local officials for many (different) things, including the issue that causes the protesting group's grievances and resistance, to lower the cost of intervention from above. Some misconduct is less tolerable to upper-level authorities than other types of misconduct. If participants are able to identify the misconduct of local governments and officials, especially the sort of misconduct that is less acceptable to upper-level authorities, they will gain new leverage over local officials. As a result, malfeasant officials will be disadvantaged. Revealing serious misconduct or even crimes (e.g., corruption) to upper-level authorities is thus a serious threat to local officials and can force them to be responsive and even make concessions. This method of resistance through issue connection is possible because, in today's China, local officials' abuse of power and corruption are anything but rare.

Another measure used by some participants in resistance is to gain extra support. Most groups of disgruntled citizens in China are weak in relation to state authorities or businesses that receive support from the government. Like weak groups elsewhere, they need to obtain extra leverage or support to strengthen their position and chance of success.[19] In China, gaining support necessitates engaging the state because of the political system that largely excludes any influential third parties that are beyond the control or heavy influence of the party-state. Citizens' chances of success will be increased if they are able to generate support from within the state. Some citizens may obtain such support because of the seriousness of their issues or their good luck in meeting sympathetic power holders or media workers.[20] In this book, I show that personal connections with people who have political power or influence are an important political asset in China where state–citizen interaction is not fully institutionalized. In China, the society is characterized by the pervasive influence of personal networks. As a result, connections with people with political power or resources can help resisters to generate support from within the state or to move their issues onto the agendas of state authorities. But the number of people able to receive such support is limited, and failures in using permitted channels are thus common.[21]

The limited effectiveness of using permitted channels is an important reason for citizens to choose more drastic and noninstitutionalized modes of action in seeking resolution to their problems.[22] The effectiveness of such action is determined by whether it involves a large number of participants, receives media coverage, and/or involves serious casualties. Because incidents that involve deaths or receive media coverage are limited, the size of the protest group is the most important indicator of the chance of success. But not all forceful resistance leads to success. The cases presented in this book reveal that the political cost of disciplining state agents has a significant impact on government behavior at both the central and local levels. The cost of concessions is seen as particularly high when higher-level local authorities are involved, in which case intervention from above becomes less possible.

The conditions for successful disruptive action also point out the problem faced by most protesters. Given that most instances of disruptive action are relatively small in scale (i.e., with fewer than 100 participants), they are generally unlikely to trigger intervention from above. Therefore, local governments assume autonomy in dealing with these instances of resistance. Suppression becomes the option when participants' demands are seen as too costly and they are unwilling to give up the resistance. Sometimes, participants may employ tactics to increase their chance of success. Innovative and peaceful tactics (e.g., directly approaching central authorities) can be helpful, but other tactics are counterproductive. This has been particularly obvious in the use of violence. To some extent, the use of violence per se implies that neither the government nor the participants are willing to back down. As a result, the participants' use of violence provides a pretext for government suppression, especially in small-scale resistance.

The cost of concessions and the forcefulness of the resistance also shape the central government's response to popular resistance in terms of policy adjustments. It is not easy to assess the impact of social protests on policy changes because of the many intervening variables.[23] This book addresses the relationship between popular contention and policy changes by comparing five cases of resistance in light of the protesters' demands and the forcefulness of their resistance. The case of peasants' financial burdens serves as an illuminating example of how the cost of concessions prevents fast policy responses. But powerful resistance may overcome the hurdle associated with such high costs. Some groups, like laid-off workers from state-owned enterprises, obtain fast policy responses because they are better able to stage powerful actions. Other groups are less able to achieve fast and significant policy responses because of their less powerful action and the high cost of accommodating their interests. As in other places,[24] less powerful groups in China need external support or extra leverage to obtain favorable policy responses. The policy adjustment regarding housing demolition reveals that the media can be a significant third party in popular resistance in China, while the case of rural land use reflects the importance of linked issues in strengthening weak groups' resistance. In contrast, laid-off workers from urban collective enterprises were able neither to stage powerful resistance nor to receive significant external support. They thus failed to provoke significant policy responses.

Popular Resistance and State–Citizen Relations in China

It has been commonly accepted that "[social] movements can and do have a range of outcomes that are essentially unintended, unanticipated, and perhaps even unwanted."[25] The changes produced by social movements (often indirectly) include macrolevel ones, such as reform, social transformation, or even democratization.[26] In China, citizen resistance does not often take the form of social movements, but their resistance has nonetheless produced changes indirectly. O'Brien and Li have analyzed the effects of resistance in rural China on policy implementation, activists or leaders, and the public.[27] In this section, I discuss the impacts of Chinese citizens' resistance on state–citizen relations in light of the similarities and differences between the central and local governments in China.

If it is difficult to establish causal relationships between resistance and direct outcomes, it is even more difficult to make connections between resistance and long-term or indirect consequences. Andrews uses the preexisting organizational strengths of movements to predict their long-term impact. In explaining black political participation in Mississippi in the United States, he writes, "The counties that established strong movement infrastructures in the early 1960s experienced significant success in expanding black political participation in the late 1960s and early 1970s."[28] In China, such movement infrastructures are largely absent. But past citizen resistance does influence state–citizen relations. The consequences of concessions and repression in previous cases of resistance affect local governments' views about citizens staging resistance and their responses.

GOVERNMENT TOLERANCE IN A TRANSITIONAL PERIOD

O'Brien and Li are right to suggest that the Chinese central government will face mounting pressure if it fails to respond to the increase in rightful resistance.[29] But at a time when instances of resistance are common, the government's responses at both the central and local levels are necessarily mixed. Governments may either extend efforts to tackle the sources of conflicts or become less tolerant of resistance. Whereas the central government sometimes uses political rhetoric to suggest that it exists to serve the people, officials of local governments are actually more practical. The many instances of repression presented in this study show that ideological constraints are largely nonexistent in many local governments and that neither government officials nor citizens believe that local government officials in China are "the people's servants."

Local officials believe that citizen resistance places serious pressure on them. Some county party secretaries complain that their jobs carry risks because of the many performance assessments. A county party secretary explained, "Like scared birds, we are on high alert everyday, worrying about production safety, sudden events, mass petitions, and other large-scale incidents that would result in punishment."[30] Therefore, there is an acknowledged "trouble-saving mentality" among local officials. After the bloody repression in Shanwei in Guangdong in December 2005, for example, the provincial party secretary, Zhang Dejiang, warned local officials in a provincial party meeting against causing further peasant resistance. His speech, which was published in the party's local newspaper, *Nanfang ribao*, indicated that the party secretary wanted lower-level officials to pay attention to the interests of peasants not because it was their duty to serve the people but because of the possible negative impact of peasant resistance on their political careers. In other words, preventing citizen resistance would reduce trouble for them.[31]

Free of ideological constraints, local officials adjust their policies by drawing lessons from their experiences in dealing with citizen resistance. In recent years, local governments have issued a number of regulations to prevent collective petitions. In Nanzhou city in Gansu province, for example, the city government declared that gatherings, demonstrations, sit-in demonstrations, and protests are not permitted in front of state agencies, and the same is the case for blocking office compounds or traffic.[32] Although some modes of resistance, including collective petitions, had been discouraged by earlier government regulations, it seems that local governments are increasingly determined to enforce these regulations. In 2006, the city government in Shenzhen held a public meeting to punish six people who had organized collective resistance in a high-profile manner. A deputy city party secretary asserted, "This public meeting is to send a signal to society that actions that break social order in Shenzhen will be seriously punished. The pursuit of any interest must be conducted within legal channels or means. Any mode that harms the interests of society, the collective, and other individuals is not acceptable."[33]

The reasons for this tough attitude are found in the undesirable consequences of past concessions. The city government in Shenzhen acknowledged that there had been repeated social disruptions in the city in recent years. Participants had the mentality that "a big disturbance lead[s] to a big solution." As a result, illegal gatherings, demonstrations, protests, and even violence occurred. The government made concessions in some cases.[34] But in the eyes of officials in lower-level governments in the city, the city seemed too weak and tolerant. These officials believed that the city government whetted the appetite of citizens and impressed on them that a big disturbance *does* lead to a big solution. The city government's tolerance created difficulties for lower-level officials in dealing with citizens' resistance.[35] As a result, the city government adjusted its attitude and policies toward citizen resistance.

Significantly, the central government has not objected to local governments' repressive regulations. Petitioners' protests in Beijing, including suicide and blocking state agencies, placed pressure on both the central and local governments. Some desperate petitioners have been punished because of their protests or for petitioning in so-called important places in Beijing, such as Tiananmen Square and Zhongnanhai, where central leaders work.[36] In 2004, the city government in Beijing issued a directive to regulate petitioners' activities, and the following activities are now prohibited: (1) making petitions in places not responsible for receiving petitioners and (2) illegal gathering in or around state agencies, blocking or attacking state agencies, blocking cars of government employees, blocking traffic, suicide, and self-injury. Those who gather or protest in important places will be sent to the complaint departments by the police. Furthermore, those who violate laws will be turned in to the state agencies of their home residence. This regulation implies that there are serious risks for those who present petitions in Beijing. Once petitioners return to their place of residence, they are very likely to be punished by local government officials.[37] Apparently, the central government is aware of the regulations made by the city government of Beijing. Therefore, the promulgation of such regulations indicates the central government's tolerance of local repression.

The autonomy enjoyed by local governments implies that they have great discretion in choosing the mode of response and that successful resistance can be highly conditional because of the high threshold of intervention from above. However, this decentralized power structure also protects the central government's image because it allows the government to distance itself from the settlement of most instances of resistance and to partly avoid the blame if suppression is used by local governments. In addition, the structure allows the central government to pretend not to know about the suppression if it does not want to intervene.[38] Under this power structure, citizens' chance of success is nonexistent if governments of different levels feel that the costs of concessions are high. This is true not only for regime-threatening acts but also for non-regime-threatening ones because there is no political space for action in this circumstance.

At a time when Chinese society is replete with conflicts, the government's less tolerant attitude toward citizen resistance is understandable because concessions tend to trigger more resistance. To be sure, by tolerating repression, the central government runs a serious risk of encouraging local officials to become more abusive. Hence, the central government has tried to make local governments more responsive to citizens' demands. The directive on petitions that took effect in May 2005, for example, requires complaint agencies to respond to citizens' petitions within fifteen days. But it is clear to both the complaint agencies and petitioners that this regulation means very little because it is beyond the ability of complaint agencies to address most of the complaints raised by petitioners.

Do local officials in China learn lessons from failed repression? Certainly. But local governments tend to have short memories about other local governments' failures, especially when they will benefit by violating citizens' rights. After all, the frequent exemption of abusive officials serves to encourage others, making them underestimate the odds of punishment—or, rather, correctly estimate the small likelihood of punishment. This is an important reason why significant violations of citizens' rights persist.

CITIZENS' PERCEPTIONS OF THE GOVERNMENT

As mentioned earlier, Chinese citizens tend to have a high level of trust in the central government, which is partly reflected in citizens' petitions. In 2003, the number of petitions directed to the National Complaints Bureau increased by 14 percent, and other central authorities received 46 percent more petitions than in the previous year. In contrast, those directed to provincial and city-level authorities increased by just 0.1 and 0.3 percent, respectively, while those sent to county-level authorities decreased by 2.4 percent.[39] In 2005, petitions to local authorities declined by about 9 percent, and the number directed at the central government remained stable.[40] However, citizens' views of the government or the political system may change as a result of their dealings with state authorities. As discussed in Chapter Three, for example, those who fail in their resistance are greatly disappointed in the government, including the central government. In the Shanwei case, villagers who "did not trust any officials in Guangdong, even the provincial government" were also greatly disappointed by the central government's refusal to intervene.[41]

Citizens' images of the government may change as a result of other people's failed experiences. In early 2004, the government in Jiahe county in Hunan province arrested three peasants for defending their homes (Chapter Six). Without a legal basis, the local government had pulled down the peasants' homes by force without providing reasonable compensation. Although the case was disclosed by Chinese Central Television, the county government refused to redress the violation. When the case was posted online, Internet users protested. Within three days, about 10,700 messages were posted on Sohu.com.[42] Some users referred to local officials as "beasts." Others were more cynical: "Do not feel surprised. These are Chinese characteristics. Cadres are not held responsible to the people."

Despite the mounting furor, higher-level authorities did not initially respond to the case. Internet users questioned the lack of intervention: "This case has been disclosed for so many days, but no higher-level officials have come out to address the problems. Why is it so hopeless in China?" They asked, "Are there any higher-level leaders who are still alive?" and "Why has the provincial party secretary of Hunan province not responded?" Others offered an explanation: "The provincial governor and the county magistrate belong to one stratum, and the people belong to another. So the governor will support the magistrate, and protecting the interests of the people in his stratum is to protect his own interests." Still others proposed "solutions": "Those poor people should unite and use class struggle to overthrow these bullies"; "The people in the county should demolish the housing of the county party secretary and then his office building." Others suggested firing the unresponsive provincial party secretary.

People who have a low level of trust in the government seem to be more sensitive to government policies that regulate citizens' behavior. This was reflected in some people's reactions to the 2005 directive on petitions issued by the State Council. When the directive was publicized, two of China's most popular websites, Sohu.com and Sina.com, reported the news and invited comments. The news was posted for one day, during which time there were about 1,500 comments posted on Sohu.com and 1,360 on Sina.com. My random selection of 100 messages from the two websites indicates that more than 85 percent of those messages mocked the new petition directive. Some questioned the policy, asking "Is there a constitutional basis for this five-person limit?" "Why does the government not simply abolish this system altogether?" and "Poor workers and peasants, do you not understand whose government this is?" Others showed disappointment with the new central leadership.[43]

In April 2006, after the new directive had been in place for one year, the Chinese National Complaints Bureau reported that the number of petitions and petitioners received by complaint agencies at the county level and above in the country declined by 8 percent in 2005, from 13.7 million in 2004 to 12.6 million. In its explanation of the decline, the bureau highlighted the enhanced responsiveness of state authorities and complaint agencies. It claimed that local complaint agencies addressed about 93 percent of the cases forwarded to them by upper-level authorities. The bureau also stated that petitioners were now more reasonable when choosing their mode of petitioning, favoring peaceful methods.[44] There is no reason to believe that the bureau's explanation is inaccurate, but the reasons for the decline may be more complex than the bureau suggested. The decline might also result, for example, from the disappearance of some important sources of conflict, such as the abolition of the agricultural tax and the completion of the privatization of most small- and medium-sized public enterprises.[45]

There could be other reasons as well. When the bureau's statement was published online, Internet users made 126 comments about the statement on Sohu.com and China.com. The limited nature of these comments makes it unlikely that they were representative, but it merits mentioning that no single comment about the bureau's explanation of the decline posted on these two sites was positive. Most comments mocked, blamed, or criticized the government or the political system. Some Internet users observed that the decline was the result of the people's loss of confidence in the petition system or because petitioners were stopped, caught, or threatened by the police. Petitioners became more reasonable, Internet users postulated, because they knew they would be punished if their modes of petition were seen as unacceptable. Some remarks on the Internet included the following: "Damn it. It is apparently the result of repression. Shame on the government that claims a decline in petitions," and "This type of self-deceiving news makes me sick." One user said, "This society is now upside down. Lawful petitions can be interpreted as making trouble, but those who really make trouble are often exempted because the government does not dare to punish them." Still others remarked that there used to be more trust in complaints agencies; but, now that the trust is gone, people do not present petitions in such great numbers.[46]

Citizen complaints matter, partly because the information flow in China is better than before, although the central party-state has time and again tightened control over the media. As Gamson suggests, mass media discourse is an important cultural impact produced by social movements.[47] In China, it is no longer rare for the media to discuss the protection of citizens' rights, a discussion that has enhanced and will continue to enhance citizens' awareness of their rights. The better flow of information also affects interactions among citizens. Authoritarian states prohibit free information flow to cover up their misconduct and weaknesses. Hence, authoritarian governments become weak when they can no longer blind their people or control information.[48] When information flows freely, citizens learn of others who resent the government, which, when the opportunity arises, may lower the threshold of participation in acts of resistance.[49] On the other hand, the information flow also influences state–citizen interactions. When citizens' grievances become the common knowledge of both the government and the public, the government must act to protect its legitimacy. There have been a number of cases in which the central government intervened to address citizens' grievances as a result of exposure on the Internet.[50] Allies online have proved to be a crucial third-party source of support for citizens seeking justice in China.

Popular Resistance and Political Development in China

The ways that popular resistance is dealt with in China demonstrate the significant flexibility embedded in the political system. The decentralized state power prevents both excessive repression that seriously damages the regime's legitimacy and unconditional concessions that lead to the "lack of discipline."[51] However, while the coexistence of resistance and political stability in China reflects the resilience of the political system,[52] challenges to the state remain. Thus far, the government's responses to citizen resistance have shown that while the "de Tocqueville effect"—minor changes leading to greater demands for the elimination or transformation of the regime—may be an old problem,[53] it has not grown any easier to solve over time. The Chinese government is trying to alleviate the dilemma by using both repression and concessions. These measures have limitations that have important implications for state–citizen relations and the institutionalization of conflict resolution in China.

As this book has shown, some citizens have been able to achieve success from staging resistance. Occasional concessions reduce social grievances and some conflicts and help protect regime legitimacy. The possibility of success, together with the limited effectiveness of permitted modes of action, determines that collective resistance has remained an important mode of political participation in China. Because of the numerous social conflicts and protests, the central party-state has set "building a harmonious society" as a top priority. For this purpose, the central party-state has revised a number of policies that had disadvantaged some weak groups in society, such as peasants and workers. A more recent example is the enactment of the new labor law in 2008. After several years of debate, the central party-state eventually decided to enact this new labor law because of numerous labor disputes and workers' grievances.

Nevertheless, accommodating citizens' legitimate interests is not the only method used by the party-state to maintain social stability. As a matter of fact, it is not uncommon for local governments to ignore or suppress incidents of popular resistance. Moreover, there is no evidence to show that the disgruntled in China are now more likely to succeed than before despite the party-state's policy of "building a harmonious society." Ironically, the call for harmony made by the central government has become a pretext for some local governments to repress citizen resistance.[54] In addition, some policies regarding citizens' rights made by the central party-state are mixed in terms of their impact on popular resistance. Some of the government's new policies favor citizens, but others do not. The 2005 directive on petitions, for example, includes items that urge complaint agencies to be more responsive, but it also discourages collective petitions. As mentioned earlier, local governments have made regulations to discourage collective petitions.

The continual abuse of power by local officials, together with the limitations of those grievance-redress mechanisms, can only foment the resentment among citizens who have encountered injustice. What complicate citizens' resentment in today's China are the many serious socioeconomic and political problems, including increasing income inequality and corruption. This is the reason for some seemingly trivial disputes triggering riots involving thousands or tens of thousands of participants, as discussed in Chapter Seven. The easy mobilization in these incidents reflects the broad social environment in which citizens are resentful about a number of issues. Moreover, there is no sign that such incidents will disappear in the near future; on the contrary, large-scale riots have continued to occur in recent years (see Appendix C). In this sense, achieving a "harmonious society" also requires legitimacy building or strengthening.

That the Chinese citizens' widespread grievances and resistance have much to do with local officials' abuse of power and the limited effectiveness of redress mechanisms has important implications for the institutionalization of state-citizen relations and conflict resolution. The transitional experience of some former socialist regimes suggests that institution building prior to the transition is crucial to the establishment of social, economic, and political order after the transition.[55] In China, popular resistance reveals the difficulty in the institutionalization of state-citizen relations and conflict resolution because it indicates that if the party-state, especially the one at the local level, has limited incentives to follow the rules that are made by itself or by upper-level authorities, the people will not follow the rules either. Given that local governments are mostly responsible for handling social conflicts in the society, future research needs to analyze the factors that lead to local governments' varied responses to popular contention or efforts in building and strengthening conflict-resolution institutions to understand the relationship between popular resistance and political development in China.

Data Collection

China General Social Survey 2005 (China GSS 2005)

This general social survey was conducted by the Division of Social Science of the Hong Kong University of Science and Technology (HKUST) in 2005. The survey used four-stage probability proportional to size (PPS) sampling consisting of the following steps: (1) selection of counties or county-level districts; (2) selection of streets (*jie dao*) and townships; (3) selection of residents' committees (*jumin weiyuan hui*) and villages; and (4) selection of households. The survey covered 10,372 people (between twenty and sixty-nine years old) in 559 residents' committees and 410 villages in 125 counties or county-level districts in twenty-eight of the thirty-one provinces or cities at the administrative level of province, excluding Ningxia, Qinghai, and Tibet (see below). Of the 10,372 respondents, 6,098 were urban residents (58.8 per cent) and 4,274 were rural residents (41.2 percent).

A survey company was hired to carry out this survey, and the survey process was monitored by another independent quality-checking company and the Division of Social Science of HKUST. The survey questions on social conflicts used in this book were designed by the author.

TABLE A.I

Distribution of Residents' Committees and Villages Covered in the Survey

Province	Residents Committee	Villages	Total Households
Beijing	40	0	407
Tianjin	40	0	405
Hebei	17	22	420
Shanxi	7	8	166
Inner Mongolia	8	8	167
Liaoning	22	18	416
Jilin	12	4	171
Heilongjiang	26	6	331
Shanghai	40	0	400
Jiangsu	26	30	615
Zhejiang	14	18	322
Anhui	24	24	524
Fujian	19	12	321
Jiangxi	11	12	241
Shandong	32	32	669
Henan	28	36	664
Hubei	18	24	491
Hunan	26	20	491
Guangdong	33	20	585
Guangxi	21	16	410
Hainan	5	2	80
Chongqing	2	4	85
Sichuan	23	38	668
Guizhou	13	18	335
Yunnan	11	16	320
Shaanxi	20	12	334
Gansu	13	10	254
Xinjiang	8	0	80
Total	559	410	10372

APPENDIX B

My Collection of 266 Cases

The 266 cases include five riots in which participants did not have specific demands, and these five cases were used only in Chapter Seven. Of the 266 cases, 257 cases were collected from secondary sources (see below), and nine were collected in my fieldwork in China. The 266 cases occurred between 1994 and 2007 in twenty-seven of the thirty-one provinces or cities at the administrative level of province, excluding Guizhou, Yunnan, Qinghai, and Tibet. Of the 266 cases, 155 (58.3 percent) occurred in the countryside, and 111 cases (41.7 percent) took place in cities. These cases generally belong to what the government calls "internal conflicts within the people," with only one exception (i.e., worker protests in Liaoyang in 2002). Because of the constraints on data collection, the cases I collected were not based on random sampling. But these cases are complete ones in the sense that there is information about their outcomes.

TABLE B.1
Distribution of the Cases

Province	Number of Cases	Province	Number of Cases
Beijing	7	Shandong	11
Tianjin	2	Henan	13
Hebei	10	Hubei	13
Shanxi	7	Hunan	16
Inner Mongolia	5	Guangdong	37
Liaoning	19	Guangxi	9
Jilin	7	Hainan	2
Heilongjiang	8	Chongqing	5
Shanghai	4	Sichuan	15
Jiangsu	11	Shaanxi	8
Zhejiang	22	Gansu	3
Anhui	10	Ningxia	5
Fujian	9	Xinjiang	1
Jiangxi	7	Total	266

SOURCES: The 257 cases were collected from the following sources.

Newspapers (49):
Beijing wanbao; Beijing yule xinbao; Chengde ribao; Chuzhou wanbao; Chongqing chenbao; Chutian dushi bao; Dahe bao; Dongfang ribao; Fazhi kuaibao; Fazhi ribao; Financial Times; Gongren ribao; Hainan jingji bao; Huhehaote wanbao; Huashang bao; Huasheng bao; Jiancha ribao; Jiangnan shibao; Jieyang ribao; Jinhua shibao; Lanzhou chenbao; Mingpao; Nanfan dushi bao; Nanfang zhoumo; Nanyang ribao; Nanfang ribao; Ningbo wanbao; Pingguo ribao; Qingyuan ribao; Shanxi fazhi bao; Shantou ribao; Shidai shangbao; South China Morning Post; New York Times; Washington Post; Wenzhou ribao; Wuhan wanbao; Xindao ribao; Xinkuai bao; Xinwenhua bao; Xibu shangbao; Xuchang ribao; Ya'an ribao; Yangzi wanbao; Zhejiang xinshengbao; Zhejiang laonian bao; Zhongguo qingnianbao; Zhongguo shibao; Zhongguo ribao

Books and Periodicals (9):
The Research Group, *Zhongguo zhuanxingqi quntixing tufashijian duice yanjiu* (Beijing: Xueyuan chubanshe, 2003); *Far Eastern Economic Review; Fenghuang zhoukan; Minzhu yu fazhi; Minqing yu xinfang; Xinmin zhoukan; Ying zhoukan; Zhanlue yu guanli; Zhongguo xinwen zhoukan*

Websites (52):
www.qtfy.gov.cn; www.new.bbc.co.uk; www.rfa.org; www.xs.gd.cn; www.washington post.com; news .qianlong.com; news.sina.com.cn; www.chinesenewsnet.com; news.boxun.com; hnfy.chinacourt.org; www .yinzi.cn; www.gx.xinhuanet.com; www.gd.xinhuanet.com; finance.people.com.cn; fy.putuo.gov.cn; news.mlr .gov.cn; en.epochtimes.com; www.fhnews.com.cn; www.chinanews.com.cn; www.lz160.net; www.gscn.com.cn; www.xinhuanet.com; www.lawon.cn; www.cq.chinanews.com.cn; www.bbzy.org; news.anhuinews.com; www .longhui.gov.cn; www.cn-doc.com; www.jcrb.com; www.gsfzb.gov.cn; www.jxnews.com.cn; lyzy.chinacourt .org; www.zhinong.cn; www.pxepb.gov.cn; www.cctv.com; www.crd-net.org; www.lirun.pdx.cn; ga.hainan.gov .cn; www.66wz.com; ycjc.gov.cn; www.hnby.com.cn; www.fsou.net.cn; www.zjol.com.cn; www.wyzxwyzx.com; www.dffy.com; www.aboluowang.com; www.cnradio.com; news.sdinfo.net; www.sociology.cass.cn; www.shm .com.cn; www.szls.gov.cn; news.creaders.net

APPENDIX C

Examples of Large-Scale Protests

TABLE C.1

Examples of Large-Scale Protests (with About 5,000 or More Participants) in China
(*N* = 44)

Year	Participants (peasants)	Location	Participants (workers)	Location
1993	15,000	Renshou, Sichuan		
1995	20,000	Yuncheng, Shanxi		
1996	10,000	Qidong, Hunan		
1997			20,000	Nanchong, Sichuan
1999			5,000[a]	Hongjiang, Hunan
1999	5,000	Daolin, Hunan	5,000	Zhangjiakou, Hubei
2000	20,000	Yuandu, Jiangxi	10,000	A factory, Liaoning
2000			20,000[a]	Panzihua, Sichuan
2000			20,000	Huludao, Liaoning
2001			15,000	Sulan Mine, Jilin
2002			10,000[a]	An unknown county
2002			5,000	A mine, Shanxi
2002			10,000	Liaoyang, Liaoning
2002			30,000	Daqin, Heilongjiang
2002			10,000	Fushun, Liaoning
2003			10,000	Xiangfan, Hubei
2004			6,000	Xianyang, Shaanxi
2004	100,000	Hanyuan, Sichuan	30,000[a]	Wanzhou, Chongqing
2004			5,000	Bengbu, Anhui
2005	10,000	Shanwei, Guangdong[b]	5,000	Fuxin, Liaoning
2005	10,000	Dongyang, Zhejiang	10,000[a]	Chizhou, Anhui
2005	15,000	Xinchang, Zhejiang	30,000[a]	Daye, Hubei
2005	5,000	Hengshan, Hunan	5,000	Shenzhen, Guangdong
2005	20,000	Jieyang, Guangdong	6,000	Huaibei, Anhui
2006	10,000	Zhongshan, Guangdong	5,000	Chendu, Sichuan
2006			5,000[c]	Zhengzhou, Henan
2007	5,000	Bobai, Guangxi	5,000[a]	Zhengzhou, Henan
2007	5,000	Yongzhou, Hunan	5,000[a]	Guixi, Jiangxi
2007	6,000	Shantou, Guangdong	10,000[a]	Dazhu, Sichuan
2007	10,000	Dahua, Guangxi	5,000[a]	Youyang, Chongqing
2007	5,000	Changshou, Chongqing		

SOURCE: Author's Collection; Note: the figures are rough estimates.

[a] They were staged by urban residents.

[b] This is not the case that occurred in Dongzhou village.

[c] By students.

Data on Collective Petitions, 1995

TABLE D.1
Collective Petitions in Twenty-Six Cities in 1995

Cities	Number[a]	Participants[b]	Location
Fushun	3.60	32	Liaoning
Harbin	3.51	38	Heilongjiang
Datong	3.29	36	Shanxi
Jinzhou	2.89	30	Liaoning
Wuhan	2.69	23	Hubei
Anshan	2.46	31	Liaoning
Dalian	1.80	36	Liaoning
Zhenjiang	1.76	25	Jiangsu
Xi'an	1.61	21	Shaanxi
Siping	1.57	31	Jilin
Zhaozhuang	1.42	28	Shandong
Yangzhou	1.28	27	Jiangsu
Zhengzhou	1.28	27	Henan
Ma'anshan	1.26	15	Anhui
Changchun	1.05	30	Jilin
Daqing	0.99	48	Heilongjiang
Nanyang	0.97	19	Henan
Qinhuangdao	0.92	24	Hebei
Changsha	0.82	18	Hunan
Yichang	0.69	20	Hubei
Hangzhou	0.65	21	Zhejiang
Puyang	0.58	25	Henan
Suzhou	0.57	19	Jiangsu
Xiangfan	0.51	—	Hubei
Kunming	0.42	13	Yunnan
Zhuzhou	0.35	30	Hunan

SOURCE: The 1996 yearbook of each city.
[a] The number is collective petitions per 10,000 citizens.
[b] The average number of participants in each collective petition.

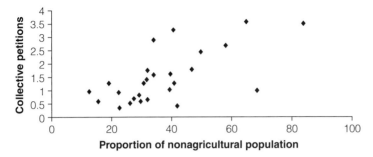

FIGURE D.I Relationship between the Number of Collective Petitions among Every 10,000 Citizens and the Proportion of the Nonagricultural Population in Twenty-Six Cities in 1995. SOURCE: The 1996 yearbook of each city.

Data on Collective Petitions, 1998

TABLE E.I

Collective Petitions per 10,000 People in Forty Cities in 1998

Cities	Petitions	Participants	Location
Fushun	21.04	25	Liaoning
Benxi	11.21	43	Liaoning
Harbin	9.99	23	Heilongjiang
Fuxin	9.43	25	Liaoning
Siping	5.67	28	Jilin
Anshan	4.82	33	Liaoning
Jinzhou	4.56	39	Liaoning
Daqing	4.12	22	Heilongjiang
Taiyuan	3.79	31	Shanxi
Jiyuan	3.78	20	Henan
Jinan	2.82	—	Shandong
Zhaozhuang	2.77	29	Shandong
Zhenjiang	2.57	21	Jiangsu
Rizhao	2.47	18	Shandong
Changchun	2.40	25	Jilin
Anyang	2.27	32	Henan
Yangzhou	2.24	28	Jiangsu
Guiyang	2.22	25	Guizhou
Qingdao	2.04	—	Shandong
Guining	1.85	16	Guangxi
Qinhuangdao	1.79	21	Hebei
Zhengzhou	1.65	31	Henan
Jingzhou	1.61	22	Hubei
Xiangfan	1.57	28	Hubei
Yichang	1.51	22	Hubei
Xuzhou	1.46	34	Jiangsu
Luoyang	1.45	31	Henan
Wuxi	1.37	22	Jiangsu
Weihai	1.32	—	Shandong
Suzhou	1.25	19	Jiangsu
Zhuzhou	1.23	19	Hunan
Xiangtan	1.23	28	Hunan
Nantong	1.22	31	Jiangsu
Weifang	1.17	18	Shandong
Weinan	1.12	27	Shaanxi
Changzhi	1.09	—	Shanxi
Changsha	0.93	24	Hunan
Yueyang	0.90	25	Hunan
Xinyang	0.60	22	Henan
Yibin	0.52	21	Sichuan

SOURCE: The 1999 yearbook of each city

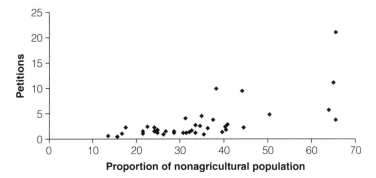

FIGURE E.I Relationship between the Number of Collective Petitions among Every 10,000 Citizens and the Proportion of the Nonagricultural Population in Forty Cities in 1998. SOURCE: The 1999 yearbook of each city.

Data on Collective Petitions, 2002

TABLE F.I

Collective Petitions per 10,000 People in Twenty-Eight Cities in 2002

Cities	Number of Petitions	Participants	Location of the City
Fushun	16.50	24	Liaoning
Fuxin	12.34	33	Liaoning
Anshan	6.23	25	Liaoning
Yan'an	5.71	21	Shaanxi
Dalian	5.23	25	Liaoning
Zhenjiang	4.54	19	Jiangsu
Jinzhou	4.26	41	Liaoning
Guiyang	3.60	17	Guizhou
Qinhuangdao	3.31	26	Hebei
Yangzhou	3.19	21	Jiangsu
Yichang	2.92	22	Hubei
Guining	2.67	20	Guangxi
Changchun	2.57	—	Jilin
Suzhou	2.43	20	Jiangsu
Wuxi	2.05	20	Jiangsu
Weihai	1.89	—	Shandong
Liuzhou	1.85	24	Guangxi
Chengdu	1.83	20	Sichuan
Zhuzhou	1.82	26	Hunan
Jinan	1.69	—	Shandong
Yueyang	1.59	21	Hunan
Xiangtan	1.56	24	Hunan
Zhengzhou	1.52	27	Henan
Nanning	1.15	16	Guangxi
Changzhi	1.11	14	Shanxi
Changsha	1.10	19	Hunan
Yibin	1.05	15	Sichuan
Jinzhou	0.99	20	Hubei

SOURCE: The 2003 yearbook of each city.

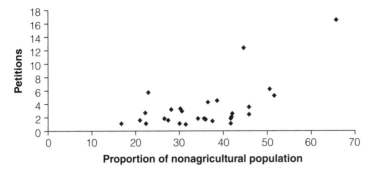

FIGURE F.1 Relationship between the Number of Collective Petitions among Every 10,000 Citizens and the Proportion of the Nonagricultural Population in Twenty-Eight Cities in 2002. SOURCE: The 2003 yearbook of each city.

Notes

Chapter 1

1. Ching Kwan Lee, *Against the Law: Labor Protests in China's Rustbelt and Sunbelt* (Berkeley: University of California Press, 2007); Kevin O'Brien and Lianjiang Li, *Rightful Resistance in Rural China* (New York: Cambridge University Press, 2006); Yongshun Cai, *State and Laid-Off Workers in Reform China: The Silence and Collective Action of the Retrenched* (London: Routledge, 2006); Thomas Bernstein and Xiaobo Lu, *Taxation without Representation in Contemporary Rural China* (New York: Cambridge University Press, 2003).

2. Jae Ho Chung, Hongyi Lai, and Ming Xia, "Mounting Challenges to Governance in China: Surveying Collective Protestors, Religious Sects and Criminal Organizations," *China Journal* 56 (2006): 1–31.

3. Peter Eisinger, "The Conditions of Protest Behavior in American Cities," *American Political Science Review* 67, 1 (1973): 11–28; William Gamson, *The Strategy of Social Protest* (Belmont, CA: Wadsworth, 1990), 81.

4. Scattered cases of successful resistance have been reported in a number of studies. See O'Brien and Li, *Rightful Resistance in Rural China*; Cai, *State and Laid-Off Workers in Reform China*; Bernstein and Lu, *Taxation without Representation in Contemporary Rural China*.

5. Yongshun Cai, "Local Governments and the Suppression of Popular Resistance in China," *China Quarterly* 193 (2008): 24–42.

6. In 2006, more than seventy desperate villagers sent a letter to *Takungpao*, a Hong Kong-based newspaper supported by the Chinese Communist Party (*Takungpao*, January 19, 2006).

7. Jack Goldstone and Charles Tilly, "Threat (and Opportunity): Popular Action and State Response in the Dynamics of Contentious Action," in Ronald

Aminzade, Jack Goldstone, Doug McAdam, Elizabeth Perry, William Sewell, Sidney Tarrow, Charles Tilley, eds., *Silence and Voice in the Study of Contentious Politics* (New York: Cambridge University Press, 2001), 179–194; Christian Davenport, "Multi-Dimensional Threat Perception and State Repression: An Inquiry into Why States Apply Negative Sanctions," *American Journal of Political Science* 39, 3 (1995): 683–713.

8. Grzegorz Ekiert, *The State against Society: Political Crises and Their Aftermath in East Central Europe* (Princeton, NJ: Princeton University Press, 1996).

9. Paul Kecskemeti, *The Unexpected Revolution* (Stanford, CA: Stanford University Press, 1961), 150.

10. For reviews, see Marco Giugni, "Was It Worth the Effort? The Outcomes and Consequences of Social Movements," *Annual Review of Sociology* 24 (1998): 371–93; and Donatella Della Porta and Mario Diani, *Social Movements: An Introduction* (Oxford, U.K.: Blackwell, 1999), chapter 9.

11. Gamson, *The Strategy of Social Protest*, 28.

12. Paul Burstein, Rachel Einwohner, and Jocelyn Hollander, "The Success of Political Movements: A Bargaining Perspective," in Craig Jenkins and Bert Klandermans, eds., *The Politics of Social Protest: Comparative Perspectives on States and Social Movements* (Minneapolis: University of Minnesota Press, 1995), 275–295.

13. Marco Giugni, "How Social Movements Matter: Past Research, Present Problems, Future Developments," in Marco Giugni, Doug McAdam, and Charles Tilly, eds., *How Social Movements Matter* (Minneapolis: University of Minnesota Press, 1999), xiii–xxxiii.

14. Doug McAdam, *Political Process and the Development of Black Insurgency 1930–1970*, 2nd ed. (Chicago: University of Chicago Press, 1999); Sidney Tarrow, *Power in Movement* (New York: Cambridge University Press, 1998); Charles Tilly, *From Mobilization to Revolution* (New York: Random House, 1978).

15. McAdam, *Political Process and the Development of Black Insurgency*, 44–47; Gamson, *The Strategy of Social Protest*, chapters 4, 5.

16. Doug McAdam, "Tactical Innovation and the Pace of Insurgency," *American Sociological Review* 48, 6 (1983): 735–754.

17. Gamson, *The Strategy of Protest*, chapter 4; Homer Steedly and John Foley, "The Success of Protest Groups: Multivariate Analysis," *Social Science Research* 8 (1979): 1–15.

18. Susanne Lohmann, "The Dynamics of Information Cascades: The Monday Demonstration in Leipzig East Germany, 1989–1991," *World Politics* 47, 1 (1994): 42–101; Charles Kurzman, "Structural Opportunities and Perceived Opportunity in Social-Movement Theory: The Iranian Revolution of 1979," *American Sociological Review* 61, 1 (1996): 153–170.

19. Donatella della Porta, *Social Movements, Political Violence and the State*. (New York: Cambridge University Press, 1995).

20. Murray Scott Tanner, "China Rethinks Unrest," *The Washington Quarterly* 27, 3 (2004): 137–156.

21. Hu Baozhen, Xie Tianchang, Chen Maohua, and Li Yanjun, "Hexie shehui goujian yu quntixing shijian falu duice yanjiu" (Research on the legal measures of constructing a harmonious society and dealing with collective incidents), *Zhongguo renmin gongan daxue xuebao* (Journal of the Chinese People's Security University) 4 (2006): 105–111.

22. Frances Fox Piven and Richard A. Cloward, *Poor People's Movements: Why They Succeed, How They Fail* (New York: Vintage Books, 1977), 27.

23. Kevin O'Brien and Lianjiang Li, "Selective Policy Implementation in Rural China," *Comparative Politics* 31, 2 (1999): 167–186; Bernstein and Lu, *Taxation without Representation in Contemporary China*, chapter 5.

24. Among the 45,330 administrative litigations that state agencies responded to in 2002, those suing county governments or their agencies accounted for more than 62 percent, while those suing city governments or their agencies and township governments accounted for a further 18 and 10 percent, respectively (*Fazhi ribao*, August 5, 2003).

25. Cai, *State and Laid-Off Workers in Reform China*, chapter 6.

26. This is also true in democratic systems. Kenneth Andrews, *Freedom Is a Constant Struggle: The Mississippi Civil Rights Movement and Its Strategy* (Chicago: University of Chicago Press, 2004); Tilly, *From Mobilization to Revolution*, chapter 4; David Meyer and Suzanne Staggenborg, "Movements, Countermovements, and the Structure of Political Opportunity," *American Journal of Sociology* 101, 6 (1996): 1628–1660.

27. To some extent, this was the case in the 1989 Tiananmen incident in China (Dingxin Zhao, *The Power of Tiananmen: State–Society Relations and the 1989 Beijing Student Movement* [Chicago: University of Chicago Press, 2001], 320–321).

28. O'Brien and Li, *Rightful Resistance in Rural China*; Cai, *State and Laid-Off Workers in Reform China*; Bernstein and Lu, *Taxation without Representation in Contemporary China*.

29. Ethan Michelson, "Peasants' Burdens and State Response. Exploring State Concession to Popular Tax Resistance in Rural China," manuscript, 2005.

30. Frank Michelman, "Ida's Way: Constructing the Respect-Worthy Governmental System," *Fordham Law Review* 72 (2003): 345–362.

31. O'Brien and Li, "Selective Policy Implementation in Rural China"; Bernstein and Lu, *Taxation without Representation in Contemporary Rural China*.

32. Long Xianlei, "Yifa tuoshan chuzhi quntixingshijian" (Sticking to rule by law and appropriately handling instances of collective action), *Gongan yanjiu* (Research on public security) 12 (2001): 50–53.

33. Goldstone and Tilly, "Threat (and Opportunity)."

34. McAdam, *Political Process and the Development of Black Insurgency 1930–1970*; Tarrow, *Power in Movement*; Tilly, *From Mobilization to Revolution*.

35. See, for example, Kurzman, "Structural Opportunity and Perceived Opportunity in Social-Movement Theory"; Doowon Suh, "How Do Political Opportunities Matter For Social Movements? Political Opportunity, Misframing, Pseudosuccess, and Pseudofailure," *Sociological Quarterly* 42, 3 (2001): 437–460; Jeff Goodwin and James Jasper, "Caught in a Winding, Snarling Vine: The Structural Bias of Political Process Theory," *Sociological Forum* 14, 1 (1999): 27–54.

36. O'Brien and Li, *Rightful Resistance in Rural China.*

37. Michael Lipsky, "Protest as Political Resource," *American Political Science Review* 62, 4 (1968): 1144–1158.

38. Craig Jenkins and Charles Perrow, "Insurgency of the Powerless: Farm Workers' Insurgency, 1946–1972," *American Sociological Review* 42, 2 (1977): 249–266.

39. O'Brien and Li, *Rightful Resistance in Rural China.*

40. See, among others, Thomas Gold, Doug Guthrie and David Wank, eds., *Social Connections in China: Institutions, Culture, and the Changing Nature of Guanxi* (New York: Cambridge University Press, 2002); Mayfair Yang, *Gifts, Favors and Banquets: The Art of Social Relationships in China* (Ithaca, NY: Cornell University Press, 1994).

41. Piven and Cloward, *Poor People's Movements*, 28.

42. Gamson, *The Strategy of Social Protest*, 81–82; Tilly, *From Mobilization to Revolution*, 111–115.

43. Edward Shorter and Charles Tilly, *Strikes in France 1830–1968* (New York: Columbia University Press, 1974), 191–192.

44. Doug McAdam, Sidney Tarrow, and Charles Tilly, *Dynamics of Contention* (New York: Cambridge University Press, 2001), 47.

45. McAdam, "Tactical Innovation and the Pace of Insurgency," 735.

46. Giugni, "Was It Worth the Effort?"

47. David Snyder and William Kelly, "Industrial Violence in Italy, 1878–1903," *American Journal of Sociology* 82, 1 (1976): 131–162; Doug McAdam and Yang Su, "The War at Home: Antiwar Protests and Congressional Voting, 1965 to 1973," *American Sociological Review* 67, 5 (2002): 696–712.

48. Shorter and Tilly, *Strikes in France,* chapter 11.

49. Steedly and Foley, "The Success of Protest Groups."

50. Li Zhilun, "Congyan zhidang zhizheng, qieshi zhuahao fanfubai renwu de luoshi" (Strengthening the discipline of party members and governance and doing a good job of enforcing anticorruption measures), *Zhongguo jiancha* (China discipline inspection) 4 (2000): 5–7.

51. O'Brien and Li, *Rightful Resistance in Rural China*, chapter 1.

52. Donatella della Porta and Mario Diani, *Social Movements*, 233.

53. Edwin Amenta and Michael Young, "Making an Impact: Conceptual and Methodological Implications of the Collective Goods Criterion," in Mark Giugni, Doug McAdam, and Charles Tilly, eds., *How Social Movements Matter* (Minneapolis: University of Minnesota Press, 1999), 22–41.

54. Edwin Amenta, Bruce Garruthers, and Yvonne Zylan, "A Hero for the Aged? The Townsend Movement, the Political Mediation Model, and the U.S. Old Age Policy, 1934–1950," *American Journal of Sociology* 98, 2 (1992): 308–339; Lee Ann Banaszak, *Why Movements Succeed or Fail: Opportunity, Culture, and the Struggle for Woman Suffrage* (Princeton, NJ: Princeton University Press, 1996).

55. Sarah Soule and Susan Olzak, "When Do Movements Matter? The Politics of Contingency and the Equal Rights Amendment," *American Sociological Review* 69, 4 (2004): 473–497; Paul Burstein and April Linton, "The Impact of Political Parties, Interest Groups, and Social Movement Organizations on Public Policy: Some Recent Evidence and Theoretical Concerns," *Social Forces* 81, 2 (2002): 381–408.

56. Giugni, "Was It Worth the Effort?"

57. Tarrow, *Power in Movement*, 162.

58. Giugni, "Was It Worth the Effort?"; Banaszak, *Why Movements Succeed of Fail*; Herbert Kitschelt, "Political Opportunity Structures and Political Protest: Antinuclear Movements in Four Democracies," *British Journal of Political Science* 16, 1 (1986): 57–85.

59. Stanley Lieberson, "Small N's and Big Conclusions: An Examination of the Reasoning in Comparative Studies Based on a Small Number of Cases," *Social Forces* 70, 2 (1991): 306–320.

60. McAdam and Su, "The War at Home"; Holly McCammon, Karen Campbell, Ellen Granberg, and Christine Mowery, "How Movements Win: Gendered Opportunity Structures and U.S. Women's Suffrage Movements, 1986 to 1919," *American Sociological Review* 66, 1 (2001): 49–70.

61. Paul Burstein, "Social Movements and Public Policy," in Marco Giugni, Doug McAdam, and Charles Tilly, eds., *How Social Movements Matter* (Minneapolis: University of Minnesota Press, 1999), 3–21.

62. Kenneth Krehbiel, *Information and Legislative Organization* (Ann Arbor: University of Michigan Press, 1991).

63. See, for example, Thomas Bernstein, "Stalinism, Famine, and Chinese Peasants," *Theory and Society* 13, 3 (1984): 339–369.

64. Annulla Linders, "Victory and Beyond: A Historical Comparative Analysis of the Outcomes of the Abortion Movements in Sweden and the United States," *Sociological Forum* 19, 3 (2004): 371–404.

65. Kenneth Andrews, *Freedom Is a Constant Struggle*, 25.

66. Kevin O'Brien and Lianjiang Li, "Popular Contention and Its Impact in Rural China," *Comparative Political Studies* 38, 3 (2005): 235–259.

67. Neil Diamant, Stanley Lubman, and Kevin O'Brien, eds., *Engaging the Law in China: State, Society, and Possibilities for Justice* (Stanford, CA: Stanford University Press, 2005).

68. Yongshun Cai, "Civil Resistance and Rule of Law in China: the Case of Defending Home Owners' Rights," in Elizabeth Perry and Merle Goldman, eds., *Grassroots Politics in China* (Cambridge, MA: Harvard University Press, 2007), 174–195; O'Brien and Li, *Rightful Resistance in Rural China*, chapter 6.

69. All the interviews conducted in China are anonymous.

70. The cases included in this collection are based on legitimate or lawful claims or, as the government claims, are "internal conflicts within the people." But nonpolitical resistance may be "boundary-spanning" or illegal according to the Chinese law (Chen Jinsheng, *Quntixingshijian yanjiu baogao* [Research report on instances of collective action] [Beijing: Qunzhong chubanshe, 2004]; Kevin O'Brien, "Neither Transgressive nor Contained: Boundary-Spanning Contention in China," *Mobilization* 8, 3 [2003]: 51–640).

Chapter 2

1. Chen Jinsheng, *Quntixingshijian yanjiu baogao* (Research report on instances of collective action) (Beijing: Qunzhong chubanshe, 2004).

2. Jerry Hough and Merle Fainsod, *How the Soviet Union Is Governed* (Cambridge, MA: Harvard University Press, 1990).

3. Tianjian Shi, *Political Participation in Beijing* (Cambridge, MA: Harvard University Press, 1997).

4. Frances Fox Piven and Richard A. Cloward, *Poor People's Movements: Why They Succeed, How They Fail* (New York: Vintage Books, 1977), 28.

5. Doug McAdam, *Political Process and the Development of Black Insurgency 1930–1970*, 2nd ed. (Chicago: The University of Chicago Press, 1999); Sidney Tarrow, *Power in Movement* (New York: Cambridge University Press, 1998); Charles Tilly, *From Mobilization to Revolution* (New York: Random House, 1978).

6. Between 1997 and 1999, the number of retrenched workers was about 10 million in each year. *China Labor Statistical Yearbooks* (1998–2003).

7. *Chinese Law Yearbook 1995*, 91; *Chinese Law Yearbook 2004*, 117.

8. Carl Minzner, "Xinfang: An Alternative to the Formal Chinese Judicial System," *Stanford Journal of International Law* 42, 1 (2006): 103–179; Isabelle Thireau and Hua Linshan, "The Moral Universe of Aggrieved Chinese Workers," *China Journal* 50 (2003): 83–103; Laura Luehrmann, "Facing Citizen Complaints in China, 1951–1996," *Asian Survey* 43, 5 (2003): 845–66.

9. Yongshun Cai, "Managed Participation in China," *Political Science Quarterly* 119, 3 (2004): 425–451; Minzner, "Xingfang."

10. Yongshun Cai, "Social Conflicts and Modes of Action in China," *China Journal* 59 (2008): 89–109.

11. Xiong Yihan, "Xinfang xiang hechuqu? (Where is the petition system heading?), *Ershi yi shiji* (21st century) 6 (2005): 91–95.

12. Diao Jiecheng, *Renmin xinfang shilue* (A brief history of people's petitions) (Beijng: Beijing Jingji Xueyuan Chubanshe, 1996).

13. Another survey of about 7,714 people found that about 6 percent (most of them peasants) reported that they had one or more grievances against government agencies in the past twenty years (Pierre Landry and Yanqi Tong, "Disputing the Authoritarian State in China," manuscript, 2005).

14. Hu Baozhen, Xie Tianchang, Chen Maohua, and Li Yanjun, "Hexie shehui goujian yu quntixing shijian falu duice yanjiu" (Research on the legal measures of constructing a harmonious society and dealing with collective incidents), *Zhongguo renmin gongan daxue xuebao* (Journal of the Chinese People's Security University) 4 (2006): 105–111.

15. Kevin O'Brien and Lianjiang Li, "Suing the Local State: Administrative Litigation in Rural China," *China Journal* 51 (2004): 53–74; Randall Peerenboom, *China's Long March toward Rule of Law* (New York: Cambridge University Press, 2002), chapter 9; Yuen Yuen Tang, "When Peasants Sue *En Masse*," *China: An International Journal* 3, 1 (2005): 24–49.

16. Cai, "Managed Participation in China."

17. Yu Jianrong, "Zhongguo xinfang zhidu pipan" (Criticisms of the petition system in China), *Zhongguo gaige* (China reform) 2 (2005): 26–28.

18. Yuezhi Zhao and Sun Wusan, "Public Opinion Supervision: Possibilities and Limits of the Media in Constraining Local Officials," in Elizabeth Perry and Merle Goldman, eds., *Grassroots Political Reform in Contemporary China* (Cambridge, MA: Harvard University Press, 2007), 300–326.

19. Yongshun Cai, "Power Structure and Regime Resilience: Contentious Politics in China," *British Journal of Political Science* 38, 3 (2008): 411–432.

20. Li Xiaoping, "Focus (jiaodian fangtan) and the Changes in the Chinese Television History," *Journal of Contemporary China* 11, 30 (2002): 17–34.

21. Shi Tan, " 'Jiaodian fangtan': yulunjiandu shinian yiyi" (Focus: 10 years of practice), *Fenghuang zhoukan* (Phoenix weekly) 4 (2005): 44–45.

22. The percentage of those who did not take action in our survey is much smaller than that reported by Landry and Tong. In their survey, they estimated that 60 percent of the citizens did not take any action (Landry and Tong, "Disputing the Authoritarian State in China").

23. Yongshun Cai and Songcai Yang, "State Power and Unbalanced Legal Development in China," *Journal of Contemporary China* 14, 42 (2005): 114–134.

24. *Chinese Law Yearbook*, various years.

25. Take the use of the law as an example. A survey of about 660 people in four cities (Nanjing, Suzhou, Nantong, and Huai'an) in Jiangsu Province in 2004 showed that about 75 percent reported that it was "difficult" to use lawsuits, as opposed to 25 percent that reported it was "not difficult." Interestingly, proportionally more people in the developed areas tended to report that it was "difficult." In Nanjing and Suzhou, the two more developed areas, the percentages who reported it as "difficult" were 90 percent and 67 percent, respectively, whereas for Nantong and Huai'an, two less economically developed cities, the percentages were 44 percent and 46 percent, respectively. The reason was that proportionally more people in developed areas had used lawsuits before, so they knew the difficulties ("Guanyu 'da guansi nan' de diaocha" [An investigation of the difficulties in lodging lawsuits], February 2004, unpublished survey by a legal department in Jiangsu).

26. Certainly, not all escalated action will take this form of collective action (Kevin O'Brien and Lianjing Li, *Rightful Resistance in Rural China* [New York: Cambridge University Press, 2006], chapter 4).

27. Kurt Schock, *Unarmed Insurrections: People Power Movements in Nondemocracies* (Minneapolis: University of Minnesota Press, 2005), 167.

28. Howard French, "Riots in Shanghai Suburb as Pollution Protest Heats up," *New York Times*, July 19, 2005.

29. *Nanfang ribao*, March 23, 2006.

30. Chen, *Quntixingshijian yanjiu baogao*, 12.

31. In some cases, participants used two or more modes of action.

32. Gregorz Ekiert and Jan Kubik, *Rebellious Civil Society* (Ann Arbor: University of Michigan Press, 1999), 113–118; Zhang Sai (ed.), *Guoji tongji ziliao 1995* (World statistics 1995) (Beijing: Zhongguo tongji chubanshe, 1996), 347–349.

33. Thomas Bernstein and Xiaobo Lu, *Taxation without Representation in Contemporary Rural China* (New York: Cambridge University Press, 2003), chapter 5.

34. Lucien Bianco, *Peasants without the Party: Grassroots Movements in Twentieth-Century China* (Armonk, NY: M. E. Sharpe, 2001), 245.

35. Donatella della Porta and Herbert Reiter, "The Policing of Protest in Western Democracies" in Donatella della Porta and Herbert Reiter, eds., *Policing Protest: The Control of Mass Demonstrations in Western Democracies* (Minneapolis: University of Minnesota Press, 1998), 1–34.

36. O'Brien and Li, *Rightful Resistance in Rural China*.

37. Cai, "Power Structure and Regime Resilience."

38. Zhou Meiyan, "Zhongguo xinfang de zhidu kunjing ji chulu" (The plight of the petition system in China and the solutions). Retrieved December 6, 2006 from www.chinaelections.org.

39. See the yearbooks of Henan, Jilin, Shandong, Sichuan, and Zhejiang (1991–2003).

40. Chen, *Quntixingshijian yanjiu baogao*, 59–60.

41. Liu Huang and Zhang Xianguo, "Chanye gongren jitishangfang shijian weihe pinpin fasheng) (Why collective petitions by workers keep occurring). Retrieved on December 25, 2003, from www.cetic.com.cn/detail/ dianlixinxi/ ling dao2002-09A.htm#_Toc19520829.

42. Zhang Chaoping, "Jiejue daguimo jiti shangfang de fabao" (Solutions to large-scale collective petitions), *Minqing yu xinfang* (People's situations and petitions) 5 (2003): 42–43.

43. The Central Complaints Bureau, *Zhongguo xinfang xiezhen* (A record of people's appeals in China) (Beijing: Zhongguo gongren chubanshe, 1998), 468.

44. See the 2003 yearbooks of Inner Mongolia, Henan, Jilin, Jiangsu, Anhui, Jiangxi, Shandong, Zhejiang, Sichuan, and Hebei. In Xi'an, the capital city of Shaanxi province, petitioners blocked traffic or the office compounds of party and government agencies 192 times in 2002, with the average number of participants being fifty-eight. In five collective petitions, the number of participants exceeded 200; and in another thirty collective petitions, the number exceeded 100 (*Xi'an Yearbook 2003*, 49).

45. *Zhengzhou Yearbook 1996*, 61.

46. Also see Kevin O'Brien, "Neither Transgressive nor Contained: Boundary-Spanning Contention in China," *Mobilizationl* 8, 1 (2003): 51–64.

47. Xi Chen, "Chinese Petitioners' Tactics and Their Efficacy," paper presented at the conference on "Grassroots Political Reform in Contemporary China," Harvard University, October 29–31, 2004.

48. The Chinese translation of this saying is "*xiaonao xiao jiejue, danao da jiejue, bunao bu jiejue*" (Dong Qingmin, "Renmin neibu tufaxing qunti maodun de tedian jiqi chuli yuanze" [The characteristics of people's internal conflicts and the principles of conflict resolution], *Lilunqianyan* [Theoretical frontiers]13 [1999]: 7–9).

49. The Research Group of the Association of Administration Studies, *Zhong-guo zhuanxing qi quntixing tufa shijian duice yanjiu* (Research on collective incidents in China during the transitional period) (Beijing: Xueyuan chubanshe, 2003), 59.

50. According to the statistics I collected for thirteen provinces, that proportion was 77.4 percent in 2002, and it reached 90 percent in two provinces (i.e., Henan and Jilin). See the 2003 yearbooks of Jilin, Henan, Inner Mongolia, Anhui, Tianjin, Jiangxi, Ningxia, Jiangsu, Shanxi, Zhejiang, Sichuan, Yunnan, and Guangxi.

51. Chang Kai, "Lun zhongguo de bagongquan lifa" (On the legislation of the rights of strikes in China). Retrieved on April 16, 2005, from: www.labournet.com.cn/lilun/fileview.asp?title.

52. Dingxin Zhao, *The Power of Tiananmen: State–Society Relations and the 1989 Beijing Student Movement* (Chicago: University of Chicago Press, 2001), chapter 8; Yongshun Cai, *State and Laid-Off Workers in Reform China: The Silence and Collective Action of the Retrenched* (London: Routledge, 2005), chapter 7.

53. Samuel Popkin, "Public Choice and Peasant Organization," in Robert H. Bates, ed., *Toward a Political Economy of Development* (Berkeley: University of California Press, 1988): 245–271.

54. Joseph Schumpeter, *Capitalism, Socialism and Democracy* (New York: Harper, 1950), 270.

55. Cai, *State and Laid-Off Workers in Reform China*, chapter 6; Kevin O'Brien and Lianjinag Li, "Popular Contention and Its Impact in Rural China," *Comparative Political Studies* 38, 3 (2005): 235–259.

56. Bernstein and Lu, *Taxation without Representation in Contemporary Rural China*; O'Brien and Li, *Rightful Resistance in Rural China*, Appendix A; for a review, see Kevin O'Brien, "Collective Action in the Chinese Countryside," *China Journal* 48 (2002): 139–154; Patricia Thornton, "Comrades and Collectives in Arms: Tax Resistance, Evasion, and Avoidance Strategies in Post-Mao China," in Peter Gries and Stabley Rosen, eds., *State and Society in 21st Century China* (London: Routledge, 2004), 87–104.

57. Cai, *State and Laid-Off Workers in Reform China*; Duan Xianju, Tan Jian, and Chen Peng, " 'Yingxiong' haishi 'diaomin' " ("Heroes" or "unlawful citizens"), *Banyue tan* (Biweekly forum) 2 (2000): 8–12.

58. Dennis Chong, *Collective Action and the Civil Rights Movement* (Chicago: University of Chicago Press, 1991).

59. Lianjiang Li and Kevin O'Brien, "Protest Leadership in the Countryside," *China Quarterly* 193 (2008): 1–23; Cai, *State and Laid-Off Workers in Reform China*, chapter 7; Elizabeth Perry and Li Xun, *Proletarian Power: Shanghai in the Cultural Revolution* (Boulder, CO: Westview Press, 1997).

60. Zhang Shengxian, "Puyang quntixing tufashijian de tezheng, chengyin ji duice yanjiu" (The characteristics and causes of collective action in Puyang and countermeasures). Retrieved on August 8, 2004, from www.puyang. gove.cn/ xfb/xf12.htm.

61. In the 1930s, for example, some peasants became rebellious leaders at the risk of their lives because of community pressure. The Office of Party History of Zhejiang Provincial Party Committee and the Political Office of the Zhejiang Military District, eds., *Zhejiang nongmin wuzhuang baodong* (Peasants' armed riots in Zhejiang) (Beijing: Dangdai zhongguo chubanshe, 1996), 97–103.

62. Ren Yanfang, *Minyuan* (People's complaints) (Bejing: Zhongguo wenlian chubanshe, 1999).

63. Yu Jianrong, "Nongmin youzuzhi kangzheng jiqi zhengzhi fengxian" (Peasants' organized resistance and political risks), *Zhanlue yu guanli* (Strategy and management) 3 (2003): 1–16.

64. Interview, China, 2002.

65. Duan et.al., "Yingxiong' haishi 'diaomin.'"

66. Yu, "Nongmin youzuzhi kangzheng jiqi zhengzhi fengxian."

67. Ying Xing, *Dahe yimin shangfang de gushi* (Story about the migrants' petitions in Dahe) (Beijing: Sanlian Shudian, 2001).

68. Marck Lichbach, "Rethinking Rationality and Rebellion: Theories of Collective Action and Problems of Collective Dissent," *Rationality and Society* 6, 1 (1994): 8–39.

69. Chong, *Collective Action and the Civil Rights Movement.*

70. The township party secretary was removed, and the township head and another official were given a party discipline (*Nongmin ribao*, March 22, 2001).

71. Author's collection.

72. Interview, China, 2004.

73. That day, some taxi drivers went to the city and provincial governments to lodge complaints, which attracted thousands of bystanders and paralyzed the traffic in some parts of the city. The city and provincial governments were shocked and promised to address taxi drivers' problems (*Fazhi ribao*, July 3, 2000).

74. The Editorial Group, *Goujian shehuizhuyi hexie shehui dacankao* (Reference on the building of a socialist harmonious society) (Beijing: Hongqi chubanshe, 2005), 102.

75. Sina.com. Retrieved on January 17, 2008, from: http://tech.sina.com.cn/i/ 2008-01-17/13231980212.shtml.

76. Radio Free Asia. Retrieved on June 3, 2007, from: www.rfa.org/mandarin/ shenrubaodao/2007/05/30/xiamen.

77. Edward Cody, "Text Messages Giving Voice to Chinese," *Washington Post*, June 28, 2007.

78. These pictures were retrieved on September 12, 2007, from: www.flickr
.com/search/?q=xiamen+px.

79. Frances Fox Piven and Richard A. Cloward, "Collective Protest: A Critique of Resource-Mobilization Theory," in Stanford Lyman, ed., *Social Movements: Critique, Concepts, Case-Studies* (New York: New York University Press, 1995), 137–167.

80. Yu, "Nongmin youzuzhi kangzheng jiqi zhengzhi fengxian."

81. Jean Oi, ""Realms of Freedom in Post-Mao China," in William Kirby, ed., *Realms of Freedom in Modern China* (Stanford, CA: Stanford University Press, 2003), 264–284.

82. Cai, "Power Structure and Regime Resilience."

83. Wang Yongqian, "Pojie qunzhong xinfang bada redian" (An analysis of the eight central issues of people's complaints), *Banyue Tan* (Biweekly forum) 21 (2003): 23–26.

Chapter 3

1. Kevin O'Brien and Lianjiang Li, *Rightful Resistance in Rural China* (New York: Cambridge University Press, 2006).

2. Ibid, chapter 2.

3. According to the police department, a collective action involving more than 500 participants is seen as a large-scale action, and an action involving more than 1,000 participants is seen as an especially large-scale action (Chen Jinsheng, *Quntixingshijian yanjiu baogao* [Research report on instances of collective action] [Beijing: Qunzhong chubanshe, 2004], 32).

4. Li Zhilun, "Congyan zhidang zhizheng, qieshi zhuahao fanfubai renwu de luoshi" (Strictly disciplining the party members and doing a good job of anticorruption), *Zhongguo jiancha* (China discipline inspection) 4 (2000): 5–7.

5. Yongshun Cai, "Irresponsible State: Local Cadres and Image-Building in China," *The Journal of Communist Studies and Transition Politics* 20, 4 (2004): 20–41. Some lower-level officials obtained promotion through bribery and could not be easily removed (Interview, China, 2004; also see Lianjiang Li, "Direct Township Elections," in Elizabeth Perry and Merle Goldman, eds., *Grassroots Politics in China* [Cambridge, MA: Harvard University Press, 2007], 97–116).

6. Yu Jintao, "Jidai gaishan de jiceng zhizheng nengli" (Grassroots governance needs to be strengthened), *Liaowang dongfang* (Oriental outlook) 39 (2004): 12–13.

7. The Central Discipline Inspection Commission, "Fanfu gongzuo baogao" (Report on anticorruption), *Zhongguo jiancha* (China discipline inspection) 5 (2000): 4–9.

8. Cai, "Irresponsible State."

9. Kevin O'Brien and Lianjiang Li, "Popular Contention and Its Impact in Rural China," *Comparative Political Studies* 38, 3 (2005): 235–259.

10. *The Yearbook of the People's Republic of China 2002*, 362.

11. See the 2003 yearbooks of Shanxi, Henan, Shaanxi, Jiangxi, Shandong, Guizhou, Hunan, Anhui, Xinjiang, Jiangsu, Liaoning, Zhejiang, Hubei, Fujian, Guangxi, Yunnan, Inner Mongolia, Tianjin, Chongqing, Sichuan, Ningxia, and Hainan.

12. Interview, China, 2004.

13. Of the 1,105 malfeasant public employees in Xinjiang in 2002, about 10 percent were fired, and 8 percent were punished through the courts. The party disciplined 2,404 members during this same period, a majority of whom (60 percent) were warned or seriously warned (*Xinjiang Yearbook 2003*, 46).

14. Lu Xingsheng, "Yu fubai yibashou de jiaoliang" (Fighting against corrupt top leaders), *Xinmin zhoukan* (Xinmin weekly) 35 (2003): 36–39.

15. In 2004, 170,850 state agents were disciplined, but only 2.9 percent were tried in courts (Li Zhilun, "Fanfu changlian biaoben jianzhi" [Fighting corruption by all means], *Ziguangge* [Ziguang attic] 9 [2005]: 4–6).

16. In Sichuan province, citizens reported 240,070 cases to discipline departments between 1994 and 1995. Only about 7.4 percent were investigated. Those cases concerning higher-level officials (that is, officials at the county level and above) totaled 29,825, or 12.5 percent of the total number of cases reported, and only 2.3 percent of these cases were investigated (*Sichuan Yearbook 1996*, 37).

17. O'Brien and Li, *Rightful Resistance in Rural China*, chapter 2.

18. Chen, *Quntixingshijian yanjiu*, 63–64.

19. Chen Lihua, "Quntixing shijian kaoyan zhongguo" (Instances of collective action challenge China), *Huanqiu* (Global issues) 15 (2005):15–18.

20. Chen, *Quntixingshijian yanjiu baogao*, 63–64.

21. For example, in Xi'an in 2002, 350 (55 percent) of the 634 collective petitions directed at the city authority were repeated petitions. On average, the number of participants in each of these collective petitions was thirty-three (*Xi'an Yearbook 2003*, 49).

22. Murray Scott Tanner, "China Rethinks Unrest," *Washington Quarterly* 27, 3 (2004): 137–156. In Fujian province between January 2001 and July 2001, six cases (1 percent) among the 597 instances of social unrest had more than 500 participants, while eight-one cases (13.6 percent) had more than 100 participants (Fu Yongkun, "Jiji yufang, tuoshan chuzhi quntixing shijian quanli weihu shehui wending" [Actively preventing and appropriately handling collective action to maintain social stability], *Gongan yanjiu* [Research on public security] 12 [2001]: 44–46).

23. He Zhuowen, "Zhengque renshi he chuli woguo xianjieduan de liyi guanxi maodun" (Properly handling the conflict in our country), *Kexue shehui zhuyi* (Scientific socialism) 2 (2005): 8–11.

24. Kevin O'Brien and Lianjiang Li, "Selective Policy Implementation in Rural China," *Comparative Politics* 31, 2 (1999): 167–186.

25. Local governments are assigned a quota of petitions that should not be exceeded. For example, the government of Qiqihaer city, Heilongjiang province (a city of more than 5 million people), was permitted to have 237 people annually present petitions to the provincial authority in the period 1988 through 1995, or five petitioners for every 100,000 citizens. The quota for the number of people presenting petitions to the central authority declined from 152 in 1988 to seventy-nine in 1995, or from 3 to 1.6 per 100,000 (*Qiqihaer Yearbook* [1989–1996]).

26. Yongshun Cai, "Managed Participation in China," *Political Science Quarterly* 119, 3 (2004): 425–451.

27. The Research Group of the Association of Administration Studies , *Zhongguo zhuanxingqi quntixing tufashijian duice yanjiu* (Study on the measures to deal with mass incidents in China during the transitional period) (Beijing: Xueyuan chubanshe, 2003), 2.

28. Ji Zhengfeng, "Yufang he chuzhi quntixing shijian de duice xuanze" (The choice of modes to deal with mass events), *Lilun yu shijian* (Theory and Practice) 16 (1999): 30–31.

29. Long Xianlei, "Jianchi 'yifazhiguo' fanglue tuoshan chuzhi quntixing shijian" (Sticking to rule by the law and appropriately handling instances of collective action), *Gongan yanjiu* (Research on public security) 12 (2001): 50–53.

30. Fan Fuming, "Quntixing lanche duandao shijian de tedian he yufang chuzhi duice" (Characteristics of collective action in blocking railways and some countermeasures), *Shanghai gongan gaodeng zhuanke xuexiao xuebao* (Journal of Shanghai Public Security Academy) 3 (2001): 30–34.

31. Tanner, "China Rethinks Unrest."

32. "Hunan sheng tuoshan chuli quntixing shijian" (Hunan province handles mass action properly), *Neican xuanbian* (Selected materials) 11 (2000): 20–22.

33. One case occurred in a village in Yujiang county in Jiangxi province in March 2001, wherein more than 600 police and riot police stormed the village, which had resisted tax collection. They opened fire on unarmed peasants, killing two and wounding at least eighteen. A more recent case took place in 2005 in Dongzhou, a village in Shanwei city in Guangdong province (Erik Eckholm, "Chinese Raid Defiant Village, Killing 2, amid Rural Unrest," *New York Times*, April 20, 2001; Howard French, "20 Reported Killed as Chinese Unrest Escalates," *New York Times*, December 9, 2005).

34. Yongshun Cai, "Power Structure and Regime Resilience: Contentious Politics in China," *British Journal of Political Science* 38, 3 (2008): 411–432.

35. Sidney Tarrow, *Power in Movement* (New York: Cambridge University Press, 1994), 95.

36. The Research Group, *Zhongguo xinfang xiezhen* (A record of people's petitions in China) (Beijing: Gongren chubanshe, 1998), 103.

37. Yongshun Cai, "Local Governments and the Suppression of Popular Resistance in China," *China Quarterly* 193 (2008): 24–42.

38. Yu Jianrong, "Zhongguo xinfang zhidu pipan" (Criticisms of the petition system in China), *Zhongguo gaige* (China reform) 2 (2005): 26–28.

39. In my collection, there was only one political crime (i.e., the worker protests in Liaoyang in Liaoning province in 2002) in which the two leaders were accused of subverting the government and were thus put in jail for four years and seven years, respectively.

40. Yongshun Cai, "Collective Ownership or Cadres' Ownership? The Nonagricultural Use of Farmland in China," *China Quarterly* 175 (2003): 662–680; Xiaolin Guo, "Land Expropriation and Rural Conflicts in China," *The China Quarterly* 166 (2001): 422–439; David Zweig, "The 'Externalities of Development': Can New Political Institutions Manage rural Conflict?" in Elizabeth Perry and Mark Selden, eds., *Chinese Society: Change, Conflict and Resistance* (London: Routledge, 2000): 120–142.

41. Wen Tiejun and Zhu Shouyin, "Zhengfu ziben yuanshi jilei yu tudi nongzhuangfei" (Government capital accumulation and the conversion of farmland for nonagricultural use), *Guanli shijie* (Management world) 5 (1996): 167–175.

42. For a discussion of land ownership in rural China, see Peter Ho, "Who Owns China's Land? Property Rights and Deliberate Institutional Ambiguity," *China Quarterly* 166 (2001): 394–421.

43. See, for example, Ren Yanfang, *Minyuan* (People's complaints) (Beijing: Zhongguo wenlian chubanshe, 1999).

44. *Guizhou dushi bao*, November 9, 2004.

45. *Wenhuibao*, May 10, 2007.

46. Other modes of compensation include reserving land for peasants or providing unemployment or pension insurance for landless peasants (Song Binwen, Fan Xiaogang, and Zhou Huiwen, "Shidi nongmin wenti shi shiguan shehui wending de dawenti" [The issue of peasants who have lost land affects social stability], *Diaoyan shijie* (Investigation and research forum] 1 [2004]: 22–24).

47. Ibid.

48. Guo, "Land Expropriation and Rural Conflicts in China"; David Zweig, "The 'Externalities of Development.'"

49. *Zhongguo qingnian bao*, July 3, 2000.

50. The Research Group of the National Land Management Bureau, "Jinnian lai woguo gengdi bianhua ji zhongqi fazhan qushi" (Recent changes in the use of farmland in our country and the development trend in the near future), *Zhongguo shehui kexue* (Social sciences in China) 1 (1998): 75–90.

51. Nationwide in 2002, the auctioned price per *mu* of land (1 *mu* = 0.067 hectares) was 357,000 yuan, but the amount of compensation paid to peasants was only 4 to 10 percent of that price (Qian Zhonghao and Qu Futian, "Guifan zhengfu tudi zhengyong xingwei, qieshi baozhang nongmin tudi quanyi" [Regulating governments land use to protect peasants' interests], *Zhongguo nongcun jingji* [China's rural economy] 12 [2004]: 4–9).

52. *Zhongguo jingji shibao*, September 2, 2003.

53. According to a survey of 2,940 peasant households that had lost most of their farmland in twenty-eight provinces in 2003, incomes of 46 percent of the households fell after they lost their land (Mao Feng, "Zhengfu gai wei shidi nongmin zuoxi shenme" [What the government does for peasants who have lost land], *Diaoyan shijie* [Investigation and research forum] 1 [2004]: 28–29).

54. Lin Wenyi, "Tudi zai shenyin" (The land is lamenting), *Fazhi yuekan* (Legal news monthly) 10 (1997): 4–7.

55. Wang Zhuo, "Chuangxin nongcun hezuo jingji de tudi chanquan zhidu" (Creating a new land property rights system for rural economic cooperation), *Nanfang nongcun* (The southern countryside) 2 (1994): 9–13.

56. Cai, "Collective Ownership or Cadres' Ownership?"

57. Samuel Popkin, "Public Choice and Peasant Organization," in Robert H. Bates, ed., *Toward a Political Economy of Development* (Berkeley: University of California Press, 1988): 245–271.

58. Approximately 8 percent of the letters were complaints about the economic development zones often set up by the government at the county level and above, and 23 percent targeted village authorities (Yu Jianrong, "Tudi chengwei zhongguo nongcun shouyao wenti" [Land use becomes the most important issue in rural China], *Liaowang dongfang* [Eastern outlook] 37 [2004]: 22–23).

59. Interviews with lawyers in China, 2005.

60. Yongshun Cai and Songcai Yang, "State Power and Unbalanced Legal Development in China," *Journal of Contemporary China* 14, 42 (2005): 117–134; Kevin O'Brien and Lianjiang Li, "Suing the Local State: Administrative Litigation in Rural China," *China Journal* 51 (2004): 53–74; Yuen Yuen Tang, "When Peasants Sue *En Masse*," *China: An International Journal* 3, 1 (2005): 24–49.

61. Shi Qinghua and Chen Kai, "Xian jieduan nongmin falu suzhi yu falu yishi fenxi" (An analysis of peasants' legal consciousness in the current period), *Zhongguo nongcun guancha* (Observations of rural China) 2 (2002): 67–75; Pierre Landry and Yanqi Tong, "Disputing the Authoritarian State in China," manu-

script, 2005; Cai, "Managed Participation in China"; Carl Minzner, "Xinfang: An Alternative to the Formal Chinese Judicial System," *Stanford Journal of International Law* 42, 1 (2006): 103–179.

62. Not surprisingly, petitions made by peasants from more developed provinces, such as Zhejiang, Jiangsu, Fujian, Shandong, and Guangdong, accounted for 41 percent of the total number of petitions (*Yunnan zhengxiebao*, November 9, 2004).

63. A survey of 632 peasants who made petitions in Beijing between June and July 2004 also showed that 73 percent of them complained about issues related to land (Yu, "Tudi chengwei zhongguo nongcun shouyao wenti").

64. See the website of the government of Inner Mongolia, retrieved on May 15, 2005, from www.nmg.gov.cn/xw1. ASP?id=4461.

65. Yu, "Tudi chengwei zhongguo nongcun shouyao wenti."

66. *South China Morning Post*, January 18, 2006.

67. Ye Jianping, Jiang Yan, Roy Prosterman, Feng Lei, Li Ping, and Zhu Keliang, "2005 nian zhongguo tudi shiyongquan diaocha yanjiu" (An investigation of rural land use in China in 2005), *Guanli shijie* (Management world) 7 (2006): 83–90.

68. *Zhongguo qingnian bao*, March 16, 2004.

69. *Xinjing bao*, April 16, 2006.

70. See Sina.com. Retrieved on July 13, 2007, from: http://news.sina.com.cn/c/2007-07-12/121513431900.shtml.

71. Lianjiang Li, "Political Trust in Rural China," *Modern China* 30, 2 (2004): 228–258.

72. According to a survey of fifty-six peasants who presented petitions in Beijing, 95 percent believed beforehand that "the central authorities sincerely want peasants to submit petitions to them." This percentage had declined to 39 percent seven days later, while the proportion reporting that "the central authorities are reluctant to see peasants presenting petitions" increased from 7 to 59 percent. In addition, the proportion reporting that "the central authorities may punish petitioners" increased from 2 to 61 percent (Yu, "Zhongguo xinfang zhidu pipan")

73. Wang Yongzhi and Chan Yanhui, "Nongmin gao 'yuzhuang' cheng dalu zhengzhi nanti" (Peasants' petitions become a difficult political issue in China), *Fenghuang zhoukan* (Phoenix weekly) 17 (2005): 31–34.

74. *Huaxi dushi bao*, June 14, 2003; Zhang Yaojie, "Shuilai chengdan zhongguo gongyehua de chengben?" (Who shoulders the burden of industrialization in China?). Retrieved on February 16, 2005, from www.dajun. com.cn/shidinm.htm.

75. Liao Yiwu, *Zhongguo shangfang cun* (The village of petitioners in China) (New York: Mingjing chunbanshe, 2005), 322.

76. Li Boguang, "Nongmin weiquan de zuihou yigen daocao" (The last straw of peasants' rights defense), *Yazhou zhoukan* (Asian weekly) 18 (2004): 47.

77. *Beijng yule xinbao*, January 17, 2005.

78. See Sohu. Retrieved on March 2, 2006, from: http://news.sohu.com/20040820/n221325586.shtml (accessed March 2, 2006).

79. Yu, "Tudi chengwei zhongguo nongcun shouyao wenti."

80. He Xiaopeng, "Zhengzhou '7.13' shangfang liuxue shijian" (The 7.13 petition event in Zhengzhou), *Zhongguo xinwen zhoukan* (Chinese newsweekly) 30 (2004): 46–47.

81. Cai, "Managed Participation in China."

82. See the website of Yinzi. Retrieved on April 2, 2006, from: www.yinzi.cn/sx/ShangLuo/news/2006/03/1910031421.html.

83. Cai, "Managed Participation in China."

84. Li Boguang, "Nongmin weiquan de zuihou yigen daochao."

85. Li Jing and Zheng Xianli, "Yimin shangfang lu" (Migrants' petitions), *Zhongguo gaige* (China reform) 2 (2003), 39–40.

86. Excluding another 2,500 yuan in settlement compensation.

87. Zhang Youren, "Hebei sheng Tangshan shi gongmin Zhang Youren xue shu" (The blood letter of Zhang Youren, a citizen of Tangshan city in Hebei province). Retrieved on May 12, 2007, from http://zhidao.baidu.com/question/1099172.html.

88. Zhang Wenjun and Wei Xiaoti, "Zhuixun 2000 wanyuan yimin zijin de xialuo" (Investigating the usage of the 20 million yuan earmarked for migrants relocation). Retrieved on November 11, 2006, from: www.audit.gov.cn/cysite/docpage/c167/ 200301/0123_167_3419.htm.

89. Yu Meisun, "Wanren lianshu yaoqiu bamian Tangshan shiwei shuji Zhang He de quanguo renda daibiao zige dongyi jishi" (A record of the 10,000 people's proposal to rescind Zhang He's membership in the National People's Congress). Retrieved on April 3, 2006, from: www.chineseunb.com/bbs/showthread.php?t=9671.

90. Ibid.

91. Zhang Yaojie, "Taolinkou shuiku huiqian nongmin de feiren shenghuo" (The hard life of the returnees in the Taolin reservoir area). Retrieved on May 22, 2005, from: http://news.boxun.com/news/gb/china/2004/03/200403210734.shtml.

92. Yu was jailed for three years between 1994 and 1997 for "releasing national secrets." He is now an activist in rights protection.

93. Yu Meisun, "Wanren lianshu."

94. Jack Goldstone and Charles Tilly, "Threat (and Opportunity): Popular Action and State Response in the Dynamices of Contentious Action," in Ronald

Aminzade, Jack Goldstone, Doug McAdam, Elizabeth Perry, William Sewell, Sidney Tarrow, and Charles Tilley, eds. *Silence and Voice in the Study of Contentious Politics* (New York: Cambridge University Press, 2001), 179–194.

Chapter 4

1. Anthony Downs, *Inside Bureaucracy* (Glenview, IL: Scott, Foresman and Company, 1967), 134–135.

2. Gordon Tullock, *The Politics of Bureaucracy* (Lanham, MD: University Press of America, 1987), chapters 15–19.

3. Sidney Tarrow, "States and Opportunities: The Political Structuring of Social Movements," in Doug McAdam, John McCarthy, and Mayer Zald, eds., *Comparative Perspectives on Social Movements* (New York: Cambridge University Press, 1996), 41–61.

4. Peter Eisinger, "The Conditions for Protest Behavior in American Cities," *American Political Science Review* 67, 1 (1973): 11–28; Frances Fox Piven and Richard A. Cloward, *Poor People's Movements: Why They Succeeded, How They Fail* (New York: Vintage, 1977), 28.

5. Yongshun Cai, "Irresponsible State: Local Cadres and Image-Building in China," *The Journal of Communist Studies and Transition Politics* 20, 4 (2004): 20–41.

6. Thomas Bernstein and Xiaobo Lu, *Taxation without Representation in Contemporary China* (New York: Cambridge University Press, 2003).

7. Maria Edin, "State Capacity and Local Agent Control in China: CCP Cadre Management from a Township Perspective," *China Quarterly* 173 (2003): 35–72; Susan Whiting, *Power and Wealth in Rural China: The Political Economy of Institutional Change* (New York: Cambridge University Press, 2001).

8. Also see Bernstein and Lu, *Taxation without Representation in Contemporary China.*

9. This is how the Chinese government calculates peasants' financial burdens (i.e., the ratio between the taxes and fees paid this year and the income per capita of the previous year).

10. Chen Guidi and Chun Tao, *Zhongguo nongmin diaocha* (Surveys of Chinese peasants) (Beijing: Renmin wenxue chubanshe, 2003): 129–130.

11. Bernstein and Lu, *Taxation without Representation in Contemporary China*, 68.

12. Liu Xiangdong and Yuan Zhiguo, "Nongmin fudan jianxiaqu le ma?" (Have peasants' financial burdens been reduced?), *Liaowang* (Perspective) 12 (1996): 16.

13. Ethan Michelson, "Causes and Consequences of Grievances in Rural China," manuscript, 2004.

14. For example, a survey of township cadres in Xinjiang found that about 70 percent reported that tax and fee collection was the most difficult job in rural areas (The Research Group of Township Organizations, "Xiangzhen dangzheng jigou he renyuan pengzhang jiqi yuanyin" [The reasons for the expansion of township organizations and employees], in the Ministry of Agriculture, ed., *Zhongguo nongcun yanjiu baogao: 1999 nian* [A research report on rural China: 1999] [Beiing: Zhongguo caizheng jingji chubanshe, 2000], 567–576).

15. Jean Oi and Zhao Shukai, "Fiscal Crisis in China's Townships: Causes and Consequences," in Elizabeth Perry and Merle Goldman, eds., *Grassroots Politics in China* (Cambridge, MA: Harvard University Press, 2007), 75–96.

16. Li Ming, "Toushi nongmin fudan" (An analysis of peasants' financial burdens). Retrieved on March 5, 2005, from www.ccrs.org.cn/newsgl/readnews .asp?NewsID=4445.

17. *Nanfang ribao*, May 9, 2003.

18. Jiang Guanhuo, "Cunji zhaiwu de xingcheng jiqi xiaohua" (The formation of villages' debts and solutions), *Zhongguo nongcun jingji* (China's rural economy) 4 (1999): 34–38.

19. Yang Ling, "Cunji caiwu" (Village financial affairs), *Diaoyan shijie* (Survey world) 10 (2001): 30–31.

20. *Guangzhou ribao*, January 2, 2006.

21. Unpublished survey by the Rural Development Research Center of the State Council, February 2003.

22. Patricia Thornton, "Comrades and Collectives in Arms: Tax Resistance, Evasion, and Avoidance Strategies in Post-Mao China," in Peter Gries and Stabley Rosen, eds., *State and Society in 21st Century China* (London: Routledge, 2004), 87–104; Bernstein and Lu, *Taxation without Representation in Contemporary China*, chapter 5; Yu Jianrong, "Nongmin youzuzhi kangzheng jiqi zhengzhi fengxian" (Peasants' organized resistance and political risks), *Zhanlue yu guanli* (Strategy and management) 3 (2003): 1–16.

23. *Chanye baodao*, November 22, 2001.

24. Bernstein and Lu, *Taxation without Representation in Contemporary China*, chapter 5.

25. Ibid, 139.

26. Kevin O'Brien and Lianjiang Li, *Rightful Resistance in Rural China* (New York: Cambridge University Press, 2006), chapter 2.

27. The state taxes included the agricultural tax, the special agricultural produce tax, the farmland use tax, and the contract tax (Bernstein and Lu, *Taxation without Representation in Contemporary Rural China*).

28. Li Maolan, *Zhongguo nongmin fudan wenti yanjiu* (Research on peasants' financial burdens in China) (Taiyuan: Shanxi jingji chubanshe, 1996), 82.

29. Leng Xiao, "Xiangguan nandang" (It is hard to be township cadres), *Nan-fengchuang* (Windows facing the south) 7 (2001): 2–5; Interview, China, 1997.

30. *Renmin ribao*, April 17, 1997.

31. He Xuefeng, *Xiangcun yanjiu de guoqing yishi* (Awareness of the country's particular situation in research on rural areas) (Wuhan: Hubei renmin chuban-she, 2004): 231–233.

32. Tom Tyler, "Why People Obey the Law," in Stewart Macaulay, Lawrence Friedman, and John Stookey, eds., *Law and Society: Readings on the Social Study of Law* (New York: W. W. Norton & Company, 1995), 474–498.

33. Cai Pengyi and Zhao Zuohuan, *Xianjieduan zhongguo nongmin fudan helixing yanjiu* (Research on contemporary Chinese peasants' financial burdens) (Beijing: Zhongguo nongye chubanshe, 2000), 78.

34. Zhang Aichun, "Yige xiangdangwei shuji yanzhong de dangqun guanxi" (Party-mass relations in the eyes of a township party secretary), *Nanfengchuang* (Windows facing the south) 11 (2001): 12–16.

35. *Renmin ribao*, April 1, 1997.

36. *Hunan ribao*, January 24, 2000.

37. *Zhongguo qingnian bao*, December 26, 2005.

38. Hence, provincial governments also passed regulations to prevent such incidents and punished those who violated the regulations (*Sichuan ribao*, October 17, 2002).

39. Fan Ping, "Nongmin jitixingdong de shehui qingjing: xuezhe de guan-cha baogao" (The social context of peasants' collective action: A report by a researcher). Retrieved on March 3, 2005, from: www.chinasociology. com/rzgd/ rzgd 041.htm.

40. He also said that when such incidents occur, the local government at the county or higher level tends to take measures to reduce the impact, hoping to prevent the news from reaching upper-upper authorities (Ibid.).

41. Zhou Wenshui, "Cong 'Sanhu shijian' kan ganbu zhucun" (Examining the role of cadres sent to villages with the Sanhu case), *Shidaichao* (Mainstream of the current times) 8 (2002): 12–15.

42. Liu Yue, "Xianxiang ganbu dui zhengce de lijie" (County and township cadres' understanding of government polices). Retrieved on March 1, 2006, from: www.world-china.org/07/0705071903 htm.

43. Chen and Chun, *Zhongguo nongmin diaocha*, 82–120.

44. Wu Yi, "Queshi zhili ziyuan de xiangcun quanwei yu shuifei zhengshou zhong de ganqun boyi" (The township and village authority and cadre–peasant interaction in tax and fee collection), paper presented at the "International Symposium on Political Science and China in Transition," Renmin University of China, July 15–16, 2002.

45. Yang Tongzhi, Zhang Hualin, and Yang Lin, "Dangqian cunji caiwu guanli zhong de zhuyao wenti jiqi duice" (Problems with the management of village financial affairs and countermeasures), *Zhongguo nongcun jingji* (China's rural economy) 8 (2000): 54–57.

46. The Joint Investigation Group, "Guanyu dangqian Henan nongcun shehui wending de diaocha yu jianyi" (An investigation of rural stability in Henan and some suggestions), *Zhongguo nongcun jingji* (China's rural economy) 12 (1998): 67–71.

47. Yi Nan, Ming Guang, and Guo Qin, "Cun ganbu jingji weiji qingkuang de diaocha yu sikao" (An investigation of village cadres' law violations in economic activities), *Zhongguo jijian* (China discipline inspection) 6 (1997): 29–30.

48. *Shekexinxi*, July 13, 1998.

49. *Fazhi ribao*, February 5, 2000.

50. Yi, Ming, and Guo, "Cun ganbu jingji weiji qingkuang de diaocha yu sikao."

51. *Dazhong ribao*, August 29, 2000.

52. The Joint Investigation Group, "Guanyu dangqian henan nongcun shehui wending de diaocha yu jianyi."

53. Guo Zhenglin, "Dangdai zhongguo nongmin de jiti weiquan xingdong" (The collective action of contemporary Chinese peasants in protecting their rights), *Xianggang shehui kexue xuebao* (Journal of Hong Kong Social Sciences) 19 (2001): 115–133.

54. Thornton, "Comrades and Collectives in Arms."

55. Xu Zhongdong, "Guanyu zhengshou nongyeshui de lingyifen diaocha baogao" (An investigation of the collection of the agricultural tax). Retrieved on April 6, 2004, from: http://news.163.com/40702/6/0q92njhk 00011211.html.

56. Lianjiang Li and Kevin O'Brien, "Villagers and Popular Resistance in Contemporary China," *Modern China* 22, 1 (1996): 28–61.

57. Wu, "Queshi zhili ziyuan de xiangcun quanwei yu shuifei zhengshou zhong de ganqun boyi."

58. Village cadres might require those who refused to pay to attend "legal education class" until they agreed to pay (Meng Liang, "Henan nongmin zifei diaocha zhenxiang" [The truth about the peasant's self-financed investigation in Henan], *Zhongguo gaige* [China reform] 8 [2004]: 30–31).

59. Interview, China, 2001.

60. This village is located in an inland province. The data were collected through my interviews conducted in 2003.

61. Also see Yi, Ming, and Guo, "Cun ganbu jingji weiji qingkuang de diaocha yu sikao."

62. Li Yelin, "Kangliang Kangshui" (Resisting turning in grains and paying taxes), *Minqing yu xinfang* (People's situation and petitions) 1 (2002): 36–38.

63. See the website of Chongqing agricultural information. Retrieved on December 10, 2004, from: www.cqagri.gov.cn.

64. Hong Xiaojing, "Heidong" (Black hole), *Diaoyan shijie* (Survey world) 3 (2005): 41–43.

65. Shi Po, "'Shuishou dilei' tuxian nongcu liyi chongtu" (The mine of tax collection reflects interest conflict in rural areas), *Zhongguo gaige* (China reform) 11 (2004): 41–42.

66. Hong, "Heidong."

67. Craig Jenkins and Charles Perrow, "Insurgency of the Powerless: Farm Workers' Insurgency, 1946–1972," *American Sociological Review* 42, 2 (1977): 249–26.

68. Interviews, China, 2003, 2004.

Chapter 5

1. See, for example, Jeff Goodwin and James Jasper, "Caught in a Winding, Snarling Vine: The Structural Bias of Political Process Theory," *Sociological Forum* 14, 1 (1999): 27–54.

2. Charles Kurzman, "Structural Opportunity and Perceived Opportunity in Social-Movement Theory: The Iranian Revolution of 1979," *American Sociological Review* 61, 1 (1996): 153–170.

3. Goodwin and Jasper, "Caught in a Winding, Snarling Vine," 53.

4. Lee Ann Banaszak, *Why Movements Succeed or Fail: Opportunity, Culture, and the Struggle for Woman Suffrage* (Princeton, NJ: Princeton University Press, 1996), 217.

5. Elizabeth Perry, *Challenging the Mandate of Heaven: Social Protest and State Power in China* (Armonk, NY: M. E. Sharpe, 2001).

6. Banaszak, *Why Movements Succeed or Fail*, 222.

7. Kevin O'Brien and Lianjiang Li, "Popular Contention and Its Impact in Rural China," *Comparative Political Studies* 38, 3 (2005): 235–259.

8. Andrew Walder, *Communist Neo-Traditionalism* (Berkeley: University of California Press, 1986); Jean Oi, *State and Peasant in Contemporary China* (Berkeley: University of California Press, 1989); Lu Xin, Lu Xueyi, and Shan Tianlun, eds., *2001 zhongguo shehui xingshi fenxi yu yuce* (2001: An analysis of Chinese society and some predictions) (Beijing: Shehui kexue wenxian chubanshe, 2001), 31.

9. See, among others, Bert Klandermans and Dirk Oegema, "Potentials, Networks, Motivations, and Barriers: Steps toward Participation in Social Movements," *American Sociological Review* 52, 4 (1987): 519–531; Gerald Marwell, Pamela Oliver, and Ralph Prahl, "Social Networks and Collective Action: A Theory of the Critical Mass. III," *American Journal of Sociology* 94, 3 (1998): 502–534.

10. Doug McAdam, *Freedom Summer* (New York: Oxford University Press, 1998).

11. Sidney Tarrow, *Power in Movement* (New York: Cambridge University Press, 1998), 23.

12. Yu Jianrong, "Zhongguo xinfang zhidu pipan" (Criticisms of the petition system in China), *Zhongguo gaige* (China reform) 2 (2005): 26–28.

13. See, for example, David Wank, *Commodifying Communism: Business, Trust, and Politics in a Chinese City* (New York: Cambridge University Press, 1999).

14. Yongnian Zheng and Guoguang Wu, "Information Technology, Public Space, and Collective Action in China," *Comparative Political Studies* 8, 5 (2005): 507–536.

15. Qiao Yunxia, Hu Lianli, and Wang Junjie, "Zhongguo xinwen yulun jiandu xianzhuang diaocha fenxi" (A survey and analysis of media exposure in China), *Xinwen yu chuanbo yanjiu* (News and communication studies) 4 (2002): 21–28.

16. Ben Dolven, "A Home Revolt at Ground Level," *Far Eastern Economic Review*, October 23, 2003, 35–37.

17. *Nanfang zhoumo*, May 29, 2003.

18. Yaping Wang and Alan Murie, "Commercial Housing Development in Urban China," *Urban Studies* 36, 9 (1999): 1475–1494; Min Zhou and John Logan, "Market Transition and the Commodification of Housing in Urban China," *International Journal of Urban and Regional Research* 20, 3 (1996): 400–421.

19. *Beijing qingnian bao*, March 15, 2003.

20. Yongshun Cai, "Civil Resistance and Rule of Law in China: The Case of Defending Homeowners' Rights," in Elizabeth Perry and Merle Goldman, eds., *Grassroots Politics in China* (Cambridge, MA: Harvard University Press, 2007), 174–195.

21. *Zhongguo jingying bao*, August 18, 2003.

22. One online survey of over 1,400 people found that approximately 93 percent reported that real estate companies violated construction plans because government officials backed these firms. See the website of Sohu. Retrieved on October 13, 2003, from: http://house.sohu.com/news/2003.8.11/54732.htmlwww.sohu.com.

23. Tianjian Shi, *Political Participation in Beijing* (Cambridge, MA: Harvard University Press, 1997).

24. Kevin O'Brien and Lianjiang Li, "Suing the Local State: Administrative Litigation in Rural China," *China Journal* 51 (2004): 53–74; Yuen Yuen Tang, "When Peasants Sue En Masse," *China: An International Journal* 3, 1 (2005): 24–49.

25. This case was first reported in a local newspaper in Guangzhou. See *Nanfang zhoumo*, March 29, 2003. Between July and August 2003, the author had

a chance to collect more data through interviews with the few major leaders of the collective action. These leaders not only disclosed the process of the event but also provided a set of materials they had kept, including a compact disc recording of their activities and the handbills they distributed. Unless otherwise indicated, the data used in this study were collected by the author through fieldwork.

26. Company L claimed that it had nothing to do with the new road, and the LG property management company was controlled by Company L. The residents' committee was supposed to be their self-governance organization, but in fact it functioned as a branch of the township government and was funded by the property management company (Interview, China, 2003).

27. Interview, China, 2003.

28. To have a legal basis, other homeowners were asked to sign an entrustment agreement that lists the fifteen members of the rights protection group (Interview, China, 2003).

29. A resident recorded the confrontation from his balcony. From the video footage, it was clear that the atmosphere at that time was tense.

30. Other problems, such as residents' disagreement over the hiring of lawyers, also made Hong feel the pressure of being a leader (*Nanfang zhoumo*, March 29, 2003).

31. Three years previously, a collective action occurred in LG due to a rise in the price of bus tickets. The resistance was partially successful, with the firm making some concessions. But the leaders of the resistance were threatened by the local government (Interview, China, 2003).

32. Interview, China, 2003.

33. In addition, they criticized the homeowners' committee for failing to advocate for them. In the video provided to us by the residents, it was shown that the residents protested in front of the office of the homeowners' committee.

34. It was *Southern Urban News*.

35. Interview, China, 2003.

36. The agreement contained the following provisions: (1) The real estate company would spend 2 million yuan on importing high-quality trees from Hainan province and plant them along the new road to beautify the landscape. (2) The company would place signs at the entrance to the road, prohibiting vehicles from sounding their horns. (3) The company would buy a watering car to reduce dust on the road. (4) The company would request the township government grant to it the right to manage the road and maintain its cleanliness. (5) The representatives of LG residents would report the company's sincerity in addressing this issue to reduce resentment among the residents of LG. (6) The representatives would persuade the residents along the road to remove the elegiac couplets, stop playing funeral music, and stop confrontational resistance (Interview, China, 2003).

37. After this agreement with Company X, Hong and other activists decided to sue Company L for violating the contract, which did not include plans for the new road (Interview, China, 2003).

38. I wish to thank Shi Fayong for his assistance in collecting the data for this case.

39. Residents in this community included blue-collar workers, white-collar workers, teachers, managers, business people, and government officials.

40. BG also enabled the X Street Office responsible for its management to win a "Model Street Office" award from the city government.

41. Benjamin Read, "Revitalizing the State's Urban 'Nerve Tips,'" *China Quarterly* 163 (2000): 806–820.

42. Fang is not the real name of this person.

43. There were about 1,300 households under the jurisdiction of this street affairs office.

44. This may be due to the influence of the traditional way of addressing one's problems through the work unit system rather than direct confrontation with the state authority. See Tianjian Shi, *Political Participation in Beijing* (Cambridge, MA: Harvard University Press, 1997).

45. Tan is not the real name of this person.

46. The strategy was to push the bureau to address their problems immediately because residents knew that higher-level authorities commonly dealt with complainants by delaying responses and undermining their momentum. Also see Ying Xing, *Dahe yimin shangfang de gushi* (Story about the migrants' petitions in Dahe) (Beijing; Sanlian shudian, 2001).

47. *Chinese Journalism Yearbook 2000*, 572.

48. According to those interviewed, fewer than 1,000 residents participated in the collective resistance over the years.

49. Benjamin Read, "Democratizing the Neighborhood? New Private Housing and Home-Owner Self-Organization in Urban China," *China Journal* 49 (2003): 31–60.

50. Dong Qingmin, "Renmin neibu tufaxing qunti maodun de tedian jiqi chuli yuanze," (The characteristics of sudden collective action and principles for resolution), *Lilun qianyan* (Theoretical frontiers) 13 (1999): 7–9.

51. The office contacted the work units of these residents, hoping that they could pressure them to refrain from making further petitions. This method did not work very well because some work units became more sympathetic to their employees when they knew the truth.

52. Jie Chen, *Popular Political Support in Urban China* (Stanford, CA: Stanford University Press, 2004); Lianjiang Li, "Political Trust in Rural China," *Modern China* 30, 2 (2004): 228–258.

53. Tan reported in an interview that he believed that a former activist betrayed him due to the persuasion of local cadres, who managed to build personal connections with this activist.

54. *Wenhuibao* is under the city party committee, and the street office was not in a position to stop its journalists from helping the residents.

55. The head of the office paid a high cost. Relatively young and with a good work record, he was in line for a promotion, but media disclosure of the illegal construction destroyed his public image.

56. Li Kuisheng, "Renmen chengwo 'fatanguaijie'" (I am called a "maverick" in the legal field), *Lushi yu fazhi* (Lawyers and law) 3 (1998): 29–30.

57. Jiang Xiao, "'Fankui'zhongde fazhi guannian" (Legal consciousness in the follow-up reports), *Xinwen Zhanxian* (News frontier) 7 (2000): 4–5.

58. Ni Ming, "'Jiaodian fangtan menwai de liangzhi gongguan duiwu," (Two lines outside the "Report on The Focal Issue," *Neibu canyue* (Reference) 8 (1999): 15–16.

59. Dennis Chong, *Collective Action and Civil Rights Movements* (Chicago: University of Chicago Press, 1991).

60. Elzabeth Perry and Li Xun, *Proletarian Power: Shanghai in the Cultural Revolution* (Boulder, CO: Westview Press, 1997); Yongshun Cai, *State and Laid-Off Workers in Reform China: The Silence and Collective Action of the Retrenched* (London: Routledge, 2006), chapter 7.

61. The term is from Robert Mnookin and Lewis Kornhauser, "Bargaining in the Shadow of the Law: The Case of Divorce," *Yale Law Journal* 88, 5 (1979): 950–997.

62. Kevin O'Brien, "Neither Transgressive nor Contained: Boundary-Spanning Contention in China," *Mobilization* 8, 1 (2003): 51–64.

63. Based on our collection, more than thirty reports on the BG case were published or broadcast by the local media.

64. Sidney Tarrow, *Power in Movement* (New York: Cambridge University Press, 1994), 18.

65. David Kowalewski and Paul Schumaker, "Protest Outcomes in the Soviet Union," *Sociological Quarterly* 22, 1 (1981): 57–68.

Chapter 6

1. He Zhuowen, "Zhengque renshi he chuli woguo xianjieduan de liyi guanxi maodun" (Properly handling the conflict in our country), *Kexue shehui zhuyi* (Scientific socialism) 2 (2005): 8–11.

2. Frances Fox Piven and Richard A. Cloward, *Regulating the Poor: The Functions of Public Welfare* (New York: Vintage Books, 1993), 456.

3. Sidney Tarrow, *Power in Movement* (New York: Cambridge University Press, 1998), 108.

4. Charles Tilly, *From Mobilization to Revolution* (Reading, MA: Addison Wesley, 1978), 183.

5. Steven Barkan, "Legal Control of the Southern Civil Rights Movement," *American Sociological Review* 49, 4 (1984): 552–565.

6. David Kowalewski and Paul Schumaker, "Protest Outcomes in the Soviet Union," *Sociological Quarterly* 22, 1 (1981): 57–68.

7. Wu Sha, "Dali jiaqiang quntixing tufa shijian chuzhi gongzuo" (Doing a good job of handling instances of collective action), *Gongan yanjiu* (Research on public security) 12 (2004): 48–53.

8. "Sheng jiansheting futingzhang Guo Chengkui de jianghua" (Talk by Guo Chengkui, a deputy director of the construction bureau of Guangdong). Retrieved on August 22, 2004, from: www.gxcic.net/nds/InfoShow .asp?InfoID=213.

9. Willaim Gamson, *The Strategy of Social Protest* (Belmont, CA: Wadsworth, 1990), 82.

10. *Nanfang dushi bao*, June 6, 2004.

11. *South China Morning Post*, January 4, 2005.

12. When the county authority wanted to punish a major peasant leader, the leader fled the village for two years (Interview, China, 2005).

13. *Jinghua shibao*, March 9, 2005.

14. Lian Xinqiao. "Miandui baiming jifang qunzhong" (Facing more than 100 petitioners), *Minqing yu xinfang* (People's situation and petitions) 5 (2001): 24–25.

15. Chen Guidi and Chun Tao, *Zhongguo nongmin diaocha* (Survey of Chinese Peasants) (Beijing: Renmin wenxue chubanshe, 2003), 82–120.

16. In several legal cases, the central government knew of the problems but refused to intervene because they involved provincial leaders (*Ershiyi shiji huanqiu baodao*, March 2, 2003).

17. Howard French, "20 Reported Killed as Chinese Unrest Escalates," *New York Times*, December 9, 2005.

18. *South China Morning Post*, December 12, 2005.

19. Tarrow, *Power in Movement*, 97.

20. *Yan'an ribao* , March 27, 2006.

21. *Nanfang ribao*, January 5, 2006.

22. Xie Li, "2000 nian Quanguo xing zheng fuyi anjian qingkuang fenxi" (An analysis of administrative reconsiderations in the country in 2000), *Xingzheng yu fazhi* (Administration and law) 6 (2001): 18–19.

23. In addition, because the top leaders (the party secretary and the magistrate, *shengguan ganbu*) in a county are directly under the management of the provincial authority, these leaders cannot be effectively disciplined unless the provincial authority intervenes (Interview, China, 2003).

24. Chen Jinsheng, *Quntixingshijian yanjiu baogao* (Research report on instances of collective action) (Beijing: Qunzhong chubanshe, 2004), 282.

25. *Zhongguo jingji shibao*, June 20, 2005.

26. *Qiaobao*, December 16, 2005.

27. Edward Cody, "For Chinese, Peasant Revolt Is Rare Victory," *Washington Post*, June 13, 2005.

28. *Jinhua ribao*, January 1, 2006.

29. *South China Morning Post*, March 3, 2006.

30. *Jinhua ribao*, December 5, 2001.

31. Zhu Yuchen, "Shaanbei youtian huchan xingdong" (A recent investigation of the oil well case in northern Shaanxi), *Zhongguo xinwen zhoukan* (Chinese newsweekly) 21 (2005): 23–27. More information about this case was retrieved on December 22, 2005 from the website of Folk China: www.folkchina.org/user1/62/archives/2005/1714.html.

32. For detailed reports, see the website of Hong Kong Pioneer Marxist Workers Movement. Retrieved on May 24, 2006, from: www.xinmiao.hk.st/trad/chinafuture1/chifu1149.htm.

33. Wang Rui, "Dui Xi'an shi quntixing zhian shijian guilu de sikao" (Some thoughts about the pattern of collective action in Xi'an), *Gongan daxue xuebao* (Journal of Chinese People's Public Security University) 5 (1999): 53–56.

34. John Chan, "Mass Protests in China Point to Sharp Social Tensions." Retrieved on June 12, 2004, from: www.socialistviewpoint.org/nov_04/nov_04_27.html.

35. Frances Fox Piven and Richard A. Cloward, *Poor People's Movements: Why They Succeed, How They Fail* (New York: Vintage Books, 1977).

36. See the website of Shandong province. Retrieved on March 4, 2005, from: http://news.sdinfo.net/72347865107660800/20040714/1289266.shtml.

37. Tang Jianguang, "Yinchuan chuzuche tingyun fengbo" (The incident of the taxi drivers' strike in Yinchuan), *Zhongguo xinwen zhoukan* (Chinese newsweekly) 30 (2004): 36–41.

38. Piven and Cloward, *Poor People's Movements*, xii.

39. Hanspeter Kriesi, "The Organizational Structure of New Social Movements in a Political Context," in Doug McAdam, John McCarthy, and Mayer Zald, eds., *Comparative Perspectives on Social Movements* (New York: Cambridge University Press, 1996), 152–184.

40. James Scott, "Everyday Forms of Resistance," in Forrest Colburn, ed., *Everyday Forms of Peasant Resistance* (Armonk, NY: M. E. Sharpe, 1989), 3–33.

41. Also see John Pomfret, "With Carrots and Sticks, China Quiets Protestors," *Washington Post*, March 22, 2002.

42. This case has been widely reported in the media outside China. But most reports failed to trace the process of the escalation of the confrontation. Unless otherwise indicated, all the materials about this case used in this book were collected by this author.

43. Ching Kwan Lee, "Is Labor a Political Force in China?" in Elizabeth Perry and Merle Goldman, eds., *Grassroots Politics in China* (Cambridge, MA: Harvard University Press, 2007), 228–252.

44. Also see Ching Kwan Lee, *Against the Law: Labor Protests in China's Rustbelt and Sunbelt* (Berkeley: University of California Press, 2007), 104–106.

45. For example, Yao Fuxin and Xiao Yunliang, were born in 1950 and 1946, respectively. They were the only two activists who were put in jail later.

46. This person used to be the city mayor and the city party secretary.

47. The reason was that the two major activists had contact with the so-called Chinese Democratic Party, although they never joined that party.

48. "Liaoyang tiehejin da'an chachu jishi" (The investigation of the case of the Ferroalloy Factory of Liaoyang), *Dangfeng yuebao* (Party discipline monthly) 5 (2003): 18–22.

49. The Research Group, *Zhongguo zhuanxingqi quntixing tufashijian duice yanjiu* (Research on collective incidents in China during the transitional period) (Beijing: Xueyuan chubanshe, 2003), 317–323.

50. In a case of a steel factory in Chongqing, the city government refused to make concessions despite the resistance of thousands of workers. Instead, the government used suppression. See the website of the Hong Kong Pioneer Marxist Workers Movement; retrieved on May 24, 2006, from: www.xinmiao.hk.st/trad/chinafuture1/chifu1149.htm.

51. The meeting was attended by the leaders from the land management bureau, the complaint office, the police department, the district government, and the provincial bureau of tourism (Chen Qingliang, "Yiqi yin zhengdi nongzhuanfei renyuan jitishangfang wenti de jiejue" [The solution of a dispute regarding peasants' being turned into urban residents]. Retrieved on November 6, 2006, from: http://finance.people.com.cn/GB /8215/72538/72539/5014493.html.

52. Frances Fox Piven and Richard A. Cloward, "Collective Protest: A Critique of Resource-Mobilization Theory," in Stanford Lyman, ed., *Social Movements: Critique, Concepts, Case-Studies* (New York: New York University Press, 1995), 137–167.

53. James DeNardo, *Power in Numbers: The Political Strategy of Protest and Rebellion* (Princeton, NJ: Princeton University Press, 1985), 35.

54. Ibid., 36.

55. This does not mean local officials have not tried to do this. In some of the cases I collected, local governments did try to hide the information but failed.

56. Interview, China, 1999.

57. Interview, China, 2000.

58. Charles Tilly, *From Mobilization to Revolution* (Reading, MA: Addison-Wesley, 1978), 111.

Chapter 7

1. Elizabeth Perry, "Rural Violence in Socialist China," *China Quarterly* 139 (1985): 704–713.

2. He Zhuowen, "Zhengque renshi he chuli woguo xianjieduan de liyi guanxi maodun" (Properly handling the conflict in our country), *Kexue shehui zhuyi* (Scientific socialism) 2 (2005): 8–11. In Guizhou province in 1999, seventeen people were killed in twenty-seven of 127 instances of disruptive action, including four police officers and government employees. A further 282 people, including eighty-one police officers and government officials, were wounded (Chen Jinsheng, *Quntixingshijian yanjiu baogao* [Research report on instances of collective action] [Beijing: Qunzhong chubanshe, 2004], 61).

3. Hugh Graham and Ted Gurr, "Editors' Introduction," in Hugh Graham and Ted Gurr, eds., *Violence in America: Historical and Comparative Perspective* (New York: Praeger, 1969), xxvii–xxxiv.

4. Willaim Gamson, *The Strategy of Social Protest* (Belmont, CA: Wadsworth, 1990).

5. Marco Giugni, "Was It Worth the Effort? The Outcomes and Consequences of Social Movements." *Annual Review of Sociology* 24 (1998): 371–393.

6. David Snyder and William Kelly, "Industrial Violence in Italy, 1878–1903," *American Journal of Sociology* 82, 1 (1976): 131–162.

7. Edward Shorter and Charles Tilly, *Strikes in France, 1830–1968* (New York: Cambridge University Press, 1974).

8. David Kowalewskl, and Paul Schumaker, "Protest Outcomes in the Soviet Union," *Sociological Quarterly* 22, 1 (1981): 57–68.

9. Myungsoon Shin, "Political Protest and Government Decision Making," *American Behavioral Scientist* 26, 3 (1983): 395–416.

10. Homer Steedly and John Foley, "The Success of Protest Groups: Multivariate Analysis," *Social Science Research* 8 (1979): 1–15.

11. This collection of 261 cases may not be representative. For example, many people who used peaceful collective petitions failed. But it is also true that peaceful action is more likely to be tolerated by the government. Of the twenty-six cases of tolerance in my collection, only two involved a small degree of violence.

12. Yongshun Cai, "China's Moderate Middle Class: The Case of Homeowners' Resistance," *Asian Survey* 45, 5 (2005): 777–799.

13. Ted Gurr, *Why Men Rebel* (Princeton, NJ: Princeton University Press, 1970); James Jasper, *The Art of Moral Protest: Culture, Biography, and Creativity in Social Movements* (Chicago: University of Chicago Press, 1997).

14. Charles Tilly, *From Mobilization to Revolution* (Reading, MA: Addison-Wesley. 1978), 183.

15. Sidney Tarrow, *Power in Movement* (New York: Cambridge University Press, 1998), 94.

16. Peter Eisinger, "The Conditions of Protest Behavior in American Cities," *American Political Science Review* 67, 1 (1973): 11–28.

17. Tarrow, *Power in Movement*, 104.

18. William Gamson, "The Success of the Unruly," in Doug McAdam and David Snow, eds., *Social Movements* (Los Angeles, CA.: Roxbury Publishing Company, 1997), 357–364.

19. Tarrow, *Power in Movement*, 96

20. Gamson, *The Strategy of Social Protest*, 81.

21. Jack Goldstone and Charles Tilly, "Threat (and Opportunity): Popular Action and State Response in the Dynamics of Contentious Action," in Ronald Aminzade, Jack Goldstone, Doug McAdam, Elizabeth Perry, William Sewell, Sidney Tarrow, and Charles Tilley, eds., *Silence and Voice in the Study of Contentious Politics* (New York: Cambridge University Press, 2001), 179–194; Christian Davenport, "Multi-Dimensional Threat Perception and State Repression: An Inquiry into Why States Apply Negative Sanctions," *American Journal of Political Science* 39, 3 (1995): 683–713.

22. Charles Tilly, "From Interactions to Outcomes in Social Movements," in Marco Giugni, Doug McAdam, and Charles Tilly, eds., *How Social Movements Matter* (Minneapolis: University of Minnesota Press, 1999), 253–270.

23. Doug McAdam and Ronnelle Paulsen, "Specifying the Relationship between Social Ties and Activism," *American Journal of Sociology* 99, 3 (1999): 640–667.

24. Frances Fox Piven and Richard A. Cloward, *Poor People's Movements* (New York: Vintage Books, 1977), xii.

25. Jeff Goodwin, James Jasper, and Francesca Polletta, "Why Emotions Matter," in Jeff Goodwin, James Jasper, and Francesca Polletta, eds., *Passionate Politics: Emotions and Social Movements* (Chicago: University of Chicago Press, 2001), 1–26.

26. Hu Baozhen, Xie Tianchang, Chen Maohua, and Li Yanjun, "Hexie shehui de jianshe he falu cuoshi" (The construction of a harmonious society and legal measures), *Zhongguo renmin gongan daxue xuebao* (Journal of Chinese People's Public Security University) 4 (2006): 105–111.

27. See Sina.com. Retrieved on December 12, 2001, from: http://dailynews .sina.com.cn/s/143438.html.

28. Also see Kevin O'Brien and Lianjiang Li, *Rightful Resistance in Rural China* (New York: Cambridge University Press, 2006), chapter 4.

29. Thirteen of the forty-four cases were not included in the 266 cases used because of incomplete information on the outcome. These large-scale protests reflect the complex causes that have generated popular resentment in China. Before 2004, all five large-scale protests in the countryside were exclusively staged by peasants to resist tax or fee collection. In urban areas, ten of the thirteen large-scale protests were staged by workers from state-owned enterprises, and the remaining three were staged by other urban residents. After 2004, the causes of large scale protests became more complex in both rural and urban areas. In the twelve large-scale protests in the rural areas between 2004 and 2007, peasants protested for land use, pollution, other people's injustice, and the family planning policy. In the fourteen protests in urban areas, the participants included workers, migrant workers, students, and residents.

30. Yongshun Cai, *State and Laid-Off Workers in Reform China: The Silence and Collective Action of the Retrenched* (London: Routledge, 2006); William Hurst, "Understanding Contentious Collective Action by Chinese Laid-Off Workers: The Importance of Regional Political Economy," *Studies in Comparative International Development* 39, 2 (2004): 94–120; William Hurst and Kevin O'Brien, "China's Contentious Pensioners," *China Quarterly* 170 (2002): 345–360; Ching Kwan Lee, "The 'Revenge of History': Collective Memories and Labor Protests in North-Eastern China," *Ethnography* 1, 2 (2000): 217–237.

31. He Zhuowen, "Zhengque renshi he chuli woguo xianjieduan de liyi guanxi maodun."

32. O'Brien and Li, *Rightful Resistance in Rural China*; Thomas Bernstein and Xiaobo Lu, *Taxation without Representation in Contemporary Rural China* (New York: Cambridge University Press, 2003); Xiaolin Guo, "Land Expropriation and Rural Conflicts in China," *China Quarterly* 166 (2001): 422–439.

33. Chen, *Quntixingshijian yanjiu baogao*, 376.

34. Cai, *State and Laid-Off Workers in Reform China*.

35. Lee, "The 'Revenge of History.'"

36. Wu Chenguang, "Fangbao jingcha: saohei jianbing" (Riot police: The vanguard of crushing crime), *Zhongguo xinwen zhoukan* (Chinese newsweekly) 7 (2001): 3–6.

37. *Chinese Statistical Yearbook 2001*, 473.

38. *Pingdingshan ribao*, January 2, 2002.

39. Doug McAdam, "Tactical Innovation and Pace of Insurgency," *American Sociological Review* 48, 6 (1983): 735–754; Karen Beckwith, "Hinges in Collective Action: Strategic Innovation in Pittson Coal Strike," *Mobilization* 5, 2 (2000): 179–199.

40. Su Quanshui, Shen Xiaochun, Yang Tie, Peng Wenjin, and Fan Wen, "Guangxi weihu shehui wending jizhi yanjiu" (Research on the Mechanisms of Maintaining Social Stability in Guangxi." Retrieved on August 15, 2004, from: www.gx-info.gov.cn/chenguo/2003-10.asp.

41. *Zhejiang xinsheng bao*, July 24, 2005.

42. Richard Felson and James Tedeschi, "A Social Interactionist Approach to Violence: Cross-Cultural Applications," in Barry Ruback and Neil Alan Weiner, eds., *Interpersonal Violent Behaviors: Social and Cultural Aspects* (New York: Springer Publishing Company, 1995), 153–170.

43. Fan Ping, "Nongmin jitixingdong de shehui qingjing: xuezhe de guan-cha baogao" (The social context of peasants' collective action: A report by a researcher). Retrieved on March 3, 2005, from: www.chinasociology.com/rzgd/rzgd041.htm.

44. When workers targeted local governments, protesting for salaries or pensions, they sought assistance from local governments. But local governments did not encroach on workers' interests directly. In recent years, the governments' certain policies regarding privatization might anger workers, but it is not common for the governments to use force to deal with workers (Cai, *State and Laid-Off Workers in Reform China*; Feng Chen, "Industrial Restructuring and Workers' Resistance in China," *Modern China* 29, 2 [2003]: 237–262).

45. Du Jingdong, "Yifa tuoshan chuzhi quntixing shijian, quanli weihu chengshihua jincheng zhong de shehui wending" (Dealing with mass incidents in light of the law to maintain social stability in urbanization), *Gongan yanjiu* (Research on public security) 12 (2004): 54–59.

46. Dai Gang, "Hongjiang quntixing shijian chuzhi yinfa de sikao" (Some thoughts about the settlement of the Hongjiang incident), *Gongan yanjiu* (Research on public security) 7 (2001): 65–68.

47. *Chutian dushi bao*, February 25, 2006.

48. Dali Yang, "Economic Transformation and Its Political Discontents in China: Authoritarianism, Unequal Growth, and the Dilemmas of Political Development," *Annual Review of Political Science* 9 (2006): 143–164.

49. James Jasper, *The Art of Moral Protest: Culture, Biography, and Creativity in Social Movements* (Chicago: University of Chicago Press, 1997).

50. Marsha Vanderford, "Vilification and Social Movements: A Case Study of Pro-Life and Pro-Choice Rhetoric," *Quarterly Journal of Speech* 75, 2 (1989): 166–182.

51. *Nanfang dushi bao*, July 2, 2005.

52. *Chongqing chenbao*, October 20, 2004.

53. Huang Huo, Duan Bo, and Zhang Xianguo, "Bugai you de 'chouguan' xintai" (Chinese entrepreneurs hate government officials), *Liaowang* (Perspective) 4 (2007): 12–13.

54. Zhong Yuming and Guo Bensheng, "Shehui maodun xinjinghao" (A new tendency of social conflicts), *Liaowang* (Perspective) 42 (2006): 10–13.

55. Luo Gan, "Zhengfa jiguan zai goujian hexie shehui zhong danfu zhongda lishi shiming he zhengzhi zeren" (Local political-legal departments take the responsibilities of achieving a harmonious society), *Qiushi* 3 (2007): 5–12.

56. Zhong and Guo, "Shehui maodun xinjinghao."

57. Ted Gurr, "A Causal Model of Civil Strife: A Comparative Analysis Using New Indices," *American Political Science Review* 62, 4 (1968): 1104–1124.

58. Gamson, *The Strategy of Social Protest*, 72.

59. Tarrow, *Power in Movement*, 95.

60. Donatella della Porta, *Social Movements, Political Violence and the State* (New York: Cambridge University Press, 1995), 211.

61. Ibid., 10.

62. Jasper, *The Art of Moral Protest*, 234.

63. Colin Barker, "Fear, Laughter, and Collective Power: The Making of Solidarity at the Lenin Shipyard in Gdnask, Poland, August 1980," in Goodwin, Jasper, and Polletta, eds., *Passionate Politics*, 175–194.

Chapter 8

1. Kevin O'Brien and Lianjiang Li, "Selective Policy Implementation in Rural China," *Comparative Politics* 31, 2 (1999): 167–186.

2. Marco Giugni, "Was It Worth the Effort? The Outcomes and Consequences of Social Movements," *Annual Review of Sociology* 24 (1998): 371–393; Donatella Della Porta and Mario Diani, *Social Movements: An Introduction* (Oxford, U.K.: Blackwell, 1999), chapter 9.

3. Paul Burstein, "Social Movements and Public Policy," in Marco Giugni, Doug McAdam, and Charles Tilly, eds., *How Social Movements Matter* (Minneapolis: University of Minnesota Press, 1999), 3–21.

4. Frances Fox Piven and Richard A. Cloward, *Regulating the Poor: The Functions of Public Welfare* (New York: Vintage Books, 1993), 456–466; Robert Albritton, "Social Amelioration through Mass Insurgency? A Reexamination of the

Piven and Cloward Thesis," *American Political Science Review* 73, 4 (1979): 1003–1011; Richard Fording, "The Conditional Effect of Violence as a Political Tactic: Mass Insurgency, Welfare Generosity, and Electoral Context in the American States," *American Journal of Political Science* 41, 1 (1997): 1–29.

5. Kevin O'Brien and Lianjiang Li, "Popular Contention and Its Impact in Rural China," *Comparative Political Studies* 38, 3 (2005): 235–259.

6. Giugni, "Was It Worth the Effort?"; Lee Ann Banaszak, *Why Movements Succeed of Fail: Opportunity, Culture, and the Struggle for Woman Suffrage* (Princeton, NJ: Princeton University Press, 1996); Herbert Kitschelt, "Political Opportunity Structures and Political Protest: Antinuclear Movements in Four Democracies," *British Journal of Political Science* 16, 1 (1986): 57–85.

7. Stanley Lieberson, "Small N's and Big Conclusions: An Examination of the Reasoning in Comparative Studies Based on a Small Number of Cases," *Social Forces* 70, 2 (1991): 306–320.

8. Paul Burstein, Rachel Einwohner, and Jocelyn Hollander, "The Success of Political Movements: A Bargaining Perspective," in Craig Jenkins and Bert Klandermans, eds., *The Politics of Social Protest: Comparative Perspectives on States and Social Movements* (Minneapolis: University of Minnesota Press, 1995), 275–295.

9. Edwin Amenta and Michael Young, "Making an Impact: Conceptual and Methodological Implications of the Collective Goods Criterion," in Marco Giugni, Doug McAdam, and Charles Tilly, eds., *How Social Movements Matter* (Minneapolis: University of Minnesota Press), 22–41.

10. The term is used by Valerie Bunce and Dennish Chong in their unpublished paper "The Party's Over." Cited in Sidney Tarrow, *Power in Movement* (New York: Cambridge University Press, 1994), 93.

11. Craig Jenkins and Charles Perrow, "Insurgency of the Powerless: Farm Workers' Insurgency, 1946–1972," *American Sociological Review* 42, 2 (1977): 249–26.

12. Michael Lipsky, "Protest as Political Resource," *American Political Science Review* 62, 4 (1968): 1144–1158.

13. David Kowalewski and Paul Schumaker, "Protest Outcomes in the Soviet Union," *Sociological Quarterly* 22, 1 (1981): 57–68.

14. The National Statistical Bureau, *Datou shi* (A comprehensive perspective) (Beijing: Zhongguo fazhan chubanshe, 1998), 33.

15. The National Statistical Bureau, *Xinzhongguo wushiwu nian tongji ziliao huibian* (China Statistics: 1949–2004) (Beijing: Zhongguo tongji chubanshe, 2005), 48.

16. Dorothy Solinger, "Labor Market Reform and the Plight of the Laid-off Proletariat," *China Quarterly* 170 (2002): 304–326; Yongshun Cai, *State and*

Laid-Off Workers in Reform China: The Silence and Collective Action of the Re-trenched (London: Routledge, 2006), chapter 2.

17. *Chinese Labor Statistical Yearbook 1998*, 431–432.

18. Zhao Xiaojian, Hu Yifan, Huang Peijian, and Zhu Xiaochao, "Shiye zhiyou" (Worry over unemployment), *Caijing* (Finance) 18 (2002): 27–53.

19. *Chinese Labor Statistical Yearbook 2003*, 134; *Chinese Statistical Yearbook 2003*, 100. The labor force of Liaoning made up 3 percent of the total labor force in the country, but its retired workers accounted for about 10 percent of the country's total number of retired workers (Mo Daquan, *Gongzhi anquanwang* [Establishing a safety network] [Beijing: jingji kexue chubanshe, 1998], 57).

20. Chen Yongjie, "Dongbei jiben qingkuang diaocha baogao" (An investigation of the basic situation in the northeast). Retrieved on December 20, 2007, from: www.chinesetax.com.cn/caishuiwenku/hongguanjingji/quyujingji/200711/5051804.html.

21. Cai, *State and Laid-Off Workers in Reform China*; William Hurst, "Understanding Contentious Collective Action by Chinese Laid-Off Workers: The Importance of Regional Political Economy," *Studies in Comparative International Development* 39, 2 (2004): 94–120; Ching Kwan Lee, "From the Specter of Mao to the Spirit of the Law: Labor Insurgency in China," *Theory and Society* 31, 2 (2002): 189–228; William Hurst and Kevin O'Brien, "China's Contentious Pensioners," *China Quarterly* 170 (2002): 345–360; Feng Chen, "Subsistence Crises, Managerial Corruption and Labor Protests in China," *China Journal* 44 (2000): 41–63.

22. Yang Yiyong, *Gongping yu xiaolu* (Equality and efficiency) (Beijing: Jiri zhongguo chubanshe, 1998), 78.

23. He Zhuowen, "Zhengque renshi he chuli woguo xianjieduan de liyi guanxi maodun" (Properly handling the conflict in our country), *Kexue shehui zhuyi* (Scientific socialism) 2 (2005): 8–11.

24. In Jiangxi, an agricultural province, 985 instances of social unrest occurred between 1998 and 1999. Collective actions by workers or retired workers accounted for 52 percent (or 507), and those taken by peasants constituted 22 percent (or 217) (Chen Jinsheng, *Quntixingshijian yanjiu baogao* [Research report on instances of collective action] [Beijing: Qunzhong chubanshe, 2004], 60).

25. In Jilin province, there were 12,200 collective petitions in 1998. While not all collective petitions were presented by workers, the yearbooks indicate that workers' failure to receive salaries, subsistence allowances, pensions, or reimbursement of medical expenditures were the most important reasons for the large number of collective petitions in the province (*Jilin Yearbook 1999*, 116).

26. See the 1999 yearbooks of Jilin, Inner Mongolia, Zhejiang, Henan, Jiangsu, Hebei, Shanxi, Anhui, and Sichuan.

27. *Heilongjiang Yearbook 2000*, 93; *Jilin Yearbook 2000*, 47.

28. *Heilongjiang gongren bao*, December 17, 2003.

29. Qiu Zeqi, "Meiyou baofadian de weiji" (Crises without identifiable triggers), *Yunnan daxue xuebao* (Journal of Yunnan University) 5 (2003): 21–26.

30. *Renmin ribao*, August 13, 1999.

31. In Jilin province in March 1998, Zhu held a meeting on reemployment work that was attended by the major local leaders of the three provinces and Inner Mongolia. He pointed out that laid-off workers' livelihood and reemployment "affected not only the success of the reform of state enterprises but also social stability and the consolidation of the socialist regime" (*Renmin ribao*, March 28, 1998).

32. *Renmin ribao*, May 28, 2000.

33. For the various policies, see the Ministry of Labor and Social Security and Document Research Office of the Central Party Committee, eds., *Xinshiqi laodong he shehui baozhang zhongyao wenxian xuanbian* (Selected important documents regarding labor and social security) (Beijing: Zhongguo laodong shenhui baozhang chubanshe, 2002).

34. Cai, *State and Laid-Off Workers in Reform China*, chapter 2.

35. Ibid., chapter 3.

36. In 1995, the number of employees in the state sector (not all of them employees of SOEs) was 109 million, whereas there were 31 million employees in the urban collective sector (most of them were in collective firms) (*Zhongguo gongye jingji tongji nianjian 1998* [China Industrial Statistical Yearbook 1998], 106–109).

37. *Liaoning Statistical Yearbook* (1999–2005).

38. Solinger, "Labor Market Reform and the Plight of the Laid-off Proletariat"; Cai, *State and Laid-Off Workers in Reform China*, chapter 2.

39. The policy was not changed until 2005 (*Zhongguo shuiwu bao*, February 14, 2006).

40. This compensation method was reiterated in a directive issued by the Ministry of Labor and Social Security in September 2003. In certain places, the practice of terminating labor relations with severance pay was put into place much earlier: In Liaoning province, it started in 2001 with the support of the central government (*Ershiyi shiji jingji baodao*, May 12, 2004).

41. *Chinese Labor Statistical Yearbook 1999*, 441–442.

42. *Chinese Labor Statistical Yearbook 2000*, 411.

43. In Fushun between 1998 and 2002, the average monthly allowance received by a worker laid off from a collective firm never exceeded 16 yuan per month (*Fushun Statistical Yearbook 2001*, 63).

44. To be sure, there is also variation across SOEs of different sizes (Cai, *State and Laid-Off Workers in Reform China*, chapters 6 and 7).

45. In the late 1970s and early 1980s, the government needed to provide jobs for 17 million young people, some of whom had previously been sent to work in the countryside. Establishing urban collective enterprises became an important way of creating employment. From 1978 to 1984, the number of employees in the urban collective sector increased by 11.2 million (The National Statistical Bureau, *Xinzhongguo wushiwu nian tongji ziliao huibian* [China Statistics: 1949–2004] [Beijing: Zhongguo tongji chubanshe, 2005], 8).

46. Simon Appleton, John Knight, Lina Song, and Qingjie Xia, "Labor Retrenchment in China: Determinants and Consequences," in Li Shi and Hiroshi Sato, eds., *Unemployment, Inequality and Poverty in Urban China* (London: Routledge, 2006), 19–42.

47. The National Statistical Bureau, *Da toushi*, 34–35.

48. *The Statistical Yearbook of Chinese Industrial Economy 1998*, 106–109.

49. Yongshun Cai, "Relaxing the Constraints from Above: The politics of privatizing public enterprises in reform China," *Asian Journal of Political Science* 10, 2 (2002): 94–121.

50. Cai, *State and Laid-Off Workers in Reform China*, chapter 7.

51. Murray Scott Tanner, "China Rethinks Unrest," *Washington Quarterly* 27, 3 (2004): 137–156.

52. For the description of data collection, see Cai, *State and Laid-Off Workers in Reform China*, Appendix.

53. Lu Xin, Lu Xueyi, and Li Peilin, eds., *2002 Zhongguo shehui xingshi fenxi yu yuce* (An analysis of the social situation in China and some predictions in 2002) (Beijing: Shehui kexue wenxian chubanshe, 2002).

54. Solinger, "Labor Market Reform and the Plight of the Laid-off Proletariat."

55. The Research Group of Laid-Off Workers' Situation, "Chengzhen qiye xiagang zhigong zaijiuye zhuangkuang diaocha: Kunjing yu chulu" (A investigation of laid-off workers' reemployment: Plight and solutions), *Shehuixue yanjiu* (Sociological Research) 6 (1997a): 24–34; The Research group, "Xiagang zhigong de shenghuo zhuangkuang jiqi shehui zhichi" (The situation of laid-off workers and their social support), *Xiaofei jingji* (Economy of Consumption) 1 (1997b): 47–51.

56. The All China Federation of Trade Unions, "Guanyu guoyou qiye xiagang zhigong jiben shenghuo baozhang yu zaijiuye gongzuo de diaocha yu jianyi" (An investigation of the living allowances of laid off workers from SOEs and some suggestions), *Shizhang cankao* (References for mayors) 4 (2000): 32–38.

57. In April 2001, when three mines declared bankruptcy in Fuxin, 4,904 workers made 196 petitions to state authorities at different levels (*Fuxin Yearbook 2002*, 108).

58. When four mines with a combined total of 13,000 employees declared bankruptcy in Jilin in 2001, they owed 553 million yuan. On average, each

worker was owed 7,070 yuan in salary and 5,750 yuan as severance pay (*Jilin Yearbook 2002*, 80).

59. The central government allocated 16.3 billion yuan to the three northeastern provinces in 2004 for the closure or bankruptcy of more than sixty enterprises, accounting for 23.3 percent of the total bankruptcy funds it disbursed in the country (*Renmin ribao*, January 16, 2005).

60. In 2001, half a million laid-off workers from SOEs were terminated from their labor relations in Liaoning. The central government provided 36.4 percent of their severance pay. In this province, 1.76 million workers from SOEs were terminated from their labor relations and paid an average of 8,700 yuan per capita in severance. The state shouldered much of the financial responsibility for this reform measure (*Ershiyi shiji jingji baodao*, May 12, 2004).

61. In Fushun city, the gap increased from 4.3 times in 1998 to 10 times larger in 2002 (*Fushun Statistical Yearbook* [1999–2003]).

62. Yongshun Cai, "Civil Resistance and Rule of Law in China: the Case of Defending Home Owners' Rights," in Elizabeth Perry and Merle Goldman, eds., *Grassroots Politics in China* (Cambridge, MA: Harvard University Press, 2007), 174–195.

63. *Fazhi ribao*, January 10, 2001.

64. For example, in Harbin, the capital city of Heilongjiang, problems arising from housing demolition were once the dominant issue of citizens' petitions. Such petitions to city authorities accounted for 40 percent of the total petitions in 1994, 61 percent in 1995, and 50 percent in 1996 (*Harbin Yearbook 1995*, p. 83; *Harbin Yearbook 1996*, p. 93; *Harbin Yearbook 1997*, p. 64).

65. *Zhongguo jingji shibao*, October 22, 2003.

66. *Nanfang zhoumo*, September 4, 2003.

67. Cai, "Civil Resistance and Rule of Law in China."

68. Changchun Party School, "Shehui zhuanxing shiqi 'quntixingtufashijian' wentiyanjiu" (Research on collective action in the transitional period). Retrieved on July 18, 2004, from: www.jlpopss.gov.cn/news/template.asp?newsid=551.

69. The newspapers included seven published by the *Nanjing Ribao* Group, *Zhongguo jingji shibao* (Beijing), *Zhongguo xinwen zhoukan* (Beijing), and *Xinmin zhoukan* (Shanghai).

70. Benjamin Page and Robert Shapiro, "Effects of Public Opinion on Policy," *American Political Science Review* 77, 1 (1983): 175–190.

71. For a detailed discussion on this issue, see Cai, "Civil Resistance and Rule of Law in China."

72. A high-profile case that caught the attention of the whole country occurred in Chongqing. In that case, a household sustained their fight against the developer for about three years until 2007 (*Yangzi wanbao*, March 21, 2007).

73. Robert Bates, *Markets and States in Tropical Africa: The Political Basis of Agricultural Policies* (New York: Cambridge University Press, 1981).

74. Kevin O'Brien and Lianjiang Li, *Rightful Resistance in Rural China* (New York: Cambridge University Press, 2006), chapter 5.

75. *Renmin ribao*, April 1, 1997.

76. Thomas Bernstein and Xiaobo Lu, *Taxation without Representation in Contemporary China* (New York: Cambridge University Press, 2003), chapter 5.

77. Ethan Michelson, "'Peasants' Burdens' and State Response: Exploring State Concession to Popular Tax Resistance in Rural China," manuscript, 2005.

78. Zhu Rongji was responsible for economic affairs at that time, but he was not aware of local governments' self-initiated efforts to reform rural taxes. In 1998, the State Council issued a directive that forced local governments to stop the reform that had already been carried out in more than sixty counties in seven provinces (Chen Guidi and Chun Tao, *Zhongguo nongmin diaocha* [Survey of Chinese peasants] [Beijing: Renmin wenxue chubanshe, 2003], 343–344).

79. The National Statistical Bureau, *Xinzhongguo wushiwu nian tongji ziliao huibian* (China Statistics: 1949–2004) (Beijing: Zhongguo tongji chubanshe, 2005), 20.

80. Interview, China, 2006.

81. Chen and Chun, *Zhongguo nongmin diaocha*, 312–330.

82. Ray Yep, "Can 'Tax-for-Fee Reform' Reduce Rural Tension in China? The Process, Progress, and Limitations," *China Quarterly* 177 (2004): 42–70.

83. Chen and Chun, *Zhongguo nongmin diaocha*, 343–344.

84. Interview, China, 2006.

85. To be sure, peasant resistance declined perhaps in many places after the tax-for-fee reform. In 1997, Anhui province was sixth in terms of the number of people who made petitions to the central government, but its standing declined to below the twentieth position in 2001 (*Anhui Yearbook 2002*, 28; *Anhui Yearbook 2003*, 39).

86. For example, among the 319 households surveyed in Hunan province, 67 percent reported that the tax burden was still heavy after the fee-to-tax reform. While 23 percent reported that the relationship between cadres and peasants had improved after the reform, 76 percent stated that there was no change in relations (Unpublished survey by the Rural Development Research Center of the State Council, February 2003).

87. The National Statistical Bureau, *Xinzhongguo wushiwu nian tongji ziliao huibian*, 34.

88. *Renmin ribao*, February 24, 2005; Interview, China, 2006.

89. Karl-Dieter Opp and Wolfgang Ruehl, "Repression, Micromobilization and Political Protest," *Social Forces* 69, 2 (1990): 521–547.

90. O'Brien and Li, *Rightful Resistance in Rural China*, chapter 5.

91. *Zhongguo qingnian bao*, December 8, 2004.

92. Li Zhaoqing, "Zhongyang yan ni quxiao suoyou kaifaqu" (The central authority is considering dismantling all the economic development zones), *Fenghuang zhoukan* (Phoenix weekly) 22 (2004): 5–6.

93. Hu Zhanfen, "Hai'an zhengdi yiyun" (Problems with land acquisition in Haian), *Xinmin zhoukan* (Xinmin weekly) 26 (2004): 32–36.

94. *Guangming ribao*, June 26, 2000.

95. *Guotu ziyuan bao*, January 2, 1999.

96. This was a common way for local governments to set up economic development zones (*Beijing yule xinbao*, December 24, 2003).

97. Li, "Zhongyang yan ni quxiao suoyou kaifaqu."

98. The National People's Congress, "Guanyu jiancha tudi guanli fa shishi qingkuang de baogao" (Report on the implementation of land law). Retrieved on May 12, 2005, from: http://news3.xinhuanet.com/fortune/2004-06/24/content_1544860.htm.

99. "Shenhua tudi guanli zhidu" (Strengthening the farmland management system). Retrieved on December 15, 2004, from: www.agri.gov.cn/xxlb/t20041215_285957.htm.

100. The first three types of complaints were not indicated (*Guotu ziyuan bao*, January 19, 2004).

101. "Shenhua tudi guanli zhidu."

102. In 2003, as demanded by the central government, local governments paid peasants 8.7 billion yuan in land-use compensation, accounting for 59 percent of the total amount owed to peasants (*Nanfang zhoumo*, January 8, 2004).

103. See http://finance.sina.com.cn/g/20041224/22241249986.shtml (accessed May 20, 2005).

104. *Xinjing bao*, August 12, 2005.

105. *Jingji ribao*, September 6, 2006.

106. Between 2002 and 2006, 8,698 people were given party or administrative discipline, 3,094 of whom (or 35.6 percent) were punished in 2006. During this period of time, 1,221 people were tried in courts, 501 of whom (or 41 percent) were tried in 2006. See http://news.sohu.com/20070917/n252194693.shtml (accessed October 17, 2007).

107. Doug McAdam, *Political Process and the Development of Black Insurgency 1930–1970*, 2nd ed. (Chicago: University of Chicago Press, 1999), 44–47.

108. Cai, "Citizen Resistance and Rule of Law in China."

109. Annulla Linders, "Victory and Beyond: A Historical Comparative Analysis of the Outcomes of the Abortion Movements in Sweden and the United States," *Sociological Forum* 19, 3 (2004): 371–404.

Chapter 9

1. Marco Giugni, "Was It Worth the Effort? The Outcomes and Consequences of Social Movements," *Annual Review of Sociology* 24 (1998): 371–393.

2. Charles Tilly, "From Interactions to Outcomes in Social Movements," in Marco Giugni, Doug McAdam, and Charles Tilly, eds., *How Social Movements Matter* (Minneapolis: University of Minnesota Press, 1999), 253–270; Sidney Tarrow, "Social Movements in Contentious Politics: A Review Article," *American Political Science Review* 90, 4 (1996): 874–883.

3. The notable exception is the 1989 Tiananmen incident (Dingxin Zhao, *The Power of Tiananmen: State–Society Relations and the 1989 Beijing Student Movement* [Chicago: University of Chicago Press, 2001]).

4. Sidney Tarrow, *Power in Movement* (New York: Cambridge University Press, 1994), 162.

5. Frances Fox Piven and Richard A. Cloward, *Regulating the Poor: The Functions of Public Welfare* (New York: Vintage, 1993), 338.

6. Jack Goldstone and Charles Tilly, "Threat (and Opportunity): Popular Action and State Response in the Dynamics of Contentious Action," in Ronald Aminzade, Jack Goldstone, Doug McAdam, Elizabeth Perry, William Sewell, Sidney Tarrow, Charles Tilley, eds., *Silence and Voice in the Study of Contentious Politics*, 179–194 (New York: Cambridge University Press, 2001).

7. James Button, *Black Violence: Political Impact of the 1960s Riots* (Princeton, NJ: Princeton University Press, 1978).

8. Myungsoon Shin, "Political Protest and Government Decision Making," *American Behavioral Science* 26, 3 (1983): 395–393.

9. See, for example, Charles Kurzman, "Structural Opportunity and Perceived Opportunity in Social-Movement Theory: The Iranian Revolution of 1979," *American Sociological Review* 61, 1 (1996): 153–170; Doowon Suh, "How Do Political Opportunities Matter for Social Movements? Political Opportunity, Misframing, Pseudosuccess, and Pseudofailure," *Sociological Quarterly* 42, 3 (2001): 437–460.

10. Jeff Goodwin and James Jasper, "Caught in a Winding, Snarling Vine: The Structural Bias of Political Process Theory," *Sociological Forum* 14, 1 (1999): 27–54.

11. Kurzman, "Structural Opportunity and Perceived Opportunity in Social-Movement Theory"; Timur Kuran, "Now out of Never: The Element of Surprise in the East European Revolution of 1989," *World Politics* 44, 1 (1991): 7–48.

12. Kevin O'Brien and Lianjiang Li, *Rightful Resistance in Rural China* (New York: Cambridge University Press, 2006), chapter 2.

13. Maria Edin, "State Capacity and Local Agent Control in China: CCP Cadre Management from a Township Perspective," *China Quarterly* 173 (2003): 35–72.

14. At the county and township levels, it is common for the party secretary to sign a so-called responsibility contract with upper-level authorities to ensure the fulfillment of assigned tasks, including achieving social stability. City-level party secretaries may not be required to sign such contracts, but they are certainly assessed on this responsibility (Dong Xueqing, Zhang Heping, and Zhang Zeyuan, "Women shishui?" [Who are we?], *Liaowang* [Perspective] 45 [2005]: 34–36).

15. It was later discovered that the party secretary was with his mistress in another city; annoyed by the phone calls, he turned off his cell phone. He was later arrested for corruption and sentenced to death with a two-year reprieve (Xiao Zhong, "Anhui fushengzhang He Minxu chezhi diaocha" [An investigation of the removal of He Minxu, a vice governor of Anhui province], *Jiancha* [Inspections] 20 [2006]: 21–22).

16. Kevin O'Brien and Lianjiang Li, "Popular Contention and Its Impact in Rural China," *Comparative Political Studies* 38, 3 (2005): 235–259.

17. Jie Chen, *Popular Political Support in Urban China* (Stanford, CA: Stanford University Press, 2004).

18. Lianjiang Li, "Political Trust in Rural China," *Modern China* 30, 2 (2004): 228–258.

19. Craig Jenkins and Charles Perrow, "Insurgency of the Powerless: Farm Workers' Insurgency, 1946–1972," *American Sociological Review* 42, 2 (1977): 249–226.

20. Kevin O'Brien, "Rightful Resistance," *World Politics* 49, 1 (1996): 31–55.

21. This has been the case in the use of petitions (Yu Jianrong, "Zhongguo xinfang zhidu pipan" [Criticisms of the petition system in China], *Zhongguo gaige* [China reform], 2 [2005]: 26–28).

22. O'Brien and Li, *Rightful Resistance in Rural China*, chapter 4.

23. Giugni, "Was It Worth the Effort?"

24. Jenkins and Perrow, "Insurgency of the Powerless."

25. Annulla Linders, "Victory and Beyond: A Historical Comparative Analysis of the Outcomes of the Abortion Movements in Sweden and the United States," *Sociological Forum* 19, 3 (2004): 371–404.

26. See Marco Giugni, Doug McAdam, and Charles Tilly, eds., *From Contention to Democracy* (Lanham, MD: Rowan & Littlefield, 1998).

27. O'Brien and Li, *Rightful Resistance in Rural China*, chapter 5.

28. Kenneth Andrews, *Freedom Is a Constant Struggle: The Mississippi Civil Rights Movement and Its Strategy* (Chicago: University of Chicago Press, 2004), 134.

29. O'Brien and Li, *Rightful Resistance in Rural China*, chapter 6.

30. Dong et.al., "Xianwei shuji shenghuo zhuangtai."

31. He said, "Now that the situation has changed, so must our working methods. It is no longer in a planned economy when the leaders decided all. The

bureaucratic working style is not feasible. You may do things with an intention to save trouble, but it may turn out that it causes more trouble" (*Nanfang ribao*, January 5, 2006).

32. The city governments in Xi'an and Shenzhen made similar regulations (*Lanzhou ribao*, September 21, 2004; *Xi'an ribao*, June 19, 2004; *Jingbao*, July 19, 2005).

33. *Nanfang dushi bao*, March 3, 2006.

34. In recent years, the city government carried out a few construction projects. Because of residents' resistance, the government made concessions by, among others, revising the construction plans (*21 shiji jingji baodao*, May 16, 2005).

35. Ibid.

36. *Beijing yule xinbao*, January 7, 2004; *Xinmin wanbao*, October 21, 2003.

37. *Beijing qingnian bao*, April 3, 2004.

38. Yongshun Cai, "Power Structure and Regime Resilience: Contentious Politics in China," *British Journal of Political Science* 38, 3 (2008): 411–432.

39. *Jiangnan shibao*, November 16, 2004.

40. See the website for Sohu. Retrieved on May 1, 2006, from: http://news .sohu.com/20060429/n243070831.shtml.

41. *South China Morning Post*, December 12, 2005.

42. The messages could actually have been more numerous: Some were blocked by the website. The comments were posted on Sohu.com on May 21 and 22, 2004. Retrieved on May 22, 2004, from: http://comment.news.sohu.com/ comment/topic. Jsp?id=220147758.

43. Retrieved on April 16, 2005, from: http://comment.news.sohu.com/ comment/topic.jsp?id=225207068; http://comment.ews. sina.com.cn/cgi-bin/ comment/comment.cgi?channel=gn&newsid=6400195.

44. Retrieved on May 1, 2006, from: http://news.sohu.com/20060429/ n243070831.shtml.

45. Yu Jianrong, "Tudi chengwei zhongguo nongcun shouyao wenti" (Land use becomes the most important issue in rural China), *Liaowang dongfang* (Eastern outlook) 37 (2004): 22–23.

46. Retrieved on May 2, 2006, from http://comment.china.com/ html/13/288/010.html; http://comment2.news.sohu.com /viewcomments .action?id=243070831.

47. William Gamson, "Social Movements and Cultural Change," in Marco Giugni, Doug McAdam, and Charles Tilly, eds., *From Contention to Democracy* (Lanham, MD: Rowan & Littlefield, 1998), 57–77.

48. Christopher Kedzie, "Communication and Democracy: Coincident Revolutions and the Emergent Dictator's Dilemma," manuscript, 1997.

49. Kuran, "Now out of Never."

50. Yongnian Zheng and Guoguang Wu, "Information Technology, Public Space, and Collective Action in China," *Comparative Political Studies* 38, 5 (2005): 507–536.

51. Federick Barghoon, *Politics in Russia* (Boston, MA: Little, Brown and Company, 1972), 308.

52. Jean Oi, "Realms of Freedom in Post-Mao China" in William Kirby, ed., *Realms of Freedom in Modern China* (Stanford, CA: Stanford University Press, 2003), 264–284.

53. Goldstone and Tilly, "Threat (and Opportunity)."

54. This is the case for the repression in Fuchuan county mentioned at the beginning of the book (*Takungbao*, January 19, 2006).

55. Herman Schwartz, *The Struggle for Constitutional Justice in Post-Communist Europe* (Chicago: University of Chicago Press, 2000).

Bibliography

Books and Journal Articles

Albritton, Robert. 1979. "Social Amelioration through Mass Insurgency? A Reexamination of the Piven and Cloward Thesis." *American Political Science Review* 73 (4): 1003–1011.

The All China Federation of Trade Unions. 2000. "Guanyu guoyou qiye xiagang zhigong jiben shenghuo baozhang yu zaijiuye gongzuo de diaocha yu jianyi" (An investigation of the living allowances of laid-off workers from state-owned enterprises and some suggestions). *Shizhang cankao* (References for mayors) 4: 32–38.

Amenta, Edwin, Bruce Garruthers, and Yvonne Zylan. 1992. "A Hero for the Aged? The Townsend Movement, the Political Mediation Model, and the U.S. Old Age Policy, 1934–1950." *American Journal of Sociology* 98 (2): 308–339.

Amenta, Edwin, and Michael Young. 1999. "Making an Impact: Conceptual and Methodological Implications of the Collective Goods Criterion." In Marco Giugni, Doug McAdam, and Charles Tilly, eds., *How Social Movements Matter*. Minneapolis: University of Minnesota Press, 22–41.

Andrews, Kenneth. 2004. *Freedom Is a Constant Struggle: The Mississippi Civil Rights Movement and Its Strategy*. Chicago: University of Chicago Press.

Appleton, Simon, John Knight, Lina Song, and Qingjie Xia. 2006. "Labor Retrenchment in China: Determinants and Consequences." In Li Shi and Hiroshi Sato, eds., *Unemployment, Inequality and Poverty in Urban China*, 19–42. London: Routledge.

Banaszak, Lee Ann. 1996. *Why Movements Succeed or Fail: Opportunity, Culture, and the Struggle for Woman Suffrage*. Princeton, NJ: Princeton University Press.

Barghoon, Federick. 1972. *Politics in Russia*. Boston: Little, Brown and Company.

Barkan, Steven. 1984. "Legal Control of the Southern Civil Rights Movement." *American Sociological Review* 49 (4): 552–565.

Barker, Colin. 2001. "Fear, Laughter, and Collective Power: The Making of Solidarity at the Lenin Shipyard in Gdnask, Poland, August 1980." In Jeff Goodwin, James Jasper, and Francesca Polletta, eds., *Passionate Politics: Emotions and Social Movements*, 175–194. Chicago: University of Chicago Press.

Bates, Robert. 1981. *Markets and States in Tropical Africa: The Political Basis of Agricultural Policies*. New York: Cambridge University Press.

Beckwith, Karen. 2000. "Hinges in Collective Action: Strategic Innovation in Pittson Coal Strike." *Mobilization* 5 (2): 179–199.

Bernstein, Thomas. 1984. "Stalinism, Famine, and Chinese Peasants." *Theory and Society* 13 (3): 339–369.

Bernstein, Thomas, and Xiaobo Lu. 2003. *Taxation without Representation in Contemporary Rural China*. New York: Cambridge University Press.

Bianco, Lucien. 2001. *Peasants without the Party: Grassroots Movements in Twentieth-Century China*. Armonk, NY: M. E. Sharpe.

Burstein, Paul. 1999. "Social Movements and Public Policy." In Marco Giugni, Doug McAdam, and Charles Tilly, eds., *How Social Movements Matter*, 3–12. Minneapolis: University of Minnesota Press.

Burstein, Paul, Rachel Einwohner, and Jocelyn Hollander. 1995. "The Success of Political Movements: A Bargaining Perspective." In Craig Jenkins and Bert Klandermans, eds., *The Politics of Social Protest: Comparative Perspectives on States and Social Movements*, 275–295. Minneapolis: University of Minnesota Press.

Burstein, Paul, and April Linton. 2002. "The Impact of Political Parties, Interest Groups, and Social Movement Organizations on Public Policy: Some Recent Evidence and Theoretical Concerns." *Social Forces* 81 (2): 381–408.

Button, James. 1978. *Black Violence: Political Impact of the 1960s Riots*. Princeton, NJ: Princeton University Press.

Cai Pengyi and Zhao Zuohuan. 2000. *Xianjieduan zhongguo nongmin fudan helixing yanjiu* (Research on contemporary Chinese peasants' financial burdens). Beijing: Zhongguo nongye chubanshe.

Cai, Yongshun. 2002. "Relaxing the Constraints from Above: The Politics of Privatizing Public Enterprises in Reform China." *Asian Journal of Political Science* 10 (2): 94–121.

———. 2003. "Collective Ownership or Cadres' Ownership? The Nonagricultural Use of Farmland in China." *China Quarterly* 175: 662–680.

———. 2004a. "Irresponsible State: Local Cadres and Image-Building in China." *Journal of Communist Studies and Transition Politics* 20 (4): 20–41.

———. 2004b. "Managed Participation in China." *Political Science Quarterly* 119 (3): 425–451.

———. 2005. "China's Moderate Middle Class: The Case of Homeowners' Resistance." *Asian Survey* 45 (5): 777–799.

———. 2006. *State and Laid-Off Workers in Reform China: The Silence and Collective Action of the Retrenched*. London: Routledge.

———. 2007. "Civil Resistance and Rule of Law in China: The Case of Defending Home Owners' Rights." In Elizabeth Perry and Merle Goldman, eds., *Grassroots Politics in China*. Cambridge, MA: Harvard University Press, 174–195.

———. 2008a. "Local Governments and the Suppression of Popular Resistance in China." *China Quarterly* 193: 24–42.

———. 2008b. "Power Structure and Regime Resilience: Contentious Politics in China." *British Journal of Political Science* 38 (3): 411–432.

———. 2008c. "Social Conflicts and Modes of Action in China." *China Journal* 59: 89–109.

Cai, Yongshun, and Songcai Yang. 2005. "State Power and Unbalanced Legal Development in China." *Journal of Contemporary China* 14 (42): 117–134.

The Central Complaints Bureau. 1998. *Zhongguo xinfang xiezhen* (A record of people's appeals in China). Beijing: Zhongguo gongren chubanshe.

Chen, Feng. 2000. "Subsistence Crises, Managerial Corruption and Labor Protests in China." *China Journal* 44: 41–63.

———. 2003. "Industrial Restructuring and Workers' Resistance in China." *Modern China* 29 (2): 237–262.

Chen Guidi and Chun Tao. 2003. *Zhongguo nongmin diaocha* (Surveys of Chinese peasants). Beijing: Renmin wenxue chubanshe.

Chen, Jie. 2004. *Popular Political Support in Urban China*. Stanford, CA: Stanford University Press.

Chen Jinsheng. 2004. *Quntixingshijian yanjiu baogao* (Research report on instances of collective action). Beijing: Qunzhong chubanshe.

Chen, Xi. "Chinese Petitioners' Tactics and Their Efficacy," paper presented at the conference on "Grassroots Political Reform in Contemporary China." Harvard University, October 29–31, 2004.

Chong, Dennis. 1991. *Collective Action and the Civil Rights Movement*. Chicago: University of Chicago Press.

Chung, Jae Ho, Hongyi Lai, and Ming Xia. 2006. "Mounting Challenges to Governance in China: Surveying Collective Protestors, Religious Sects and Criminal Organizations." *China Journal* 56: 1–31.

Dai Gang. 2001. "Hongjiang quntixing shijian chuzhi yinfa de sikao" (Some thoughts about the settlement of the Hongjiang incident). *Gongan yanjiu* (Research on public security) 7: 65–68.

Davenport, Christian. 1995. "Multi-Dimensional Threat Perception and State Repression: An Inquiry into Why States Apply Negative Sanctions." *American Journal of Political Science* 39 (3): 683–713.

della Porta, Donatella. 1995. *Social Movements, Political Violence and the State.* New York: Cambridge University Press.

della Porta, Donatella, and Mario Diani. 1999. *Social Movements: An Introduction.* Oxford, UK: Blackwell.

della Porta, Donatella, and Herbert Reiter. 1998. "The Policing of Protest in Western Democracies." In Donatella della Porta and Herbert Reiter, eds., *Policing Protest: The Control of Mass Demonstrations in Western Democracies,* 1–34. Minneapolis: University of Minnesota Press.

DeNardo, James. 1985. *Power in Numbers: The Political Strategy of Protest and Rebellion.* Princeton, NJ: Princeton University Press.

Diamant, Neil, Stanley Lubman, and Kevin O'Brien, eds. 2005. *Engaging the Law in China: State, Society, and Possibilities for Justice.* Stanford, CA: Stanford University Press.

Diao Jiecheng. 1996. *Renmin xinfang shilue* (A brief history of people's petitions). Beijing: Beijing jingji xueyuan chubanshe.

Dong Qingmin. 1997. "Renmin neibu tufaxing qunti maodun de tedian jiqi chuli yuanze," (The characteristics of sudden collective action and principles for resolution). *Lilunqianyan* (Theoretical frontiers) 13: 7–9.

Downs, Anthony. 1967. *Inside Bureaucracy.* Glenview, IL: Scott, Foresman and Company.

Du Jingdong. 2004. "Yifa tuoshan chuzhi quntixing shijian, quanli weihu chengshihua jincheng zhong de shehui wending" (Dealing with mass incidents in light of the law to maintain social stability in urbanization). *Gongan yanjiu* (Research on public security) 12: 54–59.

Edin, Maria. 2003. "State Capacity and Local Agent Control in China: CCP Cadre Management from a Township Perspective." *China Quarterly* 173: 35–72.

The Editorial Group. 2005. *Goujian shehuizhuyi hexie shehui dacankao* (Reference on the building of a socialist harmonious society). Beijing: Hongqi chubanshe.

Eisinger, Peter. 1973. "The Conditions for Protest Behavior in American Cities." *American Political Science Review* 67 (1): 11–28.

Ekiert, Grzegorz. 1996. *The State against Society: Political Crises and Their Aftermath in East Central Europe.* Princeton, NJ: Princeton University Press.

Ekiert, Gregorz, and Jan Kubik. 1999. *Rebellious Civil Society.* Ann Arbor: University of Michigan Press.

Fan Fuming. 2001. "Quntixing lanche duandao shijian de tedian he yufang chuzhi duice" (Characteristics of collective action in blocking railways and some countermeasures). *Shanghai gongan gaodeng zhuanke xuexiao xuebao* (Journal of Shanghai Public Security Academy) 3: 30–34.

Felson, Richard, and James Tedeschi. 1995. "A Social Interactionist Approach to Violence: Cross-Cultural Applications." In Barry Ruback and Neil Alan Weiner, eds., *Interpersonal Violent Behaviors: Social and Cultural Aspects*. New York: Springer Publishing Company, 153–170.

Fording, Richard. 1997. "The Conditional Effect of Violence as a Political Tactic: Mass Insurgency, Welfare Generosity, and Electoral Context in the American States." *American Journal of Political Science* 41 (1): 1–29.

Fu Yongkun. 2001. "Jiji yufang, tuoshan chuzhi quntixing shijian quanli weihu shehui wending" (Actively preventing and appropriately handling collective action to maintain social stability). *Gongan yanjiu* (Research on public security) 12: 44–46.

Gamson, William. 1990. *The Strategy of Social Protest*. Belmont: Wadsworth.

———. 1997. "The Success of the Unruly." In Doug McAdam and David Snow, eds., *Social Movements*. Los Angeles: Roxbury Publishing Company, 357–364.

——— 1998. "Social Movements and Cultural Change." In Marco Giugni, Doug McAdam, and Charles Tilly, eds., *From Contention to Democracy*, 57–77. Lanham, MD: Rowan & Littlefield.

Giugni, Marco. 1998. "Was It Worth the Effort? The Outcomes and Consequences of Social Movements." *Annual Review of Sociology* 98: 371–393.

———. 1999. "How Social Movements Matter: Past Research, Present Problems, Future Developments." In Marco Giugni, Doug McAdam, and Charles Tilly, eds., *How Social Movements Matter*, xiii–xxxiii. Minneapolis: University of Minnesota Press.

Giugni, Marco, Doug McAdam, and Charles Tilly, eds. 1998. *From Contention to Democracy*. Lanham, MD: Rowan & Littlefield.

———. 1999. *How Social Movements Matter*. Minneapolis: University of Minnesota Press.

Gold, Thomas, Doug Guthrie, and David Wank, eds. 2002. *Social Connections in China: Institutions, Culture, and the Changing Nature of Guanxi*. New York: Cambridge University Press.

Goldstone, Jack, and Charles Tilly. 2001. "Threat (and Opportunity): Popular Action and State Response in the Dynamics of Contentious Action." In Ronald Aminzade, Jack Goldstone, Doug McAdam, Elizabeth Perry, William Sewell, Sidney Tarrow, and Charles Tilley, eds., *Silence and Voice in the Study of Contentious Politics*, 179–194. New York: Cambridge University Press.

Goodwin, Jeff, and James Jasper. 1999. "Caught in a Winding, Snarling Vine: The Structural Bias of Political Process Theory." *Sociological Forum* 14 (1): 27–54.

Goodwin, Jeff, James Jasper, and Francesca Polletta. 2001. "Why Emotions Matter." In Jeff Goodwin, James Jasper, and Francesca Polletta, eds., *Passionate Politics: Emotions and Social Movements*, 1–26. Chicago: University of Chicago Press.

Graham, Hugh, and Ted Gurr. 1969. "Editors' Introduction." In Hugh Graham and Ted Gurr, eds., *Violence in America: Historical and Comparative Perspective*, xxvii–xxxiv. New York: Praeger.

Guo, Xiaolin. 2001. "Land Expropriation and Rural Conflicts in China." *China Quarterly* 166: 422–439.

Guo Zhenglin. 2001. "Dangdai zhongguo nongmin de jiti weiquan xingdong" (The collective action of contemporary Chinese peasants in protecting their rights). *Xianggang shehui kexue xuebao* (Journal of Hong Kong Social Sciences) 19: 115–133.

Gurr, Ted. 1968. "A Causal Model of Civil Strife: A Comparative Analysis Using New Indices." *American Political Science Review* 62 (4): 1104–1124.

———. 1970. *Why Men Rebel*. Princeton, NJ: Princeton University Press.

He Xuefeng. 2004. *Xiangcun yanjiu de guoqing yishi* (Awareness of the country's particular situation in research on rural areas). Wuhan: Hubei renmin chubanshe.

He Zhuowen. 2005. "Zhengque renshi he chuli woguo xianjieduan de liyi guanxi maodun" (Properly handling the conflict in our country). *Kexue shehui zhuyi* (Scientific socialism) 2: 8–11.

Ho, Peter. 2001. "Who Owns China's Land? Property Rights and Deliberate Institutional Ambiguity." *China Quarterly* 166: 394–421.

Hong Xiaojin. 2005. "Heidong" (Black hole). *Diaoyan shijie* (Survey world) 3: 41–43.

Hough, Jerry, and Merle Fainsod. 1990. *How the Soviet Union Is Governed*. Cambridge, MA: Harvard University Press.

Hu Baozhen, Xie Tianchang, Chen Maohua, and Li Yanjun. 2006. "Hexie shehui goujian yu quntixing shijian falu duice yanjiu" (Research on the legal measures of constructing a harmonious society and dealing with collective incidents). *Zhongguo renmin gongan daxue xuebao* (Journal of the Chinese People's Security University) 4: 105–111.

Hurst, William. 2004. "Understanding Contentious Collective Action by Chinese Laid-Off Workers: The Importance of Regional Political Economy." *Studies in Comparative International Development* 39 (2): 94–120.

Hurst, William, and Kevin O'Brien. 2002. "China's Contentious Pensioners." *China Quarterly* 170: 345–360.

Jasper, James. 1997. *The Art of Moral Protest: Culture, Biography, and Creativity in Social Movements*. Chicago: University of Chicago Press.

Jenkins, Craig, and Charles Perrow. 1997. "Insurgency of the Powerless: Farm Workers' Insurgency, 1946–1972." *American Sociological Review* 42 (2): 249–226.

Ji Zhengfeng. 1999. "Yufang he chuzhi qunti xing shijian de duice xuanze" (The choice of modes to deal with mass events). *Lilun yu shijian* (Theory and Practice)16: 30–31.

Jiang Guanhuo. 1999. "Cunji zhaiwu de xingcheng jiqi xiaohua" (The formation of villages' debts and solutions). *Zhongguo nongcun jingji* (China's rural economy) 4: 34–38.

The Joint Investigation Group. 1998. "Guanyu dangqian Henan nongcun shehui wending de diaocha yu jianyi" (An investigation of rural stability in Henan and some suggestions). *Zhongguo nongcun jingji* (China's rural economy) 12: 67–71.

Kecskemeti, Paul. 1961. *The Unexpected Revolution.* Stanford, CA: Stanford University Press.

Kedzie, Christopher. 1997. "Communication and Democracy: Coincident Revolutions and the Emergent Dictator's Dilemma." manuscript.

Kitschelt, Herbert. 1986. "Political Opportunity Structures and Political Protest: Antinuclear Movements in Four Democracies." *British Journal of Political Science* 16 (1): 57–85.

Klandermans, Bert, and Dirk Oegema. 1987. "Potentials, Networks, Motivations, and Barriers: Steps toward Participation in Social Movements." *American Sociological Review* 52: 519–531.

Kowalewski, David, and Paul Schumaker. 1981. "Protest Outcomes in the Soviet Union." *Sociological Quarterly* 22 (1): 57–68.

Krehbiel, Kenneth. 1991. *Information and Legislative Organization.* Ann Arbor: University of Michigan Press.

Kriesi, Hanspeter. 1996. "The Organizational Structure of New Social Movements in a Political Context," in Doug McAdam, John McCarthy, and Mayer Zald, eds., *Comparative Perspectives on Social Movements*, 152–184. New York: Cambridge University Press.

Kuran, Timur. 1991. "Now out of Never: The Element of Surprise in the East European Revolution of 1989." *World Politics* 44 (1): 7–48.

Kurzman, Charles. 1996. "Structural Opportunity and Perceived Opportunity in Social-Movement Theory: The Iranian Revolution of 1979." *American Sociological Review* 61 (1): 153–170.

Landry, Pierre, and Yanqi Tong. 2005. "Disputing the Authoritarian State in China." manuscript.

Lee, Ching Kwan. 2000. "The 'Revenge of History': Collective Memories and Labor Protests in North-Eastern China." *Ethnography* 1 (2): 217–237.

———. 2002. "From the Specter of Mao to the Spirit of the Law: Labor Insurgency in China." *Theory and Society* 31 (2): 189–228.

———. 2007. *Against the Law: Labor Protests in China's Rustbelt and Sunbelt.* Berkeley: University of California Press.

———. 2007. "Is Labor a Political Force in China?" In Elizabeth Perry and Merle Goldman, eds., *Grassroots Politics in China*, 228–252. Cambridge, MA: Harvard University Press.

Li Jin, and Zheng Xianli. 2003. "Yimin shangfang lu" (Migrants' petitions). *Zhongguo gaige* (China reform) 2: 39–40.

Li, Lianjiang. 2004. "Political Trust in Rural China." *Modern China* 30 (2): 228–258.

———. 2007. "Direct Township Elections." In Elizabeth Perry and Merle Goldman, eds., *Grassroots Politics in China*, 97–116. Cambridge, MA: Harvard University Press.

Li, Lianjiang, and Kevin O'Brien. 1996. "Villagers and Popular Resistance in Contemporary China." *Modern China* 22 (1): 28–61.

———. 2008. "Protest Leadership in the Countryside." *China Quarterly* 193: 1–23.

Li Maolan. 1996. *Zhongguo nongmin fudan wenti yanjiu* (Research on peasants' financial burdens in China). Taiyuan: Shanxi jingji chubanshe.

Li Xiaoping. 2002. "Focus (*jiaodian fangtan*) and the Changes in the Chinese Television History." *Journal of Contemporary China* 11: 17–34.

Liang Jun. 2000. *Cunmin zizhi* (Villagers' self governance). Beijing: Zhongguo qingnian chubanshe.

Liao Yiwu. 2005. *Zhongguo shangfang cun* (The village of petitioners in China). New York: Mingjing chunbanshe.

Lichbach, Mark. 1994. "Rethinking Rationality and Rebellion: Theories of Collective Action and Problems of Collective Dissent." *Rationality and Society* 6 (1): 8–39.

Lieberson, Stanley. 1991. "Small N's and Big Conclusions: An Examination of the Reasoning in Comparative Studies Based on a Small Number of Cases." *Social Forces* 70 (2): 306–320.

Linders, Annulla. 2004. "Victory and Beyond: A Historical Comparative Analysis of the Outcomes of the Abortion Movements in Sweden and the United States." *Sociological Forum* 19 (3): 371–404.

Lipsky, Michael. 1968. "Protest as Political Resource." *American Political Science Review* 62 (4): 1144–1158.

Lohmann, Susanne. 1994. "The Dynamics of Information Cascades: The Monday Demonstration in Leipzeig East Germany, 1989–1991." *World Politics* 47 (1): 42–101.

Long Xianlei. 2001. "Jianchi 'yifazhiguo' fanglue tuoshan chuzhi quntixing shijian" (Sticking to rule by the law and appropriately handling instances of collective action). *Gongan yanjiu* (Research on public security) 12: 50–53.

Lu Xin, Lu Xueyi, and Shan Tianlun. eds. 2001. *2001 zhongguo shehui xingshi
fenxi yu yuce* (2001: An analysis of Chinese society and some predictions). Beijing: Shehui kexue wenxian chubanshe.

Lu Xin, Lu Xueyi, and Li Peilin. eds. 2002. *2002 zhongguo shehui xingshi fenxi yu
yuce* (2002: An analysis of the social situation in China and some predictions).
Beijing: Shehui kexue wenxian chubanshe.

Luehrmann, Laura. 2003. "Facing Citizen Complaints in China, 1951–1996."
Asian Survey 43 (5): 845–66.

Mao Feng. 2004. "Zhengfu gai wei shidi nongmin zuoxi shenme" (What the
government does for peasants who have lost land). *Diaoyan shijie* (Survey
world) 1: 28–29.

Marwell, Gerald, Pamela Oliver, and Ralph Prahl. 1998. "Social Networks and
Collective Action: A Theory of the Critical Mass. III." *American Journal of
Sociology* 94 (3): 502–534.

McAdam, Doug. 1983. "Tactical Innovation and the Pace of Insurgency." *American Sociological Review* 48 (6): 735–754.

———. 1998. *Freedom Summer.* New York: Oxford University Press.

———. 1999. *Political Process and the Development of Black Insurgency 1930–1970*,
2nd ed. Chicago: The University of Chicago Press.

McAdam, Doug, and Ronnelle Paulsen. 1999. "Specifying the Relationship
between Social Ties and Activism." *American Journal of Sociology* 99 (3):
640–667.

McAdam, Doug, and Yang Su. 2002. "The War at Home: Antiwar Protests and
Congressional Voting, 1965 to 1973." *American Sociological Review* 67 (5):
696–712.

McAdam, Doug, Sidney Tarrow, and Charles Tilly. 2001. *Dynamics of Contention.* New York: Cambridge University Press.

McCammon, Holly, Karen Campbell, Ellen Granberg, and Christine Mowery.
2001. "How Movements Win: Gendered Opportunity Structures and U.S.
Women's Suffrage Movements, 1986 to 1919." *American Sociological Review* 66
(1): 49–70.

Meng Liang. 2004. "Henan nongmin zifei diaocha zhenxiang" (The truth about
the peasant's self-financed investigation in Henan). *Zhongguo gaige* (China
reform) 8: 30–31.

Meyer, David, and Suzanne Staggenborg. 1996. "Movements, Countermovements, and the Structure of Political Opportunity." *American Journal of Sociology* 101 (6): 1628–1660.

Michelman, Frank. 2003. "Ida's Way: Constructing the Respect-Worthy Governmental System." *Fordham Law Review* 72: 345–362.

Michelson, Ethan. 2004. "Causes and Consequences of Grievances in Rural China." manuscript.

———. 2005. "Peasants' Burdens and State Response: Exploring State Concession to Popular Tax Resistance in Rural China." Manuscript.

The Ministry of Labor and Social Security and Document Research Office of the Central Party Committee, eds. 2002. *Xinshiqi laodong he shehui baozhang zhongyao wenxian xuanbian* (Selected important documents regarding labor and social security). Beijing: Zhongguo laodong shenhui baozhang chubanshe.

Minzner, Carl. 2006. "Xinfang: An Alternative to the Formal Chinese Judicial System." *Stanford Journal of International Law* 42 (1): 103–179.

Mnookin, Robert, and Lewis Kornhauser. 1979. "Bargaining in the Shadow of the Law: The Case of Divorce." *Yale Law Journal* 88 (5): 950–997.

Mo Daquan. 1998. *Gongzhi anquanwang* (Establishing a safety network). Beijing: jingji kexue chubanshe.

The National Statistical Bureau. 1998. *Da toushi* (A comprehensive perspective). Beijing: Zhongguo fazhan chubanshe.

———. 2005. *Xinzhongguo wushiwu nian tongji ziliao huibian* (China Statistics: 1949–2004). Beijing: Zhongguo tongji chubanshe.

O'Brien, Kevin. 1996. "Rightful Resistance." *World Politics* 49 (1): 31–55.

———. 2002. "Collective Action in the Chinese Countryside." *China Journal* 48: 139–154.

———. 2003. "Neither Transgressive nor Contained: Boundary-Spanning Contention in China." *Mobilization* 8 (1): 51–64.

O'Brien, Kevin, and Lianjiang Li. 1999. "Selective Policy Implementation in Rural China." *Comparative Politics* 31 (2): 167–186.

———. 2004. "Suing the Local State: Administrative Litigation in Rural China." *China Journal* 51: 53–74.

———. 2005. "Popular Contention and Its Impact in Rural China." *Comparative Political Studies* 38 (3): 235–259.

———. 2006. *Rightful Resistance in Rural China*. New York: Cambridge University Press.

The Office of Party History of Zhejiang Provincial Party Committee and the Political Office of The Zhejiang Military District. 1996. *Zhejiang nongmin wuzhuang baodong* (Peasants armed riots in Zhejiang). Beijing: Dangdai zhongguo chubanshe.

Oi, Jean. 1989. *State and Peasant in Contemporary China*. Berkeley: University of California Press.

————. 2003. "Realms of Freedom in Post-Mao China." In William Kirby, ed., *Realms of Freedom in Modern China,* 264–284. Stanford, CA: Stanford University Press.

Oi, Jean, and Zhao Shukai. 2007. "Fiscal Crisis in China's Townships: Causes and Consequences." In Elizabeth Perry and Merle Goldman, eds., *Grassroots Politics in China,* 75–96. Cambridge, MA: Harvard University Press.

Opp, Karl-Dieter, and Wolfgang Ruehl. 1990. "Repression, Micromobilization and Political Protest." *Social Forces* 69 (2): 521–547.

Page, Benjamin Page, and Robert Shapiro. 1983. "Effects of Public Opinion on Policy." *American Political Science Review* 77 (1): 175–190.

Peerenboom, Randall. 2002. *China's Long March toward Rule of Law.* New York: Cambridge University Press.

Perry, Elizabeth. 1985. "Rural Violence in Socialist China." *China Quarterly* 139: 704–713.

————. 2001. *Challenging the Mandate of Heaven: Social Protest and State Power in China.* Armonk, NY: M. E. Sharpe.

Perry, Elizabeth, and Merle Goldman, eds. 2007. *Grassroots Politics in China.* Cambridge, MA: Harvard University Press.

Perry, Elizabeth, and Li Xun. 1997. *Proletarian Power: Shanghai in the Cultural Revolution.* Boulder, CO: Westview Press.

Piven, Frances Fox, and Richard A. Cloward. 1977. *Poor People's Movements: Why They Succeed, How They Fail.* New York: Vintage Books.

————. 1993. *Regulating the Poor: The Functions of Public Welfare.* New York: Vintage Books.

————. 1995. "Collective Protest: A Critique of Resource-Mobilization Theory." In Stanford Lyman, ed., *Social Movements: Critique, Concepts, Case-Studies,* 137–167. New York: New York University Press.

Popkin, Samuel. 1988. "Public Choice and Peasant Organization." In Robert Bates, ed., *Toward a Political Economy of Development,* 245–271. Berkeley: University of California Press.

Qian Zhonghao, and Qu Futian. 2004. "Guifan zhengfu tudi zhengyong xing-wei, qieshi baozhang nongmin tudi quanyi" (Regulating governments land use to protect peasants' interests). *Zhongguo nongcun jingji* (China's rural economy) 12: 4–9.

Qiao Yunxia, Hu Lianli, and Wang Junjie. 2002. "Zhongguo xinwen yulun jiandu xianzhuang diaocha fenxi" (A survey and analysis of media exposure in China), *Xinwen yu chuanbo yanjiu* (News and communication studies) 4: 21–28.

Qiu Zeqi. 2003. "Meiyou baofadian de weiji" (Crises without identifiable triggers). *Yunnan daxue xuebao* (Journal of Yunnan University) 5: 21–26.

Read, Benjamin. 2000. "Revitalizing the State's Urban 'Nerve Tips.'" *China Quarterly* 163: 806–820.

———. 2003. "Democratizing the Neighborhood? New Private Housing and Home-Owner Self-Organization in Urban China." *China Journal* 49: 31–60.

Ren Yanfang. 1999. *Minyuan* (People's complaints). Bejing: Zhongguo wenlian chubanshe.

The Research Group. 1997. "Xiagang zhigong de shenghuo zhuangkuang jiqi shehui zhichi" (The situation of laid-off workers and their social support). *Xiaofei jingji* (Economy of consumption) 1: 47–51.

The Research Group of the Association of Administration Studies. 2003. *Zhongguo zhuanxing qi quntixing tufa shijian duice yanjiu* (Research on collective incidents in China during the transitional period). Beijing: Xueyuan chubanshe.

The Research Group of Laid-Off Workers' Situation. 1997. "Chengzhen qiye xiagang zhigong zaijiuye zhuangkuang diaocha: Kunjing yu chulu" (An investigation of laid-off workers' reemployment: Plight and solutions). *Shehuixue yanjiu* (Sociological research) 6: 24–34.

The Research Group of the National Land Management Bureau. 1998. "Jinnian lai woguo gengdi bianhua ji zhongqi fazhan qushi" (Recent changes in the use of farmland in our country and the development trend in the near future). *Zhongguo shehui kexue* (Social sciences in China) 1: 75–90.

The Research Group of Township Organizations. 1999. "Xiangzhen dangzheng jigou he renyuan pengzhang jiqi yuanyin" (The reasons for the expansion of township organizations and employees). In The Ministry of Agriculture, ed., *Zhongguo nongcun yanjiu baogao: 1999 nian* (A research report on rural China: 1999), 567–576. Beiing: Zhongguo caizheng jingji chubanshe.

Schock, Kurt. 2005. *Unarmed Insurrections: People Power Movements in Non-democracies.* Minneapolis: University of Minnesota Press.

Schumpeter, Joseph. 1950. *Capitalism, Socialism and Democracy.* New York: Harper, 19.

Schwartz, Herman. 2000. *The Struggle for Constitutional Justice in Post-Communist Europe.* Chicago: University of Chicago Press.

Scott, James. 1989. "Everyday Forms of Resistance." In Forrest Colburn, ed., *Everyday Forms of Peasant Resistance*, 3–33. Armonk, NY: M. E. Sharpe.

Shi Po. 2004. "'Shuishou dilei' tuxian nongcu liyi chongtu" (The mine of tax collection reflects interest conflict in rural areas). *Zhongguo gaige* (China reform, rural edition) 11: 41–42.

Shi Qinghua and Chen Kai. 2002. "Xian jieduan nongmin falu suzhi yu falu yishi fenxi" (An analysis of peasants' legal consciousness in the current period). *Zhongguo nongcun guancha* (Observations of rural China) 2: 67–75.

Shi, Tianjian. 1997. *Political Participation in Beijing*. Cambridge, MA: Harvard University Press.

Shin, Myungsoon. 1983. "Political Protest and Government Decision Making." *American Behavioral Science* 26 (3): 395–416.

Shorter, Edward, and Charles Tilly. 1974. *Strikes in France, 1830–1968*. New York: Cambridge University Press.

Snyder, David, and William Kelly. 1976. "Industrial Violence in Italy, 1878–1903." *American Journal of Sociology* 82 (1): 131–162.

Solinger, Dorothy. 2002. "Labor Market Reform and the Plight of the Laid-off Proletariat." *China Quarterly* 170: 304–326.

Song Binwen, Fan Xiaogang, and Zhou Huiwen. 2004. "Shidi nongmin wenti shi shiguan shehui wending de dawenti" (The issue of peasants who have lost land affects social stability). *Diaoyan shijie* (Survey world) 1: 22–24.

Soule, Sarah, and Susan Olzak. 2004. "When Do Movements Matter? The Politics of Contingency and the Equal Rights Amendment." *American Sociological Review* 69 (4): 473–497.

Steedly, Homer, and John Foley. 1979. "The Success of Protest Groups: Multivariate Analysis." *Social Science Research* 8 (6): 1–15.

Suh, Doowon. 2001. "How Do Political Opportunities Matter for Social Movements? Political Opportunity, Misframing, Pseudosuccess, and Pseudofailure." *Sociological Quarterly* 42 (3): 437–460.

Tang, Yuen Yuen. 2005. "When Peasants Sue En Masse." *China: An International Journal* 3 (1): 24–49.

Tanner, Murray Scott. 2004. "China Rethinks Unrest." *Washington Quarterly* 27 (3): 137–156.

Tarrow, Sidney. 1994. *Power in Movement*. New York: Cambridge University Press.

———. 1996a. "Social Movements in Contentious Politics: A Review Article." *American Political Science Review* 90 (4): 874–883.

———. 1996b. "States and Opportunities: The Political Structuring of Social Movements." In Doug McAdam, John McCarthy, and Mayer Zald, eds., *Comparative Perspectives on Social Movements*, 41–61. New York: Cambridge University Press.

Thireau, Isabelle, and Hua Linshan. 2003. "The Moral Universe of Aggrieved Chinese Workers." *China Journal* 50: 83–103.

Thornton, Patricia. 2004. "Comrades and Collectives in Arms: Tax Resistance, Evasion, and Avoidance Strategies in Post-Mao China." In Peter Gries and Stabley Rosen, eds., *State and Society in 21st Century China*. London: Routledge, 87–104.

Tilly, Charles. 1978. *From Mobilization to Revolution*. Reading, MA: Addison-Wesley.

———. 1999. "From Interactions to Outcomes in Social Movements." In Marco
  Giugni, Doug McAdam, and Charles Tilly, eds., *How Social Movements Mat-*
  ter, pp. 253–270. Minneapolis: University of Minnesota Press.
Tullock, Gordon. 1987. *The Politics of Bureaucracy*. Lanham, MD: University
  Press of America.
Tyler, Tom. 1995. "Why People Obey the Law." In Stewart Macaulay, Lawrence
  Friedman, and John Stookey, eds., *Law and Society: Readings on the Social*
  Study of Law, 474–498. New York: W. W. Norton & Company.
Vanderford, Marsha. 1989. "Vilification and Social Movements: A Case Study of
  Pro-Life and Pro-Choice Rhetoric." *Quarterly Journal of Speech* 75: 166–182.
Walder, Andrew. 1986. *Communist Neo-Traditionalism*. Berkeley: University of
  California Press.
Wank, David. 1999. *Commodifying Communism: Business, Trust, and Politics in a*
  Chinese City. New York: Cambridge University Press.
Wang Rui. 1999. "Dui Xi'an shi quntixing zhian shijian guilu de sikao" (Some
  thoughts about the pattern of collective action in Xi'an). *Gongan daxue xuebao*
  (Journal of Chinese People's Public Security University) 5: 53–56.
Wang, Yaping, and Alan Murie. 1999. "Commercial Housing Development in
  Urban China." *Urban Studies* 36 (9): 1475–1494.
Wen Tiejun and Zhu Shouyin. 1996. "Zhengfu ziben yuanshi jilei yu tudi nong-
  zhuangfei" (Government capital accumulation and the conversion of farmland
  for nonagricultural use). *Guanli shijie* (Management world) 5: 167–175.
Whiting, Susuan. 2001. *Power and Wealth in Rural China: The Political Economy*
  of Institutional Change. New York: Cambridge University Press.
Wu Sha. 2004. "Dali jiaqiang quntixing tufa shijian chuzhi gongzuo" (Doing a
  good job of handling instances of collective action). *Gongan yanjiu* (Research
  on public security) 12: 48–53.
Wu Yi. 2002. "Queshi zhili ziyuan de xiangcun quanwei yu shuifei zhengshou
  zhong de ganqun boyi" (The township and village authority and cadre–
  peasant interaction in tax and fee collection), paper presented at the "International Symposium on Political Science and China in Transition," Renmin
  University of China, July 15–16.
Xie Li. 2001. "2000 Quanguo xinzheng fuyi anjian qingkuang fenxi" (An analysis of administrative reconsiderations in the country in 2000). *Xingzheng yu*
  fazhi (Administration and law) 6: 18–19.
Xiong Yihan. 2005. "Xinfang xiang hechuqu?" (Where is the petition system
  heading?). *Ershi yi siji* (21st century) 6: 91–95.
Yang, Dali. 2006. "Economic Transformation and Its Political Discontents in
  China: Authoritarianism, Unequal Growth, and the Dilemmas of Political
  Development." *Annual Review of Political Science* 9: 143–164.

Yang Ling. 2001. "Cunji caiwu" (Village financial affairs). *Diaoyan shijie* (Survey world) 10: 30–31.

Yang, Mayfair. 1994. *Gifts, Favors and Banquets: The Art of Social Relationships in China*. Ithaca, NY: Cornell University Press.

Yang Tongzhi, Zhang Hualin, and Yang Lin. 2000. "Dangqian cunji caiwu guanli zhong de zhuyao wenti jiqi duice" (Problems with the management of village financial affairs and countermeasures). *Zhongguo nongcun jingji* (China's rural economy) 8: 54–57.

Yang Yiyong. 1998. *Gongping yu xiaolu* (Equality and efficiency). Beijing: Jiri zhongguo chubanshe.

Ye Jianping, Jiang Yan, Roy Prosterman, Feng Lei, Li Ping, and Zhu Keliang. 2006. "2005 nian zhongguo tudi shiyongquan diaocha yanjiu" (An investigation of rural land use in China in 2005). *Guanli shijie* (Management world) 7: 77–84.

Yep, Ray. 2004. "Can 'Tax-for-Fee Reform' Reduce Rural Tension in China? The Process, Progress, and Limitations." *China Quarterly* 177: 42–70.

Ying Xing. 2001. *Dahe yimin shangfang de gushi* (Story about the migrants' petitions in Dahe). Beijing: Sanlian Shudian.

Yu Jianrong. 2003. "Nongmin youzuzhi kangzheng jiqi zhengzhi fengxian" (Peasants' organized resistance and political risks). *Zhanlue yu guanli* (Strategy and management) 3: 1–16.

———. 2005. "Zhongguo xinfang zhidu pipan" (Criticisms of the petition system in China). *Zhongguo gaige* (China reform) 2: 26–28.

Zhang Sai, ed. 1996. *Guoji tongji ziliao 1995* (World statistics 1995). Beijing: Zhongguo tongji chubanshe.

Zhao, Dingxin. 2001. *The Power of Tiananmen: State–Society Relations and the 1989 Beijing Student Movement*. Chicago: University of Chicago Press.

Zhao, Yuezhi, and Sun Wusan. 2007. "Public Opinion Supervision: Possibilities and Limits of the Media in Constraining Local Officials." In Elizabeth Perry and Merle Goldman, eds., *Grassroots Political Reform in Contemporary China*, 300–326. Cambridge, MA: Harvard University Press.

Zheng, Yongnian, and Guoguang Wu. 2005. "Information Technology, Public Space, and Collective Action in China." *Comparative Political Studies* 8 (5): 507–536.

Zhou, Min, and John Logan. 1996. "Market Transition and the Commodification of Housing in Urban China." *International Journal of Urban and Regional Research* 20 (3): 400–421.

Zweig, David. 2000. "The 'Externalities of Development': Can New Political Institutions Manage Rural Conflict?" In Elizabeth Perry and Mark Selden, eds., *Chinese Society: Change, Conflict and Resistance*, 120–142. London: Routledge.

Index

Note: Figures and tables are indicated by *f* and *t*, respectively, following page numbers.